VIETNAM,
A MEMOIR

VIETNAM, A MEMOIR

◆

MEKONG MUD SOLDIER

David S. Holland

iUniverse, Inc.
New York Lincoln Shanghai

VIETNAM, A MEMOIR
MEKONG MUD SOLDIER

iUniverse books may be ordered through booksellers or by contacting:

iUniverse
2021 Pine Lake Road, Suite 100
Lincoln, NE 68512
www.iuniverse.com
1-800-Authors (1-800-288-4677)

ISBN-13: 978-0-595-38036-7 (pbk)
ISBN-13: 978-0-595-82406-9 (ebk)
ISBN-10: 0-595-38036-0 (pbk)
ISBN-10: 0-595-82406-4 (ebk)

Printed in the United States of America

To those who wear, and have worn, the uniform, and their families

It's Tommy this, an' Tommy that, an' "Chuck him out, the brute!"
But it's "Savior of 'is country" when the guns begin to shoot.

Kipling

Ship me somewheres east of Suez where the best is like the worst,
Where there aren't no Ten Commandments, an' a man can raise a
thirst;
For the temple-bells are callin', an' it's there that I would be—
By the old Moulmein Pagoda, lookin' lazy at the sea—

 On the road to Mandalay,
 Where the old Flotilla lay,
 With our sick beneath the awnings when we went to Mandalay!
 Oh, the road to Mandalay,
 Where the flyin'-fishes play,
 An' the dawn comes up like thunder outer China 'crost the Bay!

From Mandalay by Rudyard Kipling

Contents

List of Illustrations

Abbreviated Glossary

Ba Moui Ba: Thirty-three, the name of the ubiquitous Vietnamese beer.

Co Van My: Vietnamese for American Advisor; "My" was pronounced "me."

Coe: Vietnamese for young woman; usually reserved by U.S. soldiers for attractive young women.

Chun Uy: Vietnamese for lieutenant, pronounced "chun we."

Dai Uy: Vietnamese for captain, pronounced "dai we."

DEROS: Date of estimated return from overseas tour; the date one was due to leave Vietnam.

Di-di-mau: The U.S. soldier's version of a Vietnam phrase meaning "go quickly."

EMs: Enlisted men.

ETS: For soldiers with a limited service obligation, which included just about everyone except Regular Army officers with an indefinite obligation, the date the limited service obligation was ended; in other words, the date one was due to get out of the Army.

Fire Team, or Fireteam: The smallest infantry unit, generally containing three to five soldiers. Two fire teams generally made up a squad, and two squads plus two machine gun teams generally made up a platoon.

LZ: Landing zone; in Vietnam, usually referring to a place where helicopters disembarked soldiers and supplies.

MACV: Military Assistance Command Vietnam; the overall U.S. military command in Vietnam, responsible for both U.S. forces and advisory activities; American advisors to Vietnamese units wore the MACV patch.

MAT: Mobile Advisory Team; the small teams the U.S. Army put together to train Vietnamese Regional and Local Forces.

Punji stick: A primitive VC booby trap; sharpened sticks, with a sharp end up, were placed in a shallow hole, which was camouflaged; a soldier stepping into the hole received a nasty wound; the VC sometimes covered the end of the stick with excrement in hopes of producing an infection in the wound.

Ruff/Puffs: Informal term of U.S. soldiers for Vietnamese Regional and Local Forces (RF/PF), which the MATs advised.

Sitrep: Situation report.

Acknowledgements

The cover and graphics are by Devon Cain.

J.B. Yowell and Rhonda Holland provided editorial comment.

NORTH
VIETNAM

Hue

Da Nang

THAILAND

LAOS

I CORPS

Dak To
Bong Song
Kontum
Pleiku   An Khe
Qui Nhon

SOUTH

CAMBODIA

Tuy Hoa
Ban Me Thout

II CORPS

Cam Ranh Bay

Mekong River

VIETNAM

III CORPS

Bien Hoa
Saigon

Cao Lanh

Can Tho

IV CORPS

100 Miles

0

100 Kilometers

They Had This War Once...

They had this war once. It was an odd war. For one thing, it went on forever, or at least it seemed to. It imprinted a generation, some members for the better, many for the worse. The truths about this war are hard to come by. Not so the myths. They called this war, Vietnam.

This is the third and final volume of a trilogy on my modest participation in what is becoming a long ago conflict, a conflict that is dimly remembered by the participants and is musty, confusing, and often boring history to newer generations. As I write, the nation is in the third year of another conflict that many are comparing, in various ways, to Vietnam. Some of the comparisons contain a degree of validity, others come across as ludicrously off the mark. For me, three similarities are compelling. First, in both instances the United States attempted to control a far corner of the planet with a relatively small number of troops. Superior technology was supposed to offset the lack of manpower. It ultimately didn't in Vietnam, and the experience thus far in Iraq has not met the initial optimistic expectations of those at the top of the command structure.

Which leads to the second similarity between the two conflicts: the top of the command structure, specifically the policy makers and implementers in the White Houses and upper reaches of the Defense Departments of Lyndon Johnson and George W. Bush. In both instances, those recommending and making policy seemed guided as much by hope for a successful outcome as by realistic, in-depth, hard-eyed, historically knowledgeable calculations of the likely costs and potential benefits. In both instances, the Department of Defense was led by a successful titan of the corporate world, an arrogant, number-crunching, efficiency expert who proved to have little understanding of the messy, nasty, brutal, dehumanizing nature of war.

And for the third similarity, in neither instance was there a universal belief that the nation was fighting for its immediate survival, as in World War II. Thus the national leadership was, and is, in a weak position to defend setbacks, apparent lack of progress, and misjudgments and mistakes that cost the lives of American soldiers. In the dark early days of World War II, Winston Churchill rallied the British people with words such as:

> *We shall fight on the beaches, we shall fight on the landing grounds, we shall fight in the fields and in the streets, we shall fight in the hills; we shall never surrender....*

And on another occasion:

> *[T]he Battle of Britain is about to begin. Upon this battle depends the survival of Christian civilisation. Upon it depends our own British life, and the long continuity of our institutions and Empire. The whole fury and might of the enemy must very soon be turned on us.... Let us therefore brace ourselves to our duty, and so bear ourselves that, if the British Empire and its Commonwealth last for a thousand years, men will still say: "This was their finest hour."*

The limited nature of their wars and the disagreements about the necessity of those wars to the survival of the nation precluded Presidents Johnson or Bush from such stirring appeals, even assuming such appeals were within their capabilities, or more accurately the capabilities of their speechwriters. Instead, rather than talking bluntly to the American people about the conflicts, rather than admitting setbacks and mistakes, all too often the motivational messages from the Johnson and Bush White Houses were, and are, when not outright distortions, little more than pabulum, centered on such phrases as "the light at the end of the tunnel," we are "making progress," we must "stay the course," and the insurgency is in its "last throes." Moreover, the messages were then and are now based on dubious domino theories: if we don't stop the commies in Vietnam, all Southeast Asia will fall under the hammer and sickle; if we don't stop the terrorists in Iraq, all Islam will fall under their sway.

Do these similarities between America's involvement in Iraq and its involvement in Vietnam mandate that the outcome in Iraq be similar to the outcome in Vietnam?

No. Significant differences exist between the two situations, differences that will likely override the common characteristic of high-level ineptness. Although in both situations America and its local ally faced an insurgency, in Vietnam they also faced a regular, main-force army, the North Vietnamese Army. That army was the ultimate victor, and then only because, after fifteen or so years of conflict, America got tired, picked up its marbles, and went home. Indeed, in Vietnam, the insurgency was, by the early 1970s, a relatively minor annoyance, just a shadow of what it had been.

In Iraq, America faces no main-force army. Its foes are an insurgency and, on a wider scale, an anti-modern, nihilistic, Islamic radicalism. America's task is complicated by its own less-than-impressive leadership, but the quality of its soldiers and diplomats on the ground may prove sufficient to offset the ineptness from above. If America were to pick up its marbles and go home, as it did in Vietnam, no modern military force is standing in the wings to fill the vacuum.

What is standing in the wings is most likely chaos. But a degree of chaos has been and is likely to remain a part of the Middle Eastern scene no matter what America does. Thus the challenge facing America is to find strategies that mitigate the chaos, that further the struggle against the real foe—which is anti-modern, nihilistic, Islamic radicalism—and that produce in Iraq itself a modicum of stability garnished with sprigs of democracy and tolerance. An ingredient of such strategies is certainly a lower profile in Iraq and a willingness to let Iraqis work out there own future, which may involve a dissolution into two or more semi-hostile semi-nations.

But I seriously digress. This trilogy is about the past. As I described at greater length in the introduction to the first volume, *Vietnam, A Memoir: Saigon Cop*, I was no hero, and no choirboy. Few of us were heroes, however, and choirboys were certainly not in the majority, so in these respects I was not unusual. What may be somewhat odd about me is that I admit to a certain liking for war. In other words, I am a form of war lover. The adrenalin rush of danger, of combat is something I wanted to experience, and after experiencing it, is something I remember with a certain fondness, a nostalgia. As Douglas MacArthur said in his farewell address at West Point:

> *I listen vainly for the witching melody of faint bugles blowing reveille, of far drums beating the long roll. In my dreams I hear again the crash of guns, the rattle of musketry, the strange, mournful mutter of the battlefield.*

Being a type of war lover is not something I'm particularly proud of. But I don't think I'm as unusual as might first appear. Ultimately, we have wars because we are drawn to them. We cloak them in purpose and patriotism, but deep down inside they appeal to something visceral and primitive in our being. Not everyone feels the appeal, but enough do to have made war a central part of the human experience.

And I am certainly not completely bereft of purpose and patriotism. I think the principles upon which this nation was founded and that we strive—with occasional success—to abide by, implement, and improve upon are the human animal at its best. I think these principles are—when the stakes are high enough—worth fighting, and dying, for.

For me in my youth, however, patriotism and high purpose were not how I viewed the growing conflagration in a far corner of the world. As described at greater length in the introduction to the first volume, genetically, educationally, and culturally I was programmed for a soldier, a somewhat rebellious soldier, not a peacetime by-the-numbers soldier, but still a soldier. A war appeared to be developing, lethargically at first, and I slowly realized I wanted to be part of it.

And after a few fits and starts, I did become a part of it. Indeed, I had an unusual war, starting off in the military police corps and ending up in the infantry. My Vietnam years were divided into four periods: August 1966 to early September 1967, when I was a military police lieutenant in Saigon; September 1967 to late January 1968, when I was an airborne infantry platoon leader in the Central Highlands, a period that included one of the most ferocious battles of the war, the Battle of Dak To; March 1968 to the last part of August 1968, when I suffered through the agony of a demanding but excruciatingly boring staff job; and November 1968 to late March 1969, when I was an advisor to a Vietnamese infantry battalion in the Mekong Delta.

Several other periods preceded or marked the boundaries of these four periods: the pre-Vietnam year; February 1968, when I was on home leave; and September 1968, when I was in Bangkok, Thailand. In addition, at times I was present in one sense but not in another. Two of these times stand out. I spent August 1967 drunker than nine skunks as I waited for an assignment to the infantry. And I spent October 1968 in the same condition as I tried to forget Bangkok and a little Thai girl and to avoid doing any work in the unit to which I had been assigned upon my return from Bangkok.

Saigon Cop, the first volume in the trilogy of my experiences, focused on the year in Saigon as a military police officer. In addition to describing the challenges, dangers, and irritations of U.S. military police work in the midst of a bustling Asian city in wartime, the volume told of my effort to join the branch of the Army that did the preponderance of the fighting, led the hardest existence, and suffered the most casualties during the Vietnam War: the infantry. That effort to transfer from the military police to the infantry was ultimately successful, and the second volume, *Airborne Trooper*, picked up the story. It was a tale that some would say exemplifies the old adage: be careful of what you wish for, you just might get it.

This final volume, *Mekong Mud Soldier*, is the story of my last Vietnam year. It begins with my first trip home in eighteen months, describes the staff officer's life I led, not very happily, upon my return to the war zone, and eventually gets to the main item: the advisory business in a little corner of the Mekong Delta. Many references in the first part of the book concern people, places, and events described in the previous volumes. Still, a reader who isn't familiar with those volumes should be able to pick up the story.

A friend who read a draft of the trilogy said that it is not a very uplifting tale. He's right. It is a story of five bs: booze, babes, bureaucracy, boredom, and occasionally battle. The tone of the trilogy—irreverent and cynical—is the tone both of a very irreverent and cynical period in the nation's history and of my own most jaded years of young adulthood. But I suspect that one group might not find the irreverence and cynicism strange: this group would consist of veterans of the current endeavors in Iraq and Afghanistan, and for that matter, veterans of the other "little" wars that the United States has engaged in over the last 30 years. Irreverence and cynicism get a soldier through the day.

Also, the tone is my personal very negative reaction to the Dudley Do-Right tone of far too many war memoirs, stories, books, movies, and television portrayals. If you want your soldiers perfect, their motivations unselfish, their conduct exemplary, their religious beliefs firm, and their leaders without flaws, this trilogy may not be for you.

Yet in spite of personal flaws and an overabundance of cynicism, sarcasm, and irreverence, I am proud, fiercely proud, of having been a soldier. I get a catch in my throat when the National Anthem, God Bless America, or a similar song is played. A fly-over by military aircraft has me yearning for a far-off battlefield. My composure is tested when a moving tribute to fallen American soldiers is read. Inconsistent you say? Welcome to the real world.

In deference to sensibilities and the privacy of individuals, most names in this narrative are fictitious. The assessments of some individuals are harsh. These assessments are subjective, the product of one whose own numerous faults and flaws have not prevented him from dwelling perhaps excessively on the perceived faults and flaws of others. Moreover, regardless of whether or not the assessments have any validity, the individuals were there, in Vietnam, in uniform, doing what their country asked of them, no matter how misguided that request may have been. Thus they are one-up on many of their contemporaries. With allowance for the usual embellishments of war stories, and subject to an occasional purposeful alteration or exaggeration, the events are as I remember them, again subjective impressions. If thirty soldiers were in a firefight, thirty different versions of what happened, of who performed admirably and who didn't, are quite possible. Finally, the dialogues are not intended to be verbatim renditions of long-ago conversations.

November 2005

PART I
REAR ECHELON FLUNKY

Home And Back

I arrived home in early February 1968. Behind me were eighteen months in Vietnam. I had been a Saigon cop and an airborne infantry platoon leader, and had survived the Battle of Dak To. Ahead was a month's leave, and then a return to the 'Nam.

Home hadn't changed much. My parents looked a little older, but being away for months at a time during college had gotten me accustomed to their aging. My sister Cary was a junior in college, at Old Dominion University in Norfolk. She was seriously dating Steve, a student at William & Mary. He had successfully wormed his way into my parents' affections, particularly my mother's. Rather than being jealous about this state of affairs, I was sort of glad. The fact that a son substitute had appeared on the scene eased my conscious a bit about returning to the 'Nam.

Most of the month at home has long faded from my memory. There was much sleeping and lounging around. The big news on television and in the papers was the Tet Offensive. The media was particularly enthralled with the attack on the embassy in Saigon and with the fighting around Tan Son Nhut and in Cholon. The events were being portrayed as a significant defeat for American forces.

I couldn't understand what the fuss was about. That the VC and NVA were able to mount sizeable offensives didn't surprise me—I had just survived a sizeable NVA offensive. That the VC were able to put forces in the middle of Saigon didn't surprise me—I had spent a year in Saigon responding to minor terrorist incidents and expecting a major one. That supposedly safe areas throughout the country were suddenly no longer considered safe didn't surprise me—I never considered much of any place safe.

What I didn't quite comprehend was that, unlike me, most of the country wanted an end to the war. Indeed, most of the country viewed war as an aberration, as something to be avoided, and if unavoidable, as something to be ended quickly. I, on the other hand, had come to view the Vietnam War as the natural state of affairs. The fact that progress toward an end was lacking was of no concern. Troopers came, spent their year, left, and the war went on. Instead of leaving after a year, some of them got wounded and left earlier. Some of them died. Whatever, it was just how things were.

Moreover, Vietnam had become my profession. I wasn't thinking beyond it, just about getting back for my next six months. And already the idea was percolating that I would put in for an additional six-month extension once I got back. My ETS from the Army was April 1969. Another extension would put me right up against the ETS. The only hurdle was that the Army had a policy of limiting the stays of officers in Vietnam to two years. I would have to plead for an exception, but such a plea might have a chance because an additional six months would fit so neatly with my remaining active duty obligation.

So the fuss about Tet was sort of lost on me. And in truth, very few people asked or talked to me about the war. Despite its omnipresence on the tube and in the papers, the war was not a topic of extensive conversation, at least among most of the people I encountered. Some of the avoidance of the subject was probably due to peoples' uncertainty about whether the topic should be raised with one who had just returned from the conflict. Some of the avoidance was probably due to the desire to get away from the pervasive, and depressing, media coverage. And some of the avoidance was probably due to an increasing ambivalence about the war. Not only was opposition growing on college campuses; it was also taking root in suburbia, among the middle classes. Those middle class Americans who had long supported without question the foreign policy of their nation were having doubts. They were disturbed by their uncertainties, and a common reaction was to bury the topic within.

I recall only two conversations about the war. The first was a brief one with my father who asked me to explain a diagram in *Life* magazine. The diagram was of the path taken by the projectiles of an exploding claymore mine. My father's familiarity with mines was limited to the World War II varieties, which generally had a circular bursting radius. He wasn't up on the principle of the claymore, which hurled pellets and shrapnel the length of a football field. The second conversation about war stuff was with the father of a fraternity brother, Nick. How I came to see Nick was the traumatic event of my home leave.

Contacting my ex-fiancée was not on my agenda when I arrived in the states. My beliefs were that the relationship was history, that no further action on my part was necessary, and that revisiting the past was something neither of us needed. In short, I had not intended to look JoAnn up, just to sneak in and out of the country as quietly as possible. My mother did suggest that I had some obligation to bring the relationship to a formal closure, but disappearing for 18 months in the 'Nam seemed formal enough to me.

Somebody snitched, however. About mid-way through my stay, I answered the phone and found myself talking to JoAnn's mother. Jesus H. Christ, just what I needed! "David, we heard you were back in town."

You did, huh? Well, who was the sonuvabitch that squealed? It mighta even been my own mother. "Yes ma'm. I'm only here for a few weeks. I'm going back shortly."

"Are you planning to talk to JoAnn? She's still at Mary Washington."

"Wellll, yuh know, I'm not here long. I'm goin' back very shortly."

"You ought to talk to her, David. She's dating someone fairly seriously, but you and she need to resolve your relationship." Hell, I thought it was resolved. I didn't need anyone to remind me what a bastard I was. "Why don't you come down for lunch? We can talk about it, and then you can decide whether you should see her or not." God, see the mother of my ex? Couldn't I get back to the 'Nam tomorrow? But being the coward that I was in the personal relationships area, I didn't have the balls to refuse a direct request to report and explain. So we made a luncheon date for her home, which was about 50 miles away. JoAnn's father would also be there. Great.

To say the lunch was awkward in the extreme is probably unnecessary. Small talk was the order of the day. JoAnn's father was polite but cool, like in cold. JoAnn's mother moved the meal along quickly, got the father back to work expeditiously, and settled in for a serious heart-to-heart. This was her specialty. She was of the complete openness school of personal relationships and conversation. She was Oprah before there was Oprah. And she was undeterred by the obvious Neanderthal across from her. Indeed, she appeared challenged. It isn't often that an advanced amateur psychiatrist can corner an insensitive lout for an extended examination.

It was a good thing I wasn't being charged for the analysis. The session lasted a good two hours. I adopted the approach I had taken in the letters to JoAnn when I first arrived in Saigon—the war lover approach—as she and I struggled with how to end a relationship we both knew was over. The adventure of Southeast Asia had completely captured me. Love for the action, the excitement, the adrenalin-rush had overridden any feelings I had for individuals. I was making a career of Vietnam and had no idea when I would be giving it up, assuming it didn't get me killed first. Although I didn't use the word, I tried to give the impression I was no better than a merc, a mercenary, a soldier of fortune, a killer for money. The portrayal certainly contained a considerable degree of accuracy, how much accuracy I didn't know at a conscious level, and still don't.

Mrs. Burdock didn't give up easily, but eventually my effort to convince her I was irredeemable appeared to be successful. I knew the inquisition was about over, and that she had written me off, when she asked, "Have you considered getting professional psychiatric help, David?"

I put the nail in the coffin: "No, Mrs. Burdock. I know it sounds bad, but I like the way I am, the way I feel. Vietnam hasn't changed me. It's just been an outlet for who I am. If it hadn't been Vietnam, it would eventually have had to be something else. I got things inside me that Vietnam satisfies." It was melodramatic, but it did the trick. She sighed, and there was a long silence as we both pondered my insanity. Finally she said:

"Well, I think you need to see JoAnn before you go back. She deserves that, to have the relationship formally ended. Will you promise me you'll see her?" Shit. I suspected this was much more about her than about JoAnn. But anything to get this session over with. I needed a beer bad.

"Yes, I'll do that."

"Good. And I hope you come through this okay, David. I hope you overcome whatever it is that's devouring you."

I didn't think anything in particular was devouring me, but she was the analyst. I was just happy to be outta there. We parted. I toyed with the idea of not doing what I promised, but I feared Mrs. B. would track me all the way back to the 'Nam. So in a day or so I found myself on the phone with JoAnn. The call was obviously not unexpected. She knew about the lunch with her family, and even seemed to evince a little sympathy regarding the grilling I had undergone. She knew her mother well. We made a date for a few days hence.

In the meantime, I had been contacted by Nick, who lived in Washington, D.C, and was attending law school at George Washington University. He was getting married in the summer and wanted me to be part of the festivities. He had learned earlier from my mother that I might be back sometime around February, and had called. I thanked him for the invite but told him I would be over in the jungle when he was engaged in the nuptials. I told him of my pending visit with JoAnn in Fredericksburg, and he said, "Why don't you continue on to D.C. for a day or so?"

So I set off for my visit—date doesn't sound like the proper term—with JoAnn and a stay with Nick. She kept me waiting in the dormitory lounge area for a considerable time. Several of her friends paraded through, giving the sonuvabitch the once over. Maybe if they could identify a tell-tale characteristic, they could avoid JoAnn's fate of getting involved with a shithead. The girls of Mary Washington were a bit closer to the war than were students at many other colleges. The Marine Corps platoon leaders course was conducted at Quantico, just 25 miles up the road. A number of Mary Washington girls dated jarheads, and there had been more than a few tearful goodbyes. The ultimate price of the war, death, had a much greater presence than at the typical U.S. institution of higher learning.

Finally, JoAnn appeared. Her hair was different, shorter and not as girlish, but she looked awfully good. The next few hours were awkward, but not excruciating like the session with her mother. JoAnn seemed to have long since accepted the situation and had no desire to rekindle anything. As her mother had said, she had a serious boyfriend and spent a good deal of the time talking about that relationship. Which was fine with me. I didn't have to put on the war lover act, or fact, as I did with her mother, but it was comforting to know that the defense was readily available.

On the surface, our parting did not approach what a reader of romance novels or watcher of tear-jerker movies would want. We simply said goodbye. And as much as I hated to admit it, her mother was right: the meeting was something we needed to have done. I left with ambiguities and uncertainties. Only in novels and the movies are things clear cut.

I went on to D.C. and Nick's place. He was living with his parents while attending law school. His father had been a Marine in World War II. I arrived about 10 p.m., and Nick, his father, and I settled in for some heavy drinking. It was Chivas Regal, well beyond my usual alcohol of choice, beer. The stuff went down like water, and I was soon drunker than nine dogs. We talked about the war. Nick's father and I got into a discussion about the relative merits of the 81-mm mortar versus the 60-mm mortar. The latter weapon was standard with the Marines, and had been back in World War II. It was much lighter than the 81, a fact that I had thought about a number of times as Oscar—the Weapons Platoon—wrestled its tube, base plate, and cumbersome heavy rounds over hill and dale. So late into the night, a pompous earnest young drunk talked mortars with a bemused old drunk, two businessmen discussing the tools of their trade. I became so snookered that when I finally retired I went into the wrong bedroom and attempted to crawl in bed with Nick's mother. It was an understanding household, however, and I was directed in the proper direction.

The next day Nick drove me around D.C. on a few errands, his and mine. He showed me his law review office at George Washington. I was too ill-informed to realize that being on the law review was an honor. I missed meeting his bride-to-be, Carol. It would be several years before I met her and had to cope with the question, what great thing had Nick done to be rewarded with someone so obviously above him?

Nick had beaten the draft by joining the D.C. National Guard. He made no bones about his motivation, having zero desire to go to Vietnam or to spend any but the minimum required amount of time in uniform. But he had been called to active duty several times to guard against anticipated disturbances and other shenanigans. And we of course didn't know it at the time, but he still had the Martin Luther King assassination riots ahead of him. His stories of protecting D.C. from hippie anti-war protestors had made him something of a military expert at the law review. He introduced me around as a real combat veteran, but there was obviously a disconnect. To these law students, what happened on the streets of D.C. seemed of much greater interest than events on the other side of the world.

Next we went to a military personnel office, the assignment office for infantry officers. I wanted to see if I could get a feel for where I might be assigned for my final six months if I came home after the upcoming six months. Naturally, no one would venture a likelihood. The office was pretty much pandemonium, and I left dissatisfied, both informationally and emotionally. I suppose I thought a visitor from the combat zone should be accorded a bit more attention, maybe even a little reverence. But I was just another clown demanding time.

I returned home the next day. And after another week, it was time to leave the Land of the Big PX. Although I hadn't paid a great deal of attention to the war news, one item in my final days at home grabbed me. In response to the Tet offensive, President Johnson was ordering more troops to Vietnam. One of the units was a brigade of the 82nd Airborne Division from Ft. Bragg. The 82nd was the home unit for many Army paratroopers. They might rotate to another unit for a tour, but they always returned to the 82nd. In addition, for those young paratroopers not making the Army a career, those two-year draftees and three-year enlistees, the 82nd was often where they started off and finished up even if most of their time was spent elsewhere. Thus paratroopers completing their tours in Vietnam—both lifers and short-timers—were likely to end up in the 82nd. Many of those who had left the 173rd Airborne Brigade during my months there—Harold Campton, for example—were at Ft. Bragg.

Not many of these guys wanted to return to the 'Nam. The newsreel footage of Johnson reviewing the troops at Ft. Bragg showed a lot of grim visages. Reportedly, Johnson was greatly affected. I scanned the brief shots of the ranks, looking for familiar faces. The vague thought began to intrude into my thick skull that perhaps the nation was lurching toward some sort of decision point regarding its Vietnam involvement.

The disquiet I felt watching the brigade of the 82nd preparing to depart contributed to a growing ambivalence I was developing about my own return. For one thing, I didn't have a job and would likely end up in some staff position. About the only field position available was company commander, and given the competition for these slots, getting one was pretty much out of the question for me. For another thing, I had gotten used to sleeping late, to having no responsibilities. But the option of staying home didn't exist, so one day at the beginning of March 1968 I said goodbye to the family and boarded a flight to McCord Air Force Base outside Seattle. I stayed there overnight and then flew on one of the civilian charters to Cam Ranh Bay. The passengers weren't actually somber, but they were certainly more subdued than those on my flight of a month before going the other way. I was kind of subdued myself.

At An Khe, there was disturbing news. Gary Kline was still the Alpha Company XO. He now operated from the 173rd base camp at An Khe itself. I ran into him shortly after I arrived. He said that the month since my departure had been a bad one for Alpha Company. The main trouble occurred one long afternoon near Ban Me Thuot, in central Vietnam. The company had gone to the area from where I had left it south of Pleiku. On the day in question, the company had moved a short distance and set up a laager site before noon. Mike, the Second Platoon, was sent on an afternoon patrol. A crucial mistake was made right off when apparently no one took any smoke grenades. A few clicks from the laager site, Mike stumbled into a bunker complex—an occupied bunker complex. The platoon became pinned down and unable to extract itself. Because of the absence of smoke grenades, it could not mark its position for an air controller and an airborne artillery forward observer. The number of wounded, some seriously, gradually mounted. Mike was in deep shit.

Wolfowitz, the new Company Commander, called in the other rifle platoons, which were also on patrols, and mounted a rescue attempt. Whether he acted with sufficient alacrity was a matter of dispute. Apparently some at battalion felt he needed considerable prodding.

Even if that judgment was unfair, Wolfowitz's lack of command presence certainly contributed to a general impression of indecisiveness.

One of Wolfowitz's decisions regarding the rescue attempt was the subject of considerable second-guessing. The laager site was abandoned, with everyone heading for Mike. Leaving packs and supplies was one thing, but the mortar and its ammunition were also left behind, although an effort was made to hide them. It wasn't clear why the mortar couldn't have made the journey. In any case, the 15 or so mortar men of Oscar became reluctant riflemen. I can imagine their anger and frustration. The mortar was their reason for being, and they had proved its usefulness and effectiveness on Hill 882, although that apparently wasn't generally recognized. The one person who would probably have argued forcefully and convincingly enough for an alternative course of action was not there. Harold Campton had DEROSed.

So the rest of Alpha Company went charging to the rescue. Kline had been at the laager site on business and went along. For him, I think the day partially made up for the action he did not see at Dak To. When the rescue column got close to Mike, a rough line was formed. It inched forward. Mike wasn't being charged by the Charlies, but it was subject to fire from a number of automatic weapons and couldn't pull back without help. The rescue line reached Mike without too much difficulty. The more seriously wounded were extracted from the immediate front. The plan then apparently became to advance into the bunker complex, both to aid in the complete extraction of Mike and to beat Charlie's butt. First Sergeant Duckett called for a "mad minute" of fire before the advance. Only Charlie responded with a "madder minute," which inflicted a number of casualties. Several were in Lima, the First Platoon and my first command in the field. Henderson, the Indiana farm boy who was one of the M-60 machine gunners, died instantly with a round in the forehead. The idea of advancing was abandoned, and the company beat a retreat, leaving the field to Charlie.

All in all, it had been a worse day for Alpha Company than November 18, 1967, on Hill 882. The casualties were at least as great, and there was nothing to show for it. At day's end, Charlie controlled the ground. The standard exaggerated body count of enemy dead was even more problematic than usual. One outcome of the fight was that Wolfowitz was relieved of command. The new battalion commander—Shafter had departed—flew out several days later with one of the captains who had been on the battalion staff when I first arrived at the 173rd the previous September. Wolfowitz was summarily told he was finished, and departed on the same chopper.

The day at Ban Me Thuot was not the only bad one for my former company. Montdragon, the tough little guy who Captain Jerome had prodded me into defending back in Tuy Hoa when he didn't unass a chopper quickly enough, had been killed by a nervous FNG—fuckin' new guy. The company had been on the move. At a stop, Montdragon went a few meters off the trail to crap. As he was returning, the FNG put a burst into him. Then there was my old semi-nemesis, Sgt. Hikaey. He had DEROSed to Hawaii. Within two weeks of leaving the 'Nam, he bought the farm in a car accident. And there were others. Perhaps for the first time, the war seemed depressing to me.

I reacted by throwing a memorable drunk. Kline introduced me to An Khe's most notorious feature, one that had been the subject of news and commentary all the way back in the World. A small town existed outside the base. It contained the usual collection of Vietnamese lives and businesses, buttressed by those attracted to serve the vast home of the First Air Cav. At the edge of town stood a large structure that resembled a fort, more particularly a Spanish or southwest U.S. style fort. Its outside surface or wall was an adobe-appearing material, burnt-orange in color. The wall was actually the rear of a number of small side-by-side buildings that were arranged in a square. Another group of connected buildings stood in the center of the square. A single large entrance-way controlled ingress and egress. The entrance-way was guarded by MPs, giving a seal of semi-official approval to the place.

What the An Khe fort provided were booze and babes, lots of both. The buildings inside were bars and whorehouses. One of the functions of the MPs was to keep out drugs. I don't know how successful they were. I didn't see any drugs during my couple of visits, but as an officer I wouldn't have ordinarily been offered hallucinogenics.

Kline and I spent a long afternoon sampling the wares. He limited himself to the booze, and that sparingly. I was more glutinous. We got a few mean looks from troopers who resented what they considered to be their turf being invaded by officers, but a small number of other commissioned gentlemen were also making the rounds. Most were lieutenants with the dirty and disheveled look of those just out of the field. As a captain, I seemed to be the highest ranking guy around. I felt that put a special burden on me, and I responded by showing the other patrons how to raise hell.

The fort ceased operations before dusk. Unlike some of the metropolitan areas of the country, An Khe and environs closed down to U.S. troops at night. The Americans retreated to the relative safety of the base. Kline and I made it back just as the gate was closing. We went to his quarters, which had an extra cot, and on which I promptly passed out. Several hours later I was revived by the sound of voices. Kline, a conscientious workaholic, was sitting at a desk, apparently interrupted from an evening of paperwork. The guy hadn't had near as much to drink as I did, but he'd still imbibed generously. How he could work after an afternoon of debauchery was beyond me. The voices were his and a trooper from Lima, my first platoon.

I recognized him as Ross, a rifleman. He had been one of those who had defended PFC Moste those many moons ago in Tuy Hoa when I expressed unease about the mutilation of a dead VC. Back in those days, he was a gung ho, cold, steely-eyed, hard-charging paratrooper hankering for action. Now he looked tired, beaten. He had been through Dak To and Ban Me Thuot. Of the approximately 30 members of Lima when I became platoon leader, over 20, probably close to 25, had been killed or wounded. Fortunately, the ratio of wounded to killed was high, but still an 80 percent casualty rate was pretty damn stiff. Ross had seen Baum, Washington, Montdragon, and Henderson killed. The wounded included his buddy Moste. Not much thinking was required to realize that what the MACV press people looking at the big picture would call a modest contact could be the decimation of a platoon. Ross had obviously figured that the odds of him surviving another contact were not good. As I regained consciousness, I heard him say, "I don't wanna go back to the field, Lieutenant. My luck's not gonna last much longer. Ain't there somethin' I can do back in the rear?"

"We might be able to do something. Why don't ya just hang 'round An Khe for a couple 'a days. I'll see what we can come up with."

"Thanks, Lieutenant. I don't think I could survive another firefight." At about that time, I groggily struggled up from my prone position on the cot. "How ya doin' Lieutenant Holland, oh, it's Captain now? You ain't lookin' too good."

"Well, that's cuzz I ain't feeling too good. Lieutenant Kline there got me drunker'n nine dogs. How you doing, Ross?"

"Okay. Lieutenant Kline's gonna get me outta the field. We've had a bad run 'a luck, Sir. Didja hear about Montdragon?"

"Yeah, that's bad, damn bad. Gettin' greased by an FNG ain't no way to go. Just piss poor."

"Yeah, well I gotta run. Thanks a lot Lieutenant Kline. I really 'preciate it."

"Okay. Just lay low and check with me in a couple'a days."

After he left, I said to Kline: "Damn, he's changed. They musta really been hammered. How'd he get outta the field?"

"R&R. He just got back."

"Can you find him a job back here?"

"Yeah. There's a lot of these guys around. You find nooks and crannies for 'em. A year in the field only works if you get no contact. Stuff like the company's seen over the last four months shouldn't be suffered by these guys. You get them outta the field if ya can."

The next day I flew to the brigade's forward base camp, which was now at Pleiku. The brigade had been given a small corner of another large hunk of transplanted Americana—the 4th Infantry Division's base camp. As with An Khe, the 4th Division's base camp was a place of permanent structures, paved roads, and mowed lawns, although the 173rd's temporary portion of it was a bit less permanent. The brigade's forward elements were housed mostly in large tents with wooden floors. I located the 1st Battalion's small enclave. A captain was in charge. He was vaguely aware of who I was and my status. He implied that there was an over-abundance of captains and finding a place for me might take a little time. In the meantime, I should just plan on hanging around for a few days.

Running Alpha Company's forward area was Sgt. Hernandez, my last platoon sergeant, of November, the Third Platoon. He had recently left the field in preparation for his DEROS, which was about six weeks away. His job was to push A Company's supplies forward, and to control the company's transients. I found an empty cot in his bailiwick and settled in for what looked like a good little wait.

During our conversations over the next couple of days, he elaborated on the fight at Ban Me Thuot and on Wolfowitz's brief tenure as company commander. According to Sgt. Hernandez, Wolfowitz just couldn't get it right. He made lousy decisions about laager sites, had great trouble with the map, and didn't have anyone's confidence. One example of the bad laager site decisions particularly had Hernandez shaking his head. Wolfowitz put the company in the middle of a field that was surrounded on all sides by woods. Although the fields of fire for the 25 or so meters to the tree lines were good, anything beyond that was well hidden. And the company's actions and movements were in full view of any prying eyes. The normal course would have been to laager in the trees, at least partially, with the field as one side of the laager site. As for the Ban Me Thuot action, Sgt. Hernandez wasn't particularly critical of Wolfowitz, except for leaving the mortar behind.

Hernandez was more vituperative about Mike's getting itself pinned down in the first place, and about the platoon not having any smoke grenades to mark its position.

During one of my nights with Sgt. Hernandez, Charlie put on a show, conducting a prolonged rocket attack on the base. Hernandez, myself, and several Alpha Company transients were sitting around the tent's entrance when a siren began blaring. Hernandez yelled, "Incoming! Hit the bunker!" In back of the tent was a large sandbag-covered bunker. We all grabbed our steel pots and weapons and ran for cover. Only no one actually went inside. The bunker had been dug a long time previously, and any number of strange tropical varmints could have taken up residence inside. So we lay on the ground or on the bunker's top.

A few explosions rumbled from distant parts of the base. The impacts continued intermittently. Since nothing was landing nearby, we relaxed and began taking in the setting. The night was exceptionally clear, with the stars bright against the black sky. The brigade's area was on a small rise, and no trees hindered visibility. We had an unobstructed view toward the nearest portion of the perimeter, and to the rolling country beyond. Charlie's firing positions turned out to be in that rolling country. As we watched, trails of sparks and fire rose into the sky. The trails began a high, lazy arch toward us before the propellants of the rockets burned out. After a pause of some seconds as the warheads sliced silently and invisibly through the night, the sounds of explosions far to our rear, near the center of the camp, reached us. Eventually, helicopter gunships arrived in the vicinity of the VC firing positions. Red tracer rounds began a downward journey in search of fabric and flesh.

Surprisingly, the appearance of the gunships did not bring an immediate halt to the incoming rockets. The firing positions were separated by up to a click, and it took the choppers a bit of time to discourage the operators at each one. Eventually, the show was over. It was a long time, however, before the desire for sleep overcame the beauty and mystery of the tropical night.

After a few days, I finally was instructed to report to the battalion fire support base. I was to be the battalion S-2, the staff intelligence officer. I didn't have the training for it, but battalion S-2s didn't have a real demanding job. An energetic ambitious guy could make something of it, but someone lacking the motivation could get by with doing very little. The vast amount of intelligence analysis work was done at brigade and higher levels. Battalion S-2s were barely even conduits for intelligence findings, most of the stuff coming down through the S-3, or operations, channels. So I wasn't particularly excited about the prospective job.

A chopper carried me out to the battalion. The fire support base was in a large open field. I had never really paid much attention to the organization of the battalion field headquarters and TOC—tactical operations center—so I was now having my first good look. The nerve center was a semi-buried conex container that had been outfitted with shelves for communications and related equipment. The radios were in contact with the line companies, with the next higher headquarters, and with supporting artillery units. At least two soldiers monitored the radios, with shifts operating around the clock. The entrance to the TOC was a stairway cut into the ground. When the fire support base was moved, a Chinook slung-loaded the conex container to the new location.

Because the TOC was so small, much of the staff work was done in a five-sided tent, which was surrounded by a three-foot high sandbag wall. The tent contained a few field desks and chairs, and maps on easels. The main map showed the current locations of the battalion's combat elements. Small radios in the tent enabled the occupants to overhear the radio traffic and permitted the S-3 or the battalion commander to break in if he saw fit. As units called in sitreps to the TOC, the maps in both the TOC and the tent were updated.

Housed near the TOC and the headquarters tent was the fire direction center. It contained the brains of the Four-Deuce Platoon and the
artillery battery—the radios and calculation equipment for providing
fire support. Often the fire direction center was also a two-element
affair, with a buried conex container and a sandbagged tent.

Sleeping arrangements varied. This was the dry season, so overhead
shelter was not a major concern. The members of the battalion headquarters group were haphazardly dispersed, some under large tarps,
some just in the open. The artillery and four-deuce people also seemed
spread out, although a portion were congregated in large field tents.
The battalion commander had his own five-sided tent. He slept on a
cot, the only one among the headquarters group. A few of the artillery
and four-deuce people, however, also had cots.

The new battalion CO, LTC Shafter's replacement, was out in his
chopper when I arrived. Maj. Sills was the S-3, the operations officer,
and as such the guy who was the operational second in command. Sills
had been around for awhile, since at least before Dak To, where he had
performed admirably. Another member of the headquarters group was
Lt. Charlie Jones, formerly of Charlie Company and now the S-3 Air.
The artillery liaison officer was a ring-knocker, a West Point graduate.
He had been the quarterback of the football team. One of the University of Virginia's memorable, and few, football victories during my
days there had been over Army, and he had been Army's quarterback. I
probably mentioned the game more than I should have.

Maj. Sills gave me a briefing on the battalion's situation and my
duties, such as they were. As I suspected, battalion S-2 did not appear
to be a demanding position. Sills also hinted that the new battalion
commander left something to be desired. Later Charlie Jones was less
circumspect: "The guy's a fuckin' idiot." It seemed that the new CO
had little concept of what movement was like in the jungles of Vietnam
and little familiarity with basic map-reading. According to Charlie
Jones, the CO gave orders that had companies traversing the sides of

mountains and attempting impossible distances. Contour lines were apparently Greek to him.

With this introduction, I awaited the arrival of the man himself. His chopper came in about mid-afternoon. From out of the door strode an overweight middle-aged man in a baggy uniform. The first thought that went through my mind was that a lot of buttons had been pushed to get this guy the command of a paratroop battalion in combat. As the Army started the fourth year of the involvement of ground combat units in Vietnam, it must have been running out of battalion commanders. Those needing to get their tickets punched to enhance their promotion possibilities were coming out of the woodwork, and resisting their entreaties for their shot was apparently becoming more and more difficult. My interview with the CO only enhanced the impression of a guy totally out of his element. He belonged back in the bowels of the Pentagon, counting the commas in defense contracts.

And that wasn't just my opinion. Within a few days of my arrival, LTC Blimp was gone, relieved of command. Whether there was a precise infraction, I don't know. I suspect his general incompetence was so obvious that brigade wanted him out of there before any of the battalion's companies had a significant contact.

In the meantime, I slumped into boredom and depression. The days were interminable, the minutes dragging and the hours creeping at a snail's pace. The S-2 job consisted of nothing I could sink my teeth into. I have never been good with ill-defined jobs, and the S-2 job was about as ill-defined as you could get. Moreover, I in truth had no desire to sink my teeth into much of anything. The fresh memory of the month at home sleeping late with no responsibilities made me pretty much of a basket case. The only thing I could concentrate on was, "six more months of this shit? How the hell will I handle it?" Sitting around the operations tent in the heat with nothing to do made sleep the most attractive thing in my existence by far, and within a day I began to indulge the desire for shut-eye by sneaking off to my air mattress. The problem was that the air mattress was in full view of everyone.

On the second or third day, the arrival of a Mike Force at the fire support base served to accentuate my unhappiness. Mike Forces were the Special Forces-led Montegnard or Chinese Nung units that performed various missions, mostly of a reconnaissance nature, in out-of-the-way corners of the country. This particular Mike Force appeared on foot. It had been on a patrol of several weeks duration in the nearby mountains. It consisted of three or four Americans and 75 or so ethnics. The force, including the Americans, were dressed in tiger suits—black and green camouflaged fatigues with the camouflage pattern being sharp horizontal streaks. Tiger suits wagged my needle in the extreme. What I wanted to be doing was sneaking around in a tiger suit leading a bunch of cut-throat Chinese mercs, not sitting on my butt in the middle of a hot field, watching the situation map being updated.

The battalion was only at the fire support base in the field for five or six days, but it seemed like an eternity. It was to be a prelude for the next six months, however. I was destined to spend a full half year as a staff flunky, although most of the time was in a position requiring beaucoup work. That position was a few weeks hence. In the meantime, I made half-hearted efforts to come to grips with my non-job.

Our departure for a new locale and the arrival of a new battalion commander occurred pretty close to simultaneously. LTC Blimp had been visited by the brigade commander and told of his relief. Blimp packed his things, got in his chopper, and departed without any good-byes. Maj. Sills oversaw the move to a new fire support base. It was located some distance away, in a broad valley near the Cambodian border. The valley contained a Special Forces A Camp and a runway that could accommodate two-engine Caribous. The fire support base was situated at the opposite end of the runway from the Special Forces camp, which was off-limits to the paratroopers. The Sneaky Petes didn't want anyone to see how well they lived.

The new fire support base was on a bare little hillock. The ground was rock-hard, making digging in extremely difficult. Consequently, many of the facilities that were normally below ground were practically unprotected. Some sandbags were filled on the other side of the airstrip and trucked to the fire support base, but not enough to shield everything. The sleeping quarters for the headquarters group were randomly located around the conex TOC, which was protected by no more than a two-foot layer of sandbags.

As the base was being set up, the line companies were deploying into the surrounding area. Alpha Company unloaded from Chinooks landing on the runway. The troopers had a wait before Hueys would carry them out to an AO, and I went down to say hello. A number of new faces peppered the group, but a lot of the old guys were still around. I saw that Stucky, a black trooper, was an RTO in November, and that was when it dawned on me how "white" the platoon headquarters had been during my tenure. I didn't stay long. I felt out-of-place, and envious. These guys were doing what soldiers were supposed to do, and I was a rear echelon flunky. I trudged back up the hill, more than ever despairing of my non-job.

LTC Gundersen was the new battalion commander. He had been the brigade S-1. He was a bundle of energy, a type A+ personality. Since at the moment I was the antithesis of a type A personality, a conflict was highly probable. And it came quickly. About the third afternoon, I was sacked out on my air mattress 15 or so meters down the hill from the TOC and the headquarters tent. A tarp partially concealed the sleeping area, but my jungle boot-clad feet were prominently visible to anyone walking by. LTC Gundersen walked by. I learned this because a short time later Charlie Jones was kicking my boots: "Get up Cap'n Holland! The CO saw ya down here and is mad as hell. He don't want no sleepin' in the afternoon." I stumbled up, wondering what the point of being awake was if I didn't have anything to do.

So for the next few days I tried to keep regular hours. The desire for sleep, however, was overpowering, and there was nothing to keep my mind off it. A few times I traveled to far corners of the fire support base for a little shut-eye. When I was around Gundersen, I tried to look busy, but it was difficult, and he seemed to have already pegged me as a dullard. One day one of the companies came across a large cache of clothes and equipment. The stuff was about two Huey-loads worth and was transported to the fire support base. I figured the S-2, the intelligence officer, should have some interest in such items. Therefore, I made a pretense of going through it, but I fooled neither Gundersen nor myself. I soon pulled out a few possible souvenirs for my own use and went in search of a nap spot.

An attack on a supporting fire support base a few nights later probably sealed my fate. Our location was such that we were out of artillery range of any other U.S. unit. Therefore, to provide for a little artillery support, the Four-Deuce Platoon was separated from the 105-mm howitzer battery and placed on a nearby mountain top. That way, the Four-Deuce Platoon could provide close-in fires for the main fire support base, which in turn could provide close-in fires for the Four-Deuce Platoon's base. "Mutually supporting" was the concept. A problem was that there wasn't much to the four-deuce's base. It consisted only of the four mortars, the platoon's headquarters and fire direction center, and a small perimeter guard. Moreover, the nature of the base was such that secrecy suffered. The registering of the guns and the subsequent H&I firing resulted in the location being known to even the densest NVA commander in the area. A little reconnaissance would quickly reveal the base's minuscule size and bare-bones defenses.

A couple of nights after the base was established, I was scheduled to be the TOC duty officer. I didn't have a good grasp on what this task required, and no one was particularly forthcoming. When I asked the RTOs in the conex container whether the duty officer remained with them all night, one said, "Ah, you don't have'ta do that, Sir. We'll come get ya if anything happens."

"Well, okay. I'm gonna move my air mattress right outside. Just get me if the shit hits the fan." I also figured that even if they didn't get me, I would hear any commotion and be on top of the action, or at least appear to be.

I figured wrong. NVA sappers hit the four-deuce base shortly after midnight, getting inside the perimeter and causing a number of casualties, including Lt. Storch, formerly of Charlie Company and now the Four-Deuce Platoon leader, and his platoon sergeant. The TOC RTOs went directly to the S-3 and the battalion commander. The desultory 105-mm H&I fires were replaced with a heavy prolonged bombardment of the slopes of the four-deuce's hill. Flares lit up the whole valley. Traffic into and out of the TOC conex was heavy and continuous as the battalion leadership sought information and strove to contain the situation. The entire fire support base was awake and engaged in activity with one exception. Young Captain Holland was zonked on his air mattress a few feet to the side of the conex but in more than plain view.

Finally, a hurrying figure stumbled over me. I groggily awoke, slowly becoming aware of all the action. The conex door banged each time someone entered or left, usually at a trot. I struggled up, put on my steel pot, grabbed my weapon, and entered the conex. I soon grasped the details of what was happening. I also grasped that by sleeping through much of it, I had most likely closed the door of the doghouse I was already deeply in. During a brief lull in the activity, I whispered to one of the RTOs: "Why didn't you guys wake me?"

"Sorry, Sir. We just got the battalion commander right away." But he didn't sound very sorry.

The four-deuce base made it through the night. By shortly after dawn, the few NVA who had gotten into the perimeter had been killed, and those outside faded away. Choppers arrived with reinforcements and to evacuate the wounded. Comfort had been the cause of the wounding of Lt. Storch and his platoon sergeant. They had been sleeping on cots, the only two in the Four-Deuce Platoon. A mortar round or a grenade exploded on the ground near their sleeping area, and the shrapnel caught anything a few feet in the air in the immediate vicinity. The Alpha Company trooper who died in his jungle hammock back in Tuy Hoa some months before had also been a comfort casualty. Fortunately for Storch and his platoon sergeant, their wounds weren't life-threatening or permanently disabling, just multiple holes in the body. It was Storch's sixth Purple Heart. I was envious.

I was also gone. No one said anything, but the coldness radiated in my direction by LTC Gundersen and the rest of the battalion staff, even the enlisted men, told the story. Gundersen's opportunity to rid himself of his do-nothing sleep-addicted captain came only a day or so later in the form of a levy from brigade. An assistant to the brigade S-1 was needed, 1st Battalion was tapped, and I was on a chopper back to Pleiku. No one was happier that I was on my way than me. The downside was that I was headed for another staff job.

Assistant S-1

At Pleiku, I left the 1st Battalion area in search of my new home. It wasn't impressive, a five-sided tent with several field desks and cots. The occupants were Capt. Dennis Hemp and PFC John B. Sweat. Hemp was the acting brigade S-1. LTC Gundersen had been the brigade S-1 before taking over the 1st Battalion, and Hemp had been the assistant S-1. Hemp's branch was Infantry. Before coming to the brigade staff, he had been a platoon leader in B Company of the 1st Battalion. He was due to DEROS shortly. A replacement S-1 was expected but the arrival date was uncertain. Thus there was a chance that I might end up as the acting S-1, an unappealing prospect.

Hemp was an enthusiastic staff guy. In fact, he let it be known fairly early that he had a branch transfer to the AG Corps pending. When I learned this, my opinion of him went down a notch, but what the hell, I was now a staff guy too, just not an enthusiastic one. Although Hemp had been on the line, and sported a CIB, he apparently hadn't seen a lot of action. This became apparent when the clerk, John B. Sweat, started grilling me about Dak To. I told a few war stories that Hemp feigned disinterest in, even irritation with, and that Sweat ate up. Sweat increased Hemp's irritation by saying, "Captain Hemp spent Dak To guarding a fire support base."

John B. Sweat was a wise guy, an extremely likable wise guy, but a wise guy nevertheless. He was also one of the top three or four memorable characters of my Vietnam years. A slender guy from New Jersey, he barely looked his 18 years. He had signed up right out of high school to avoid the draft. The fact that he went to jump school showed that he had a degree of gung-honess, but it was a constrained, ambivalent gung-honess. He was lovesick over his high school honey, and that might have had something to do with his attitude. He was also extremely bright, which maybe meant he realized more than some other 18 and 19 year-olds just how precarious was the life of an infantryman.

And that was the source of much mental agony on the part of John B. Sweat—he was trained as an infantryman. When he had arrived in-country and at the brigade the previous October, he fully expected to be in a rifle company. His record, however, indicated he had typing ability, and he was side-tracked to fill a clerical vacancy in the S-1 shop. A part of him welcomed the reprieve. But a part of him was the guy who volunteered for jump school and knew he was missing the Great Adventure, an Adventure that could get him killed but an Adventure nevertheless. Over the months ahead, these two parts of John B. Sweat were to battle for control. At times, these internal battles were violent enough to make John B. Sweat, though an interesting character, a real pain in the ass.

In general, the brigade S-1 was the staff section responsible for personnel matters. The brigade had a large AG Company that did the massive amount of administrative paperwork required to keep the unit running. The AG Company was headed by a Major and was located at An Khe. The S-1 had staff supervision of the AG Company but didn't really get into its business. The S-1 was more of a firefighter office, putting out such fires, mostly in the personnel area, as the brigade commander saw fit to focus on. The S-1 could also be viewed as a conduit, routing personnel-related requests of the brigade commander to the proper place.

An important daily duty of the S-1 was to compile the foxhole strength for the late afternoon briefing for the brigade commander. The foxhole strength was the number of line company troopers actually in the field—not the theoretical or TO&E (table of organization and equipment) strength, not the morning report strength, but the number of bodies physically out humping the boonies. The revealing thing about the foxhole strength was the relatively small proportion of troopers who were performing their assigned jobs at any one time. The TO&E strength of a line company might be 175. If 110 troopers were actually in the field, however, most company commanders would be content. If a long-time company commander had 125, he would feel Herculean. The shortfalls between the TO&E and foxhole strengths were due to in- and out-processing, R&R, malaria and other ills, casualties, short-timers hiding in rear-echelon jobs, you name it.

The foxhole strength was posted by battalion. During this period, the battalions were generally operating with four line companies. A low battalion foxhole strength would be below 400. A high strength would be above 500. Getting the foxhole strength was no mean task, and my introduction to the process was also an introduction to a focal point of my life for the next five months. That focal point was the field telephone.

Other than operational communications, most communications in Vietnam outside the semi-permanent bases were via the field phone. This was a hand-cranked instrument that required the user to spin a little handle to get the operator's attention. The user then gave the operator the destination of the call, and the operator attempted to make the connection. The telephone was connected to the operator's switchboard by wire. From the switchboard to the destination, the call might be routed completely through wire—or "land line" as it was called—or might go to a radio and then through the air. The radio route was the more difficult, and sometimes unavailable for several days. Even a land line connection was frequently hard to establish.

The upshot was that making phone calls from the S-1 tent was not like making a call back in the World. Considerable cranking was usually necessary just to get the operator. And then the operator had to struggle to find an appropriate free path. Crossed lines, wrong connections, and interruptions were common. The word "working" became second nature. A completed connection was constantly being broken into, and to let the new parties know they were horning in on an ongoing conservation, one said "working." The term was also used when an operator pulled your plug in his switchboard to see if your call was finished.

Getting the daily foxhole figures was rarely easy. Usually, the effort went down to the wire, which was 1700, the time of the briefing. The numbers were posted with a grease pencil on an acetate board. The posting was often done as the board was being carried to the briefing location. The foxhole strength was John B. Sweat's responsibility, but if he was on another mission, Hemp, and now I, pitched in.

The briefing itself was mostly given to operational matters. An S-3 representative, usually a captain, summarized activity over the last 24 hours. An S-2 representative described the enemy situation. An S-4 representative discussed logistics. Then the S-1 said, "Sir, the brigade strength is on the board." That was about it, at least for the briefings I attended or took part in. During my time at Pleiku, which was less than a week, there were only a couple of briefings. The brigade's forward-forward CP—where the brigade commander operated from—was elsewhere. What was at Pleiku was a sort of forward staging area, and the brigade CO wasn't there much. The staff elements made a pretense of an evening briefing, but without the general, no one was greatly motivated.

Dennis Hemp couldn't have been much impressed with my initial efforts. I was still subservient to the sleep god, and the presence of the cots in the tent was just too tempting. More than a few times during the day, I lay down with a piece of paper as if I were reading and promptly started cutting Zs. Some of the problem was Hemp's own fault because he was not a delegator. Evidently, I was supposed to ease into the job by watching what was happening, by asking questions, and by volunteering for tasks. I've rarely done well in those kinds of situations, however. My attitude has usually been, "Hey, if someone else is doing the job, let them do it. When it becomes my job, then I'll do it." As one might expect, this attitude has limited my upward mobility in this world.

John B. Sweat seemed to take considerable enjoyment in my don't-give-much-of-a-shit attitude, which only egged me on. My Dak To experience and my obvious lack of interest in staff work stood in marked contrast to Hemp's scarcity of actual combat and the serious-ness with which he took the paperwork aspects of war. Being the smart aleck that he was, Sweat couldn't resist occasional comments tinged with admiration for Captain Holland's apparent unconcern about the S-1 office and its functions.

Our situation was in too much flux, however, for Hemp and me to get locked onto a collision course. Within a week, orders came to move to Kontum, where the brigade forward CP was settling in. Much of the forward-forward trains would go north by convoy. The S-1 shop had a jeep and a trailer. The tent, desks, cots, and other equipment fit in the trailer, so we could actually claim to be mobile. Sweat and I were to go up in the jeep. As the acting brigade S-1, Hemp merited a ride on a chopper. The day before we departed, Hemp and I drove out to the U.S. hospital that was located at Pleiku to visit Lt. Storch, the wounded 1st Battalion Four-Deuce Platoon leader. Hemp knew Storch from Hemp's 1st Bat days. Except for complaining about his six Purple Hearts, Storch was in good shape and expected to be released shortly. His DEROS was only a few weeks away, but that was probably enough time for him to get number seven.

On the morning of the move to Kontum, we packed up and set off, John B. Sweat driving, me riding shotgun. About 25 miles separated Pleiku and Kontum. Much of the route was through hilly terrain with heavy vegetation. Bulldozers and Rome plows had created a 50-meter wide buffer between the road, which was packed dirt for the most part, and the jungle's edge. The convoy was preceded and followed by armored machine gun jeeps and watched over by choppers. In addi-tion, armored personnel carriers were parked at intervals and various trouble spots. This was a remote area of the Central Highlands close to the Cambodian border, and an ambush was more than a possibility. Emphasizing this point were occasional bursts of automatic weapons fire in the distance and a few dead bodies on or near the road. The bodies were fresh-killed NVA. I suspect the ones on the road had been dragged there by the killers in order to impress the rear echelon flunkies who made up the convoy. And indeed, for a few Vietnam veterans, the most vivid recollection of the war could be a semi-flatten oriental on a dusty stretch of road deep in the Central Highlands.

John B. Sweat certainly seemed impressed. When we swerved to avoid the first body, his eyes bugged. "Didja see that, Captain Holland? That was a dead gook!"

"Yeah, musta had a firefight 'round here," I said as nonchalantly as possible, but I had a firm grip on my M-16 and my vision glued on the distant tree line. I was ready to bail into the ditch at the first burst of incoming.

But the trip was uneventful, and we pulled into Kontum shortly after noon. The forward CP was just outside of town. Between the location and the town was a Special Forces headquarters camp. The Kontum airfield was nearby. The 173rd's headquarters commandant—the guy responsible for the physical layout and operation of the CP—was a major, an MP officer. In a month or so, he would become the Provost Marshal. For the time-being, however, an important part of his job was to tell the staff sections where to put their tents. He was a fat semi-serious type with a large degree of bluster but not much bite.

John B. Sweat and a couple of troopers from the postal unit put up the S-1 tent and the postal tent, which was adjacent. It was toward the end of the dry season, and the ground was rock hard. Most of the wooden stakes for the guy ropes splintered before penetrating the surface, so thick metal rods were used. The ground was covered by a very short coating of grass. A number of mounds of dirt, three feet or so high by about six feet long, were scattered about the area. It turned out that these were make-shift graves. Kontum had been the objective of a major NVA offensive during Tet, a month before. A particular target was the Special Forces camp, and the field where we were located had been a principal axis of attack, meaning that a bunch of poor NVA slobs had charged across it. They remained where they fell. Instead of attempting to dig graves or a burial pit, the U.S. or South Vietnamese forces responsible for doing something with the bodies had simply trucked in some dirt and dumped a load over each stiff. Only the loads weren't all centered. Thus a number of the departed were separated from the air by only a few inches of soil. A bit of limb even protruded from a few of the mounds. A result was that the sweet nauseating smell of decaying humans pervaded the area.

Among the responsibilities of the brigade S-1 shop was an ill-defined oversight of the commanding general's mess. Actually, the oversight duties seemed to be limited primarily to a bar fund and inventory. The CG's mess was open to the CG's staff, not lower flunkies like me but the S-1 himself and his peers. The cook of the mess, an E-7 sergeant first class, also kept a few bottles of booze that the CG and his boys could unwind with. The booze was paid for by collections from the staff. Under BG Sweitzer, the CG's mess was a pretty austere affair. This was probably partly due to the many moves the 173rd had been making since leaving Bien Hoa and the II Corps area the previous year. Most likely as important, however, was the personality of General Sweitzer. He was not a flamboyant man. His tastes were simple, and he seemed to be a line-doggie at heart. At Kontum, where I first encountered it, the CG's mess was simply a tent with a few long field tables. The liquor was resorted to sparingly. Hemp turned over to me, as the assistant S-1, responsibility for the booze and the fund. The duty didn't seem like much, and I thought little of it. Things were to change, however.

The forward CP was at Kontum for about two weeks. Two or three of the 173rd's battalions were operating in the surrounding mountains. The period for me was marked by three events. First, the brigade got a new commanding general. Second, the S-1 shop got a new S-1. Third, reluctantly, with little enthusiasm, I got into the job of assistant S-1.

To start with the last, Hemp was at Kontum only part of the time. The remainder of the period he was on errands in Pleiku or An Khe. Or maybe even he, as serious as he was about his job, was developing a belated case of short-timer's attitude. In any event, I was stuck as the MFWIC of the S-1 shop and had to come to grips with some of the demands of the job. When the general sends over a message to do something, one best damn well do it.

One small incident during this period brought home to me that I was no longer a line-doggie, and the realization may have contributed to my reluctant acceptance of my fate. I was walking across the area during an early evening. A group of jovial jiving black troopers passed about ten meters to my left. In the growing darkness, I recognized one of them as Doc, the medic from Alpha Company's Mortar Platoon, my old Oscar. I shouldn't have said anything, but I yelled out, "Hey Doc, howya doing?"

The group slowed and went silent. I felt a definite coldness, even hostility. This was a headquarters, and the closeness and camaraderie of a line company was far away. In addition, there was the black-white thing. During my brief time in the rear, I had noticed that race was becoming an important divider. Some black troops were becoming borderline insubordinate of any white authority. After a pause, Doc said quietly, "I'm doing okay." The group continued on its way, returning quickly to its jiving and juking. I felt the way I suppose they wanted me to feel, as a despised member of both the lifer Army and the honky establishment. Maybe at that moment my subconsciousness said: "Well, you ain't part of the troops no more, Cowboy. Time to get on with what you're stuck with."

Nevertheless, I was still taking every opportunity to avoid paperwork and related requirements of the S-1 job. Filling sandbags was often good for a break from the office. A huge pile of dirt had been trucked in for the use of headquarters personnel in constructing above-ground bunkers. When Hemp was around, I would often drag Sweat up to the pile for an hour or two of sandbagging. Hemp obviously disapproved of an officer performing manual labor, but the pressure from the headquarters commandant on up to the general was to get bunker facilities constructed. Consequently, Hemp kept his unhappiness mostly to himself. A period of sandbagging would steel me for another bout with the paper.

Brigadier General Sweitzer had been the brigade commander for a number of months. He was due for rotation, and his replacement arrived while we were at Kontum. A change of command ceremony and a reception were scheduled. These events were to occur in the Special Forces compound. The ceremony was to be in a field, and the reception was to be in the Officers Club in the compound. I was given the task of arranging the reception—a social chairman in a combat zone. As befitted a Special Forces facility, the club was a plush affair. The managers were two Vietnamese girls, and I felt right at home, sweet-talking coes—the Vietnamese word for young women—in a house of booze. In between the smooth words, I made the arrangements for a change of command drunk.

The change of command ceremony was presided over by the Big Cheese himself, General William C. Westmoreland. Beside the four-starred, tall, jut-jawed, well-built Westmoreland, BG Sweitzer came off as a bespectacled middle-aged school teacher. His jungle fatigues engulfed him. Though cleaned and pressed, they were no match for the starched, flat-as-a-board fatigues sported by The Man. Sweitzer's appearance might have contributed to his somewhat controversial reputation. Some were critical of his decisions at Dak To. The only negative thing I was personally familiar with was his insistence on extracting the media people from Hill 882 almost before the wounded.

On the other hand, Sweitzer was a troopers' general. His headquarters was lean and without pretense. His general's mess was not much more than what could be found at a battalion rear area. His quarters were virtually indistinguishable from the quarters of other officers of the brigade staff. Some members of that staff, Hemp being one of them, virtually worshipped the old guy. Initially, I was ambivalent. As I gradually became familiar with his successor, however, Sweitzer's stature rose.

The successor was BG Richard Allard. He was a short hard-looking man, and as the brigade staff was to find in the months ahead, the hardness was more than skin deep. A little incident at the start of the ceremony said something about both Westmoreland and Allard. Generals are differentiated from the masses by more than stars. One of the differentiations is a belt. Generals get to wear a black leather belt with a round buckle. In field and combat conditions, a holster with a pistol is attached to the belt. BG Allard showed up for his change of command ceremony with his general's black pistol belt at a considerable angle, sloping down to the holster riding low on his hip. He looked like your generic western gunfighter. On the raised platform, in full view of the assembled multitudes, Westmoreland said something to Allard. The words didn't carry, but the tone did, as did Westmoreland's irritated visage. The subject of Westmoreland's ire was quickly discernable as Allard's hands went immediately to his belt. He yanked the pistol off his hip and tightened the belt so that it was horizontal.

That Allard was dense enough not to know how to wear his general's belt didn't say much for him. You would think that by the time a guy had played the game long enough and politically enough to get a star, he would have noticed how to dress. As for Westmoreland, that he would publicly reprimand a new brigade commander didn't sit real well with me. Maybe that's how a four-star maintains fear in his subordinates, but the action made many of those in attendance more than a little uncomfortable.

After this inauspicious start, the ceremony proceeded uneventfully. Westmoreland said how proud he was of the 173rd, Sweitzer, and Allard, although Allard hadn't done anything yet. Sweitzer said how proud he had been to lead such an outstanding unit. Allard said how proud he was to be taking command of such an outstanding unit. After all this proudness, everyone adjourned to the Special Forces club, where amid the crowd of lifers trying to get close to the generals, I again tried to sweet-talk the coes.

The last significant event during the brief stay in Kontum was the arrival of a new S-1, Major Robert Tree. Squat, heavy-set, balding, a semi-chain smoker, Major Tree did not come to the 173rd with the grateful attitude most professional officers displayed on getting a plum assignment. Being an elite unit, the 173rd was looked upon by much of the officer corps as a real career enhancer. Major Tree, however, was an armor officer who had little use for airborne gung-honess. Back at the beginning of his career, he had gotten his basic jump wings, but his true love was tanks, and tanks were where he had spent most of his career.

Moreover, after a month in the 'Nam he had been unceremoniously jerked from one of the few bona fide tanker assignments of the war—in the S-3 shop of the 11th Armored Cav, the Blackhorse Regiment. The exact details of the transaction were murky, but apparently he had come to Vietnam slotted for the 173rd's S-1 job. Once in-country, however, he had wangled, or lucked into, the 11th Armored Cav position. But with the movement of LTC Gundersen to the 1st Battalion, the 173rd was without an S-1. Consequently, the brigade insisted that USARV produce the slotted Major Tree even though lower level field grades arriving in Vietnam were often diverted from their tentative slots without anybody objecting. The 11th Armored Cav resisted mightily, and the final decision was made way, way up the totem pole. So Major Tree, a tanker by preference, at heart, and in looks shuffled into Kontum, still hoping against hope for a reprieve.

His first few days at the 173rd's forward CP and in the S-1 tent had to have been depressing. From bouncing around in a big armored vehicle, plotting the movement of gas-guzzling columns, he comes to a little five-sided tent in a dismal field smelling of death. His command consists of a wise-guy teenager and a new captain with a sleeping problem—maybe also a head problem seeing as how he was on his 19th month in the 'Nam—and a preference for filing sandbags over shuffling papers. The acting S-1, the only guy who seems to be at least semi-competent and to have a handle on the job, is leaving within hours. His peers on the brigade staff are all long-time paratroopers with senior and master jump wings and much shared time in the Army's airborne community.

Fortunately for Major Tree's mental state, he didn't have long to dwell on his depression. The orders came for a major move, a part of a large-scale reshuffling. Long the MACV fire brigade, the unit that traveled light and went to the hot spots for General Westmoreland, the 173rd's mission was changing. It was to have a semi-permanent AO in the area around Bong Song on the coastal plain. North of Quin Nhon, northeast of An Khe, Bong Song had been under the care of the 1st Cav since that division's arrival in Vietnam in the summer of 1965. With the Cav's move north to I Corps, the 173rd was given the responsibility.

Bong Song was heavily populated. The area was one of the breadbaskets of Vietnam. Numerous small villages and hamlets dotted a landscape of vast rice paddies. Dikes crisscrossed the paddies, controlling the water supply and providing pathways. To the west, all the way to the Laotian border, lay mountain wilderness. To the east were isolated clumps of mountains and the South China Sea. In addition to being a major food producer, Bong Song also produced VC. The history of guerrilla activity stretched back to French days, and during its sojourn there the Cav had fought a number of bloody engagements.

The brigade forward CP was to move to LZ English, just north of the town of Bong Song. The forward brigade trains were also to close on English. As it turned out, the brigade CP would be at English for some time, until well after my departure. Indeed, the brigade was to be focused on eastern II Corps for the remainder of its time in Vietnam, until mid-1971, three years hence. The 1st Cav was completely abandoning An Khe, making the 173rd the principal occupant, and the major combat unit. Other occupants were combat service support units—transportation outfits, maintenance groups, and the like. Over the months ahead, at least one of the brigade's battalions would be operating on the Bong Song plain. Another would be in the An Khe area, a third would be south of Quin Nhon at Tuy Hoa, my old stomping ground, and a fourth would be in south-central II Corps, near Ban Me Thuot.

For the immediately preceding few months, a battalion or battalions from the 4th Division had been operating in the Bong Song area. As part of the general reshuffling, this unit or units were taking over the 173rd's responsibilities in northwestern II Corps. The headquarters element was to occupy the field we were vacating, so we were instructed to leave our bunkers in place. I was sorely tempted to drag one of the decaying bodies from the mounds and stuff it in the back corner of our bunker as a present for the 4th Division. Discretion prevailed, however, but a little part of me has always regretted not undertaking the project. The mental vision of the first time some leg staff flunky crawled in with Nguyen Stiff still brings a smile to my warped self.

For me, the last night in Kontum was one of those times when nothing extraordinary occurs but that nevertheless for some reason stand out in memory. The air was nippy, the sky was brilliantly clear, and the stars shown enticingly in their remoteness. From the postal tent nearby, a plaintive song of the 60s by someone like Dionne Warwick drifted over the area. Dennis Hemp had gone ahead with the advance party. John B. Sweat, Major Tree, and I were sitting out on sandbags. Major Tree was in the depths of his depression over leaving his beloved fellow tankers and unburdened himself of much of the story. There wasn't much John B. Sweat or I could say, so we just listened.

Perhaps one reason the night stands out in my memory is that it came to mark the end of the brigade as I knew it. The 173rd was under new management and had a new sort of mission. It was on the road to becoming top-heavy and settled. Although much combat and hard living were ahead, few of the line units would henceforth spend months humping the boonies without a break. There would be no more Dak Tos. The brigade staff, of which I was now a part, would shortly be virtually indistinguishable in appearance, procedures, attitude, and outlook from the staff of a state-side unit. The gap between the grunts playing the game for real and the rear echelon flunkies, half of whom didn't realize there was a war on, would grow exponentially.

Bong Song

Our new life began the next day. Having done it once, packing the S-1 trailer was now old hat to me. The plan was to fly from Kontum to Quin Nhon and drive north from there the 50 or so miles to LZ English. I decided to play convoy. I would drive the S-1 jeep. Major Tree would ride with me. John B. Sweat would ride in the postal unit's three-quarter ton. Major Tree was obviously a bit uneasy at the thought of an officer driving, but he probably felt too new to make an issue of the matter. For all he knew, officers driving in the 173rd might be standard procedure.

I drove the half mile to the Kontum airfield but turned the vehicle over to John B. Sweat for loading on the C-130. The vehicle and trailer were to be backed on, and a number of Army and Air Force enlisted folks were standing around. I wasn't confident enough about my backing ability to perform publicly. Let them laugh at John B. Sweat. I had the dignity of the officer corps to protect.

The flight across Vietnam wasn't long, and we were soon off-loading at one of the islands of American suburbia, the Quin Nhon air base. The buildings were permanent, the roads were paved and maintained, the uniforms were cleaned and pressed, the boots were shined. Our motley little group of dirty dented vehicles, rumpled jungle fatigues, and worn boots stood out. We reveled in our boniness. The base had a stateside-quality PX where we stocked up, having been warned that LZ English was without amenities. After a few more 173rd vehicles had arrived, we formed a small convoy and headed north.

Allegedly, the route was less perilous than, say, the Pleiku-Kontum road. The route was Highway 1, the road that ran pretty much the length of South Vietnam. In some places, it traversed pacified areas. In other places, it was virtually closed. The 50-mile Quin Nhon-Bong Song portion was relatively safe and often driven in daylight by single vehicles. Convoys were preferred, however, and nighttime travel was a no-no. Our small convoy was preceded by an MP gun jeep and watched over by choppers. In addition, U.S. and ARVN units were conducting security operations at several points close to the road. We were stopped briefly as one such unit shot up a nearby patch of woods, probably more to impress us than because of any actual threat.

After close to two hours of rice paddies and stretches of rolling hills, we entered Bong Song. It was a small town that was not unattractive, at least compared to the dingy, ram shackled Kontum. Brightly painted masonry and wooden structures lined the main street. Large trees provided shade, and multi-colored flowers added to the visual appeal of the many-hued buildings. A thick coating of dust churned up by the heavy truck traffic lay over everything, however, considerably subduing the colors. The dust also hung in the air, giving one the impression of observing the town through a film of thin gauze.

LZ English was a mile or so beyond the town, situated on a series of small knolls rising from the surrounding paddies. The initial area inside the perimeter was occupied by a sizeable ARVN contingent. The ARVNs did not bother with construction niceties, slapping together wood and tin in whatever rudimentary shape that appealed at the moment. Square corners were generally avoided in favor of more personalized angles. In this little nook of the country at least, the arrangement of buildings in rows to create recognizable streets was apparently one of those foreign concepts that American advisers had not yet been able to impart. Fortunately for the well-being of the precise linear paratrooper minds who were coming to share the base, the main road within the perimeter skirted the sprawling ARVN complex. We thus did not have to contend with the unorganization of our allies close up.

The 173rd and various U.S. supporting units had the western portion of LZ English. The 4th Division had just vacated the facilities, and the 1st Cav had been there before that. A few semi-permanent structures existed, including a heavily sandbagged TOC, but the Ivy Division guys had taken most of the other stuff with them. Thus we began the same way we had left Kontum, in tents.

Improvement was quick in coming, however. Within a few weeks, most of the headquarters was situated in webtocs—wooden framed structures overlaid with canvas tents. Initially, the S-1 shop shared a webtoc with the postal section, but Major Tree soon moved the latter next door. He converted the former postal area to his private office, leaving John B. Sweat and I to share the main area. The S-1 webtoc was eventually one in a group of twelve arranged in two rows of six each. The S-1 webtoc was the first in one of the rows. Directly across from us, the first webtoc in its row, was the S-4 shop. The placement of the two, the first in their respective rows, equidistant from the commanding general across the street, turned out to be symbolic. Major Tree and the S-4, Major Turner, eased into a rivalry that matched the best in office political brouhahas.

Four major structures were across the street, which itself was just a packed dirt track. One was the TOC. The second was a briefing building. The daily briefings were about to become full-scale productions. The third was the general's mess. The general's evening meals were also about to become elaborate shows. The final structure arrived about a month after we settled in. It was indicative of what the brigade—at least the headquarters portion of it—was becoming. The structure was General Allard's personal quarters. It was a massive house trailer, elegantly furnished, and air-conditioned.

One other structure, a small one, was nestled among others. It was the office and sleeping quarters of the brigade's executive officer, LTC Johnson, who was to be one of the few ties to the old brigade. LTC Johnson had been the commander of the 4th Battalion at Dak To. One of his companies had come to the rescue of McNever's Charlie Company, and the whole battalion had saved the 2nd Battalion on Hill 875, eventually being the principal part of the force that took the hill. During Tet, the 4th Battalion had seen heavy action near Tuy

Hoa. At one point, Johnson had landed his command chopper in the middle of a VC bunker system, leading an attack that overran the enemy. For this action, Johnson had received the DSC, and by all accounts the award was deserved. As the brigade XO, Johnson would be highly respected, extremely competent, and a superb tasker and coordinator. In essence, he ran the brigade headquarters. Yet he appeared to remain a soldier's soldier. One reason he was popular with such individuals as John B. Sweat and myself was that he seemed to view with distaste the pomp and circumstance, and the office politics, that came to dominate the headquarters of the formerly elite 173rd Airborne Brigade.

Our sleeping quarters were separated from the office, another indication of permanence. The quarters also were webtocs and were located about 50 meters up the road, toward the center of the camp. Major Tree and I shared one end of a webtoc. Sometime during the next few months, our end was subdivided, giving Major Tree and me private rooms of sorts. A rudimentary shower and washing area was nearby. The sleeping area was adjacent to a small POW transient compound. A few bushes and small trees stood between the compound and the webtocs. The compound was surrounded by a barbed wire fence and several strings of concertina wire. It wasn't always occupied, but from time to time a few Vietnamese could be seen squatting in isolation. The guards, who were in a tower and at the gate, didn't allow any mingling of prisoners. On the other side of the POW compound and the road was the mess hall for the headquarters.

These four points—the S-1 webtoc, the headquarters buildings across the street, the sleeping webtoc, and the mess hall—were my life for most of the next five months, April through August 1968. I made occasional trips into Bong Song, increasingly fewer as time went by, and there was a brief attempt to work out of An Khe, a trip to Saigon, a trip to Quin Nhon, and a memorable R&R to Bangkok, but by and large my world was very small, and very boring.

The moments of excitement were few and far between. One occurred within a few days of our arrival. It was late afternoon, and the evening briefing was just getting underway. I was to give the S-1 portion—this was before Major Tree relieved me of this job—and was waiting behind the stage. The briefing building had one large room, with a stage in front. Behind the stage was a small corridor that served as a waiting area for the flunkies giving the briefing. A separate entrance connected the corridor to the outside. The entrance way had a screen door, so the outside was visible from inside. A trench about four feet deep lay about five meters beyond the door.

Three or four individuals were standing in the corridor waiting their turn to brief when a heavy automatic weapon sounded in the distance. It was the thudding of a .50 caliber. We glanced at each other, but there didn't seem to be anything to be concerned about. The sounds of a few more bursts rolled over the area. The briefing continued, however. I was looking down the corridor through the screen door when the sound of another burst came. Unlike the previous bursts, the sound of this burst came accompanied. Several small explosions of dirt jumped into the air just outside the door. The next thing I knew, I was in the trench. I had no recollection of racing down the corridor, pushing open the door, and diving into the trench. I was just there. And I wasn't alone. The other briefers were right behind me, and from the end of the building, the assembled staff was scattering in all directions.

The moment of excitement was soon over, however. Someone ran into the TOC and put a call to the source of the firing, which was a gun jeep of E Troop of the 17th Cav, the 173rd's small semi-armored unit. A platoon of E Troop was operating in the area a mile or so away, toward Bong Song, and just got a little disoriented. I'm sure the troopers had few regrets when they learned they had scattered the general's evening briefing.

After some fits and starts, the routine of the S-1 shop soon solidified. One of the fits was an attempt to have me operate out of An Khe.

Soon after the move to Bong Song, we received a senior NCO, MSG Robert Brotzman, a truly outstanding personnel man. He had a Special Forces background, much time in Germany, and many helpful connections throughout the Army. We also had in the rear a Spec. 5 clerk, Specialist Freund, who Sweat took great delight in harassing. Much of the S-1 business consisted in prodding, pushing, and tweaking the 173rd's AG operation, a company-sized unit located now at An Khe. Major Tree's initial idea, originating with Captain Hemp, was that Sgt. Brotzman would operate from the rear, serving as our direct link with the AG people and as our rear area gofer.

But Bob Brotzman seemed at first to be overwhelmed. He was jumping out of his butt running from one errand to another. The phone connections between An Khe and Bong Song were bad on a good day, and he spent half his time trying to get us on the phone. Of course, we were spending half our time trying to get him on the phone. After about a week of us not being able to get much out of An Khe or Sgt. Brotzman, Major Tree decided I should join the rear area gofers. So I went back to the exotic pearl of the Central Highlands. The S-1 rear was in a one-story wooden building with a concrete floor. It was luxury compared to LZ English, and I quickly settled in, running errands for S-1 forward.

It was a good thing the settling in was quick because the settling out was quicker. Not five days had gone by before Major Tree called one morning with a blunt message: get my butt back out to Bong Song. I talked to Sweat after the good major left the phone and got the flavor of the previous few days. He and the major had been run ragged by the various demands of General Allard. Major Tree determined that Sgt. Brotzman being run ragged was preferable to him being run ragged. And in truth, Bob Brotzman turned out to be more than enough S-1 presence in An Khe. He quickly learned what levers to pull and buttons to push, and provided us all the support we needed. The communications difficulties, however, were never fully overcome. We could sometimes go hours before getting through to An Khe.

In my short stay in the rear, I did have the opportunity to visit the TOC of the 1st Battalion, which was now operating out of An Khe. Life had definitely changed. The TOC was situated in permanent, almost palatial facilities. Shined boots and clean uniforms complete with insignia and name tags were standard. Charlie Jones, the former C Company platoon leader who was now the battalion S-3 Air, was putting on weight. Two other C Company alumni, Cpt. McNevers and Lt. Cedric, were now on the battalion staff, and occupying themselves with various plots. One was to get McNevers a Distinguish Service Cross for, a sarcastic cynic would say, leading Charlie and Delta Companies into the ambush at Dak To. Cedric had received the DSC, and McNevers figured he was entitled to one also. Cedric was actively supporting the effort, whether out of loyalty, expediency, politics, or what I don't know. The two had never given me the time of day before, but now that I was the assistant brigade S-1, maybe I had a use. So for a few minutes we were bosom buddies, discussing shared times in the Dak To maelstrom. They even refrained from criticizing Alpha Company for not coming to their rescue that fateful day.

During this brief period, another meeting with a former comrade from the 1st Battalion was more pleasant. I was doing some paperwork early one evening when November's Sgt. Hernandez stumbled into the office. Stumbled is the correct word because he was drunker than nine dogs. He was leaving the next day for home, a year in the 'Nam done, and had been celebrating at the nearby NCO club. He was one of the finest NCOs I encountered during my stay in Southeast Asia. We reminisced for a bit and then parted, telling each other how great we were. Outwardly, what was said was no different than what a lot of parting company officers and NCOs said to each other, except that I truly meant it. And I was honored that he had gone to the trouble of tracking me down.

And there was one further meeting, a sad one, with a former 1st Battalion acquaintance. Captain Wolfowitz, having been relieved of command of Alpha Company shortly after its firefight in February near

Ban Me Thuot, was in An Khe as the company commander of the Replacement Company. It was a non-job. The Replacement Company's NCOs largely ran the unit, and a good thing, as Wolfowitz had gone to hell in a hand basket. In the two and a half months since I had last seen him—two months since he had left the field—he had put on 25 pounds and looked as if he had consumed a good portion of the inventory of the An Khe booze store.

Being relieved of command is a devastating experience, particularly for someone who thought the military was to be his life-long profession. Wolfowitz was obviously taking it particularly hard. We exchanged a few pleasantries, he made a lame joke about the morning November had been diverted from the airlift back to Kontum to baby sit a downed Huey, and we parted. In my view, he was not the type of officer to take over a unit that had been in combat. He didn't have the presence, and he was much too unsure of his abilities. Still, you had to feel sorry for what had become of him. He was falling hard and fast. He would be going home shortly. He is another one whose future I have occasionally pondered in the years since Vietnam. If he had trained as a company commander with a unit and had brought that unit to Vietnam, I think he would have had a much better chance of succeeding. I hope he stopped his freefall and found a niche in this world.

I arrived back at Bong Song in the afternoon of the day Major Tree called and immediately started work on some hot project. And that was about what the next four months consisted of: one hot project after another. The only relief from hot projects was routine work. There were no days off, and the work day stretched from 7:30 in the morning to past 7 in the evening. Much time was spent on the phone trying to get some distant locale, or even some not-so-distant locale. Four beers every evening were what passed for recreation. I didn't have the freedom to investigate the possibility of local brothels. My trips to exotic downtown Bong Song were limited to laundry runs—when I tried unsuccessfully to make time with the launderer's teenage daughter—and to picking up plaques from a local engraver. Every Swinging Richard who visited the 173rd's headquarters got a plaque memorializing the event, and it was my job to see that all names were spelled correctly.

These plaques were usually presented during a luncheon or dinner at the general's mess. From the utilitarian and humble facilities of General Sweitzer's time, the general's mess under General Allard quickly became a place of ostentatious elitism. A screened-in wooden structure in the approximate center of the headquarters area was refurbished. Padded chairs, table clothes, and fancy plates and utensils were added. A seating arrangement was adopted. And a social hour when the staff and the general hobnobbed over cocktails was scheduled. Out in the field, the line doggies were living like slime. At the headquarters of the supposedly hard-charging 173rd, the senior staff was pretending it was stateside fun and games.

Attendance at the general's mess was limited to the senior staff, which meant mere captains like me were excluded, which was just as well. The whole concept sucked. I did have a responsibility, and that was to supervise the liquor inventory. I collected a "donation" from each of the members of the mess, kept a record of the "donations," and turned the funds over to the mess sergeant, who incidentally sported a CIB that had been awarded for service in the Dominican Republic in 1965. Dom Rep CIBs were generally considered to be a joke. Otherwise, the guy wasn't a bad sort. He used the funds I gave him to buy the liquor in An Khe or Quin Nhon. Probably a goodly portion of the booze ended up being imbibed by the sergeant and his cooks.

An ostentatious mess was not the only grossly inappropriate thing BG Allard brought to the 173rd. He also had that humongous trailer lifted into LZ English. The trailer was placed beside the mess. It had several rooms and was air-conditioned. The furniture was upscale. I was only in the place once, with Major Tree to brief the general on some personnel matter. Major Tree and I sat on an upholstered couch.

The general sat in an easy chair on the other side of a coffee table from us. Magazines were neatly arranged on the table. Curtains shielded the windows, and rugs covered the floor. Reality was nowhere to be seen.

The general instituted a policy of pulling a squad out of the field every Sunday, feeding them in the mess, and entertaining them for an hour or so in the trailer. Exposure to this out-of-place piece of luxury had to have had an effect opposite to what the general desired. Instead of having their morale boosted, the grunts undoubtedly returned to the mosquitoes, leeches, snakes, heat, and death hating the rear-echelon muthafuckers even more.

As the weeks went by, the environs of the trailer became an oasis of beauty amid the dust and dirt of LZ English. A stone walkway leading to the door was laid down. Small flower gardens were planted on each side of the walkway. An awning was constructed out from the door. It was all very tasteful and attractive—and an obscenity.

My involvement in the general's mess did not go unnoticed. If the S-1 office was that close to the man, it must be getting an advantage. Staff jealously asserted its ugly self. Specifically, the S-4 wanted a piece of the action.

Major Turner had been in the 4th Battalion with LTC Johnson. That was in his favor. In his debit column was the fact that he was a jerk, a staff politician of the first order. He objected to Major Tree concerning the S-1's lone role in the general's liquor business. Surely the S-4 had a responsibility regarding the general's care and feeding. After much arduous negotiations, Major Tree and Major Turner arrived at an agreement. The S-4 would be responsible for table placement and seating arrangements. Turner apparently believed this would be a high profile duty entailing little actual work.

Well, in one of life's rare moments of justice, I stuck it to Major Turner just a few days later. One of the traveling road shows of visiting dignitaries was coming through, a sizeable group. Prior to Turner's assumption of table placements and seating arrangements, the responsibilities had really been performed by the E-7 mess sergeant. He would ask me if things were okay, and not knowing any better, I would say: "Yeah, sure, fine." But this particular group was different, and the general's aide, another of the world's jerks, came to me with a seating plan. A gleam entered my eye. Hot damn, time for a little fun.

I took the list and hauled ass over to the S-4's webtoc. Major Turner was sitting in his office, his feet propped up on his desk, most likely plotting his next power play. "Sir, here's the seating arrangement for tonight's shindig." I dropped the paper on his desk. He picked it up, scowled, swung his feet to the floor, scowled again, and growled:

"What the fuck didja say this was?"

"The seating arrangement, Sir. For tonight's dinner."

"What the fuck am I supposed to do with it?"

"The seating arrangement, Sir. I understood you took over responsibility for seating in the general's mess."

"Well, who the hell is supposed to do this?"

"I don't know, Sir. The mess sergeant has been handling it, but I understood you wanted it."

He didn't say anything more for a moment, so I exited: "Got to run, Sir. See ya later." I scooted across the way to the S-1 hooch and settled behind my desk. I had barely gotten seated when Major Turner came charging through the door, head in front of his body by a good foot. Without a glance at myself or Sweat, he stomped past to Major Tree's office. There was no door, so Sweat and I heard the whole conversation.

"What the hell is Holland trying to pull? What is this seatin' crap? I haven't got time for this."

"I thought you said you wanted part of the responsibility for the mess, the seatin' and placement stuff." I could tell Major Tree was going to enjoy this.

"But this means I've got to have one of my men go over to the mess hall and see that things are arranged. That's what Holland does, doesn't he?"

"Not anymore. That's what you wanted to do. Now you got it."

"How often does this crap go on? I've got a lot better stuff to do than this."

"Oh, it's not much. But if you don't want it, Holland will take it back. It's no big deal."

There was a long pause, then: "No goddammit. We'll do it. There just better not be much of this crap."

Major Turner came charging out of Major Tree's office, still leading with his head. He bore across the space separating the S-1 and S-4 webtocs and flung open the screen door of the latter. In less than a minute, one of his captains—he had several, none of whom appeared to do any real work—came briskly out of the webtoc and made his high-stepping way to the mess tent. Major Tree, who by this time had come out of his office, watched him go. Tree was chortling with obvious glee: "We win this one, Dave. Good job." His ebullient mood lasted well into the next day.

Observing staff politics was one of the few diversions from the never-ceasing work load. Another was the periodic visits of the Donut Dollies.

"Donut Dollies" was the soldiers' term for the Red Cross girls who devoted a year of their lives to serving and entertaining the troops. Stationed in base camps, one of which was An Khe, Donut Dollies made forays to various forward support areas, sometimes getting as far as fire support bases. LZ English was a regular stop for the An Khe Dollies. Sometimes they stayed at LZ English. Other times they went on to a fire support base. During their visits, the Dollies talked to the troops, played little games, and provided a look at a round-eye.

The troops' reaction to the Dollies varied. Some were unreservedly appreciative. Some felt a degree of unease, even resentment. This was the pre-woman military. Female soldiers were confined to special branches, WACs in the Army. The Women's Army Corps provided clerical jobs for females, and that was all. The number of WACs in Vietnam was minuscule. There were nurses, but they were limited to major bases. Thus Vietnam was a man's war, and many of those men felt that women were intruders. Consequently, the Donut Dollies often played to an undercurrent of hostility.

Exacerbating the situation was that the Dollies were often monopolized by officers, especially the lower field grades—majors and lieutenant colonels. These gentlemen were still young enough to be governed by their hormones. The combination of hormones, rank, and the scarcity of round-eyes could make some of them blithering idiots around the Dollies. The general contributed to the problem by invariably inviting the Dollies to lunch in his mess. There, the senior staff would do their best to impress the girls who, despite the best of intentions about entertaining lowly grunts, found themselves warding off lecherous assholes with rank.

Of course, lowly grunts could also pose problems for the Dollies. During one visit, a Dolly found out just how much of a problem.

Latrine facilities at LZ English matched the standard for long-term fire support bases. The facilities consisted of crude outhouses. The receptacle for the human deposits was a third of a 55-gallon drum. After the drum had received a goodly supply of urine and feces, it was dragged from the back of the outhouse through a hinged panel. A mixture of gasoline and kerosene was poured in the drum. The shit and piss were then burned away. Smoky shit drums are one of the images engraved in the minds of a goodly proportion of Vietnam veterans.

While visiting forward areas, the Dollies had to use the facilities of the troops, or hold things for a long, long time. One morning shortly after two Dollies arrived, one of them used a latrine near the headquarters area. Soon after she entered, she emerged screaming, with her panties around her ankles. That location for the garment severely constrained her movement, but she was still making pretty good time. As she was running one way, a furtive figure was seen departing from the vicinity of the rear of the outhouse.

Gradually, the story came out. Shortly after she sat down, the rear panel was raised, a hand snaked in through the opening, up through the hole in the seat—and grabbed a handful of snatch. For all future visits of the Donut Dollies, an MP was discretely stationed in the rear of the outhouse designated for their use.

Time moved much too slowly at LZ English. I realized shortly after we settled in that I was looking at a good four months of long, heavy days. It was extremely easy to fall into an anguish of overbearing proportions. The minutes slowly gave way to hours, the mornings gave way to the afternoons, the afternoons faded into the evenings. I was in a combat zone, but I was stuck in a paperwork job. I hated my fate but saw no way out. I would have to suffer the months. The period was a lesson in trying to deal with boredom, with desperate desires to be elsewhere, with longing for something different. I experienced the feelings, but I did not find a way to immunize myself against them.

At one point, the boredom and a latent machismo got to John B. Sweat. He became semi-determined to go to the field. The hours of typing, of wrestling with the phone system, of filing, of responding to all the crap floating around a headquarters, temporarily overcame his desire to go back to his girl in one piece. He wanted to experience the war. Only he wanted a selective experience. Humping the boonies with a 60-pound rucksack was not for him. What he wanted was E of the 17th Cav, the 173rd's small reconnaissance force.

E Troop of the 17th Cav was a company-size unit, about 125 individuals. It was commanded by a captain. In June of 1968, a new captain took over. He was a tall friendly guy who had worked in the S-3 shop. Since he came out of the headquarters, Sweat knew him. E Troop's mode of transportation was armored jeeps. With sandbags on the floors and armored doors, the jeeps could withstand a minor amount of pounding. In the Bong Song area, E Troop traveled the back roads, performing security and reconnaissance missions.

Oh, one other thing—E Troop wore camouflaged uniforms. This was in the days before the standard Army field uniform was camouflaged patterned. The multi-hued uniforms added exponentially to E Troop's allure.

Sweat was going through a particularly bad time in late May and early June. The days were dragging, the duty sucked, Major Tree was hopping from one General Allard-initiated crisis to another. The general was a screamer. On more than one occasion, he came to the middle of the road running through the headquarters area and bellowed for Majors Tree or Scott, who would then have to emerge for a full-scale dressing down. Traffic would have to stop while the show went on. During the late May-early June period, Major Tree was the recipient of more than his share of these tirades.

Major Tree was good about not passing the animosity on to Sweat and myself. But the damage to his emotional well-being was showing. He was haggard and not in a mood to be sympathetic to the needs and concerns of his subordinates. And Sweat was in need of some sort of attention. He evidenced that need by being a bit more insubordinate than usual. The atmosphere in a small office such as ours was informal, with a fair amount of banter, some of which could get quite sharp. Sweat was always on the edge of acceptable behavior, and one day in June he stepped over the boundary.

The spark was the daily foxhole strength board that was the focal point of Major Tree's portion of the late afternoon briefing. I had long since been relieved of briefing duties. Maybe my fear and nervousness at being in the presence of a general showed too much. Maybe Major Tree just wanted the spotlight. In any event, I was out of the evening lineup. But the change in the person of the briefer had not changed the difficulty of getting the numbers together. The 173rd was now spread all over II Corps: a battalion in Bong Song, a battalion at An Khe, a battalion near Tuy Hoa, and a battalion way down south, near Ban Me Thuot. In addition, a leg mechanized battalion, the 1st of the 50th Infantry, had been assigned to the brigade and was operating in the Bong Song plain. Making phone contact with these widespread units generally took Sweat a good part of the afternoon. Often, I was required to help out with the phone calls.

On this particular afternoon, Sweat began smart-ass-answering more than usual when Major Tree started easing into his pre-brief panic mode. "Don't bust a gut, Sir. I'm getting it." "Just calm your liver down, Sir. The numbers are a'coming." "You're getting your liver in a quiver, Sir. It's bad for ya."

And so it went. I could see Major Tree was getting more and more irritated. As often happened, the numbers hadn't all arrived before the briefing began. On such days, Major Tree would go to the briefing, and Sweat would bring the board over at the last possible minute. Only on this day, Sweat just sat there after Major Tree left. He made no effort to make additional phone calls, and he made no move to getting the board across the street. I finally said, "You better get yer butt in gear. Major Tree is gonna be pissed."

"I'm tired of this shit. I wanna go to the Cav."

"Well, that's real nice. But I suggest you get that board over to Major Tree first."

"Bull-fucking-shit. I want to go to E of the 17th."

I should have done something, but a certain part of me wanted to let Major Tree handle this revolt himself. Besides, I sympathized with Sweat's expressed desire to go to E of the 17th. I wasn't sure, however, that Sweat was truly certain about what he wanted to do. Maybe he viewed insubordination as a way to get to the field without actually having to take the affirmative steps of putting in the paperwork.

Major Tree emerged from the briefing building and jogged to the road separating it from the S-1 webtoc. "Sweat, where is that goddamn board!" he yelled.

Sweat finally got off his butt, grabbed the board, and went out to the middle of the street. He shoved the board at Major Tree. They exchanged a few words that I couldn't hear. Then each stomped off in their separate directions. "What'd he say?" I asked as Sweat entered the building.

"I want to go to E of the 17th," he non-responded.

"Well, that's real good. I think ya oughta. Maybe ya just got your wish."

When Major Tree returned, he closeted himself with Sweat for a good hour. After he finished with Sweat, he called me in. "Sweat seems to really wanna go to E of the 17th. I told him that if that was what he wanted, I would try to arrange it. He has to think it over for a day before I do anything."

The Major went on to say a few things that showed he was disappointed in my non-participation in the little drama. He certainly had a point. As his assistant and as an officer, I had certain responsibilities. But I didn't feel too badly about letting him down. I was too much of a fuck-up myself.

Unfortunately from some perspectives, but perhaps fortunately from the standpoint of Sweat's long-term existence, he said no more about E of the 17th. His 24-hour period to think it over passed. He must have done the thinking and decided in favor of discretion versus youthful exuberance. I wonder if in later years he ever regretted his decision.

Major Bryant, the chief of the 173rd's support company—and my official greeter when I had joined the brigade back in September—received a less-than-honorable sendoff in the early summer of 1968. He was in charge of the move of the brigade rear area from Bien Hoa to An Khe. This was a monumental task. The brigade had been in Bien Hoa since 1965. The junk it had accumulated was considerable and defied easy culling. Consequently, a large number of conex containers stuffed indiscriminately with crap were trucked and flown north. At some point in the process, a number of secret documents were found in one of the containers. This was not the proper way to store secret documents, but the harm was much more in theory than in actuality. The secrets in secret documents could often be read in the newspapers, heard on the radio, or seen on television. And if they were secret when first put on paper, the necessity to maintain the secrecy classification usually evaporated quickly.

But the secret papers in the conex were found by a zealot who felt compelled to make an issue of the matter. The Inspector General of the 173rd conducted an investigation. The conclusion was that the ultimate responsibility for the security violation rested with Major Bryant, the AG Company commander and the individual in charge of the move of the brigade rear to An Khe. So Major Bryant, who had so enjoyed his status as the "Major of Bien Hoa," who had in fact overseen a Herculean task—the aforementioned move—became the fall guy. The Legion of Merit that a field grade staff officer could expect upon the completion of a successful Vietnam tour was downgraded to a Bronze Star. The incident was probably noted in the poor major's efficiency report, a sure career-killer. The really unfair aspect of the situation was that if BG Sweitzer had still been the brigade commander, the matter would probably have been ignored. BG Allard, however, gave the impression of enjoying a subordinate's downfall.

As the weeks went on, it dawned on me that I was getting out of shape. The sedentary life, in conjunction with four beers a night, was not conducive to maintaining the lean, mean profile of an infantry officer. In addition to just being generally concerned about my condition, I also was beginning to develop a specific reason for not getting too plump. When my current six months was ended, I would still have six months left in the Army. Why spend my last six months in some stateside non-job when I could be enjoying a combat zone? Maybe I could even get a company command. For an officer, staying longer than two years in Vietnam was generally not allowed, but I figured a request based on the implied threat that I would present a crazed-war-veteran problem if I had to spend my last six military months stateside might warrant an exception.

So I attempted a little running. Near the headquarters area was a section of road that, together with a side road into a gasoline fueling area, formed a small circle of about a fifth of a mile. The fueling area was in a very small valley, meaning the prospective course had a nice little hill. Much to John B. Sweat's amusement, I tackled the track one evening after Major Tree had gone for the daily ritual at the general's mess. Running in boots and jungle fatigue pants, ample love handles undulating with each step, I managed several laps before succumbing to the desire for rest and my evening grog. But I continued the routine. Four or so times a week, I struggled over the little course or continued following the road, which became tangent to the base perimeter for about a third of a mile. The only problem with running along the perimeter was the guard bunkers, which were usually occupied by a unit having a small break from the field. The troopers thoroughly enjoyed watching an out-of-shape rear echelon muthafucker plod past. More than a few of them spent their perimeter time on booze or pot, meaning any inhibitions they might have had about harassing someone who might be an officer were well stifled.

John B. Sweat even ran with me several times. He and I also played a few games of catch. Some office in the headquarters complex had a small number of baseball gloves, including a catcher's mitt. Sweat fancied himself a pitcher, even claiming to have aspirations of playing in college when he left the Army. He did have a helluva fast ball, but the number of times he got it to me was not promising for a college scholarship. I spent considerable energy chasing the balls across the road to the vicinity of the general's mess, a route that would produce a few disapproving glances from behind the drink glasses.

Regarding one of the motivations for the running, I eventually did put in that ten-forty-nine to do a final six months in the 'Nam. In it, I noted that I had an ETS—expected termination of service date—and no plans to make the Army a career, but I did have a desire to spend my final six months where I might be of the most value. Returning to the states for those months would result in little benefit to the Army. I could best put my two years of 'Nam experience to use by staying in the 'Nam. I hoped that the approving authority back in the Pentagon would read between the lines and say: "We don't need this time-bomb at some state-side post, drinking and looking for trouble. Let him spend his final six months in the 'Nam. If he manages to survive, he'll be someone else's problem when he comes home as a civilian."

One of the recurring tasks in the S-1 shop was to fill quotas for MACV Mobile Advisory Teams. The quotas first started coming down from MACV shortly after I arrived in the S-1 office, and the frequency of their appearance quickly increased. Unbeknownst to me at the time, I was participating in my own future.

The Mobile Advisory Teams were part of the effort to turn the war over to the Vietnamese—Vietnamization was the term. The process started in early 1968, even before the U.S. troop buildup stopped and before Richard Nixon became President. As advisors, of course, had been how Americans first entered the war in the early 1960s. The advisory effort had been focused on the provinces and districts and on regular units of the Vietnamese military forces. Now the focus was being expanded to the Vietnamese "irregular" forces, the RF/PFs, for Regional Forces/Popular Forces. The acronym gave rise to the term, "Ruff-Puffs." The goal of the Mobile Advisory Teams, or MATs, was to advise the Ruff-Puffs.

Regional and Popular Forces were somewhat akin to the National Guard in the United States. Many of the units were part-time, although this was less likely to be the case with the Regional Forces, which were generally organized at the province level and were closer in organization and training to regular military units. The Popular Force units were usually organized at the district level and often manned by peasant-farmers who worked the fields during the day and guarded their villages at night. The Popular Force concept had been around for a long time. Since at least the early 1960s, U.S. Special Forces had been experimenting with one form or another of local force units. Now the idea was apparently for the U.S. to make every Swinging Richard in the country a soldier and then di-di mau (leave quickly).

The MATs were to perform the task of converting peasants to soldiers, and initially the U.S. units in-country were to provide the personnel for the MATs. So every few weeks MACV would send down another levy for warm bodies to become advisors to our Vietnamese brothers. All major combat units—divisions and separate brigades—were subject to the calls, which would indicate the required rank and MOS—military occupational specialty—of acceptable candidates. Basically, combat arms lieutenants, captains, and E-6, -7, and -8s were what was wanted.

Now stop and think about this for a moment. If you are a commander and you get a requirement to give up one of your officers or NCOs, who are you going to give up, your best or something else? Yes, the something elses were given the task of Vietnamization. This is not to say that the potential MAT members supplied by in-county units were all duds, just that the levy procedure was not guaranteed to result in the best and the brightest. The levies were filled with transients, with those not in key jobs, with individuals on some commander's shit-list, and yes, with duds.

My job was to take the brigade requirement and divvy it up among the battalions. I developed a rotational approach, going from battalion to battalion, thus ensuring that a particular battalion would have several months between levies. As might be expected, the battalions fought the levies vehemently. Giving up people is not something that a commander does readily. Several of the levies were appealed by the battalion commander to the brigade XO and a couple to even the brigade commander. My one visit to General Allard's air-conditioned abode was occasioned by the necessity to explain why I was picking on a particular battalion. I showed the general my chart indicating that the pain was being evenly spread, which seemed to satisfy him. But every levy required a Herculean effort to pry the required bodies out of the battalions.

Another subject also hung around for much of my S-1 time. Actually, there were two separate situations, but they both could be viewed as falling within the topic of MIAs—missing in action—the topic that gave rise to a profession in the decades following the U.S. withdrawal from Vietnam. One situation originated at Dak To. A wounded trooper was evacuated—one of the many—to a hospital in the Central Highlands, probably at Pleiku, but died while waiting to be examined. He had no identification on him, at least none that was found. His body was caught up in the rush of the Dak To dead and wounded and was shipped, without being identified, to the mortuary at Tan Son Nhut. There, it was put in the cooler pending a determination of who the poor guy was.

Meanwhile, the trooper's unit assumed he was just wounded and carried him as such on its records. Indeed, the unit members who had been involved in his evacuation recalled only a minor wound and had no reason to suspect that he was doing anything more than recuperating. And this is what the unit reported to the trooper's parents when they began questioning why they hadn't heard from him. Initially, they wrote to the brigade, which went down through the battalion to the company for a response. That response was, "He's okay. He had a minor wound and was evacuated. He's someplace in the medical system now."

As might be expected, this was not a satisfactory answer for parents who had not heard from their son in a war zone. Consequently, they went to their congressman, triggering a dreaded Congressional. Inquiries from members of Congress were treated with great respect and accorded priority treatment. A well-established procedure existed for investigating the subject of a Congressional inquiry, verifying the findings, and preparing and forwarding the response. In this instance, however, the well-established procedure resulted in the same response: "He's okay. He had a minor wound and was evacuated. He's someplace in the medical system now."

For almost three months, the 173rd continued to claim that the trooper was alive, just misplaced. And in truth, and as difficult as it might be to comprehend in this age of almost instant global communication, getting lost in the Green Zoo was not impossible. The guy could have been alive in any number of places, from in-country medical facilities, to hospitals in Japan, to replacement battalions. But he was dead in a freezer at Tan Son Nhut. Finally, someone put the missing soldier and the unidentified body together, solving the mystery—and devastating the family who not only had lost a son but had been the butt of some horrible bureaucratic joke.

Now the Congressionals and the letters from the Pentagon were to explain how such a thing could have happened. These requests for explanations and the responses flowed through the S-1 shop during my tenure. We didn't really have a role to play, merely serving as a conduit between the AG section, which coordinated the responses, and the general, who had to sign most of them. But we did have a ring-side seat to a government trying to explain an immense screw-up to two of its constituents who had just suffered the most tragic of losses. Being young and cynical, I couldn't help being caught up in the black humor of the situation, and Sweat and I spent far too much time composing the macabre responses we would make if we were in charge. Our attitudes will likely result in considerable purgatory time for us, assuming we don't fall into the hell-for-all-eternity category.

The second MIA situation was more of a mystery, and I never did learn how it ended. Shortly after the 173rd moved to the Bong Song area, a platoon of the 2nd Battalion had a trooper disappear. The platoon was operating on its own, patrolling a mountainous area above several isolated fishing villages on the seacoast. The scenery was spectacular: from the slopes of the lush dark green mountains, the platoon looked down on the picturesque villages, the broad white beaches, the deep blue-green of the South China Sea, and the surf breaking in long gentle bands of frothy foam. Viet Cong activity was minimal. The purpose of humping the mountain trails with a weapon and a 60-pound pack easily receded to a remote corner of the mind.

One morning, the platoon moved out from its laager site, setting a course up a steep trail. After a half-hour sweat-producing climb, the platoon leader called a break. During this pause, someone noticed that a trooper was missing. He had been the last one in the column when they left the laager site. Now he was nowhere to be seen.

Immediately, the platoon leader led a patrol back toward the laager site. They found no sign of the missing trooper, nor any evidence of foul play. The platoons in adjacent AOs were notified. For several days, the entire company scoured the vicinity. A Vietnamese military unit was brought in to search the villages. No sign.

The missing trooper was a relatively new guy, having been with the unit a little less than two months. He had been a loner, with no close friends. On the other hand, he hadn't been completely uncommunicative. He had engaged to an extent in the usual banter and conversations. And he hadn't shown any recent mood swings or acted odd or out of sorts.

One of four things could have happened. As the last man in the column, he could have been silently ambushed by the VC and taken either dead or alive. There was no evidence of this, however. Moreover, if such a thing occurred, it would have been a most unusual event. Bona fide instances in which the VC tried to pick off surreptitiously a single individual in a column are hard to come by. A second possibility is that the trooper could have had an accident, falling off the trail and into a ravine or down a hillside. The extensive search, however, would seem to preclude this outcome. A third possibility is that for some reason the platoon did the guy in. This, however, would have had to involve a sizeable conspiracy. I met some of the platoon members. Maybe I was naive, but they didn't strike me as a murderous group capable of killing one of their own and then keeping it a secret.

That leaves the fourth possibility, the one I think the most likely. The trooper awoke that morning, had a view through the mountainside jungle canopy of the villages, the beach, and the ocean, turned to see the column moving out of the laager site up the trail, the packs creaking, the breathing already heavy, and said, "Fuck this noise." He proceeded in the opposite direction, to the villages. Several things could have happened on his arrival. The villagers, VC sympathizers if not actual VC, could have done him in on the spot. Or they could have taken him prisoner and moved him gradually westward, toward the Laotian border. Or the guy could have found a home.

The incident was under investigation throughout my months in the S-1 shop. Several times, platoon members were brought to LZ English for interviews with various authorities, once even by the general himself. In my brief conversations with them, they seemed genuinely perplexed. My own musing is that today, on a little stretch of beach by the South China Sea, a stretch isolated from the Bong Song plain by a crescent of rugged mountains, an aging deeply tanned Caucasian leisurely plies his trade as a fisherman, surrounded by a passel of kids, the oldest now parents themselves. He talks and thinks in Vietnamese, only occasionally finding himself puzzling over a bit of English that has popped into his consciousness. In a far corner of his thatched home sits a mildewed rucksack, its frame almost as rusty as the M-16 on which it rests.

Before leaving the topic of the coastal mountains, there is one other recollection to impart. A clump of these mountains was visible from LZ English. For much of the early summer of 1968, this clump was subject to assault by defoliant-dispensing C-123s and helicopters. Sometimes, great pink clouds of liquid could be seen descending onto the mountains. Other times, there was no visible dispersion, just an aircraft making numerous passes over the heights. LZ English was too far from the mountains for its occupants to see the effects of the defoliant campaign, but later in my Vietnam stay I was to see the results of such attacks on nature. What was likely being used, of course, was Agent Orange, the chemical that gave rise to another post-Vietnam profession.

Much of the correspondence that came through the AG Company and S-1 shop for the general was about casualties. "How did my son-husband-brother die?" The AG Company had a standard response for most of the inquiries, and the general usually just signed what was presented to him. Being young and cynical, I didn't take much notice of this category of correspondence. One letter, however, gave me pause. A mother was asking about her son who had been killed at Dak To. Ostensibly, she wanted details on the death. But mostly she seemed to want to tell someone about what a fine young man her son had been: good student, active in high school service organizations, church-goer, athlete. He had wanted to go to college but concluded that he should serve his country in Vietnam first. He had enlisted, volunteered for the airborne, and ended up with the 173rd. The letter was not that different from many others, perhaps a little more moving but you got inured to "moving" pretty quickly.

I looked at this letter much longer than usual, however. And its memory has remained with me over the years. You see, the soldier's name was Douglas Baum, my first radio operator when I became an airborne infantry leader in Alpha Company of the 1st Battalion the previous year.

Will It Ever End?

Diversions at LZ English were few and far between. One brief respite was provided by a visiting USO-sponsored band. LZ English was spread over a number of small hills, and one of the hillsides and adjacent valley had been turned into an amphitheater of sorts. A crude wooden stage was in the small valley, and the hillside provided a vantage point for the audience. The facility didn't get much use during my months at LZ English, but there were a few movies and a couple of USO groups. One of the groups was a rock and roll band of no great distinction. On a clear night, with the stars innumerable and brilliant against a black sky, I sat down with a few beers and listen to the group wade its way through some of the songs of the sixties. It finished with the anthem of the U.S. soldier in Vietnam—"The Green, Green Grass of Home."

As the nostalgic strains wafted away and the band members moved to end their desultory performance, their escort jumped onto the stage. He was a Spec. 4 based in An Khe. He had been out to LZ English a couple of times to arrange USO visits. And that night he showed he was one helluva performer. He grabbed the drum sticks and began pounding away. The drums came alive, the pounding bouncing off the hillside and pulsating across the base, out over the perimeter wire, and into the surrounding rice paddies. As the electricity of the performance jumped from battery level to 220 volts, he began a line of patter into a microphone. His voice was deep and overpowering as he said, "Now let's do a little real rock and roll."

The result was about 30 minutes of gut-churning music. The guy beat hell out of the drums and sang in a deep bass that sent shivers down the spine. The problem was he couldn't do it alone. Some members of the USO band stayed on the stage and attempted to play along, but they weren't in his class. The session eventually wound down as he ran out of steam. The onlookers drifted off to their hooches, reveling in the taste they had of real music but feeling unfulfilled because the taste had been so small.

During my stint at Bong Song, two reminders of my days in the boonies briefly crossed my path. One was Johnny Pots, the November machine gunner who had been shipped to the 3rd Battalion as part of the personnel reshuffling to avoid that unit having a DEROS budge—a bunch of people leaving at the same time. Pots, loud and only semi-controllable, had been gleefully offered up by Sgt. Parker and had last been heard and seen cursing a blue streak as he flung himself on a Huey in a clearing on a jungle-covered hillside.

The 3rd Battalion moved several times during my months at LZ English, but for a portion of the period its headquarters was on a far corner of our dusty little world. I had occasion one day to visit the battalion S-1 on business. I walked the third of a mile to the battalion's area, conducted the business, and was about to return when the S-1 offered me a ride. He was headed to the brigade's area on business of his own. We went outside his webtoc and got in his jeep. And who should be driving but Johnny Pots. He greeted me quietly, "Hi, Captain Holland."

I was so surprised that I barely acknowledged his hello. He didn't say anything else on the short ride to the brigade, and truth be told, I was a little apprehensive about asking him how things were. He was certainly not the loud, boisterous guy who had been such a distraction during that long-ago night move in the mountains above Dak To. He had apparently avoided being assigned to the line in the 3rd Battalion. Instead, he had fallen into a cushy, safe job as a headquarters driver. Maybe the vastly increased odds that he would return to the Land of the Big PX had changed his attitude about his departure from Alpha Company. They dropped me near the brigade S-1 shop, and I entered the webtoc wondering at the ways of the world. Because of his disruptive behavior, Pots ends up spending only half a tour in the boonies. A quiet trooper, one who caused his NCOs and officers no problems, is rewarded with a full year of potential death. It seemed unfair. But if it were my unit, I would most likely opt to get rid of a disrupter if the opportunity presented itself.

The other Alpha trooper I ran across was also from November. Spec. 4 Markey was at LZ English to get a Silver Star. During the short period I was with the 1st Battalion headquarters, sleeping extensively and getting on the wrong side of LTC Gundersen, Markey had been performing heroics. The event occurred in the mountains surrounding the large valley near the Cambodian border where the battalion had been set up near a Special Forces camp and its airstrip. It was the location where the battalion's Four-Deuce Platoon got whacked.

Over a several day period, Alpha Company had been in sporadic contact with a North Vietnamese unit. Late one afternoon, the company thought that it had located an enemy laager site. That night, the company sent out a patrol from November. Markey volunteered to conduct a stealthy recon. He actually crept passed several North Vietnamese fighting positions into the unit's perimeter. What happened next—a firefight, an artillery strike, or nothing—I never did learn, but Markey was getting a Silver Star for sneaking into the enemy camp.

I talked briefly to him prior to his appearance before the general. He had acquired the attitude of calm assurance tinged with a bit of haughtiness, even arrogance, that was characteristic of those who had recently separated themselves from their peers by an act of derring-do. I was envious. Such reminders that I was stuck in a rear echelon job were not welcome.

In late June, time began to speed up a bit. The reason was travel. A little change of pace can do wonders for a clock slowed by boredom. First, I took a two-day trip to Quin Nhon. The purpose was to check out the in-country R&R facility there. General Allard had apparently finally gotten the message that bringing the squad of the week to his air-conditioned quarters had some negatives. So his idea was to send them for a 3-day in-country R&R. I caught a hop to Quin Nhon. Much of the area was typical of U.S. rear-echelon bases in Vietnam: air-conditioned offices and quarters, reasonable work hours, shined boots, and pressed uniforms. The beach wasn't anything to write home about, but a few days there sure beat, to my way of thinking, an afternoon with the general in his trailer. After a couple of evenings soaking up the suds at a quiet U.S. club in a French-era massive masonry building, and an afternoon at the beach, I reported back to LZ English.

Another trip was a one day affair by chopper down to Tuy Hoa. The brigade had been given a Deputy CO. He was an overweight, rumpled, middle-aged colonel who had as much business in a combat zone as the 1st Battalion commander who had been relieved shortly after my return from home leave. The colonel was a grandfatherly type, assuming your grandfather was an asshole. He had taken General Allard's lead and acquired himself an air-conditioned trailer to live in. Exactly what he did was unclear, but on one particular day he was to visit the 4th battalion at Tuy Hoa. Representatives of each staff section were to go with him to meet personally with their counterparts at the battalion.

The trip down was uneventful. The 173rd area at Tuy Hoa had become a much more permanent place since I had last seen it, in October of the previous year. Wooden structures with concrete floors had replaced tents. My staff interfacing took all of 15 minutes, and then I just hung around. We departed before lunch for a province headquarters to the west. This was my first exposure to the world of the MACV adviser. It was a world with a fairly high comfort quotient. The billets and offices at this province headquarters were in a square around a courtyard and were basically one continuous structure. Breaks at a couple of the corners provided entry and exit points. Several buildings were in the center courtyard, one of them a mess hall. All of the structures were permanent, constructed of masonry and wood.

I hung around the mess hall drinking coffee, somehow impressed by the stainless steel serving tables. The colonel had some business with the province people. After he was finished, we returned to the chopper and were off. Shortly after we were airborne, a rainstorm of tremendous velocity enveloped us. The Huey bounced and rocked. Looking past the pilots out the front windshield, I could see absolutely nothing. The chopper's window-wipers were beating furiously, but to nil effect. An uneasiness spread through the machine. Even the pilots seemed worried. They glanced at one another several times, and moved forward and sideways as if they were trying to see around the raindrops. All I could think of was a mountainside. I wondered if I would see it for a split second before we plowed in. We were in the grip of the storm for at least 10 minutes, and they were 10 minutes that seemed like 10 hours. Finally, the rain slackened and the ground below became visible. Eventually we broke into sunshine. LZ English actually looked good.

Yet another bit of traveling finally exposed me, after almost two years in Vietnam, to what R&R was really all about. The previous year, in my waning days with the 716th MPs, I had been to Singapore. The trip wasn't bad, but Singapore was a fairly straight-laced place. In late July of 1968, I spent five days in the then, and maybe still, sin capital of the world, Bangkok, Thailand.

Before arriving there, however, I had a little in-flight adventure. To get to Bangkok from An Khe, one first went to Cam Ranh Bay. There, one caught a civilian charter, such as a Boeing 707, complete with stewardesses. The plane would be jam-packed with a bunch of rowdy guys looking forward to a few days of fun. A few would be coming straight from the jungle. More would be from some rear echelon base, maybe a luxurious place like Quin Nhon—in which case you wondered why they needed an R&R in the first place—maybe a backwater like An Khe, or maybe a hole like LZ English. Wherever they were from, as a group they were raring to go.

A formality of military flying was that there always had to be an aircraft troop commander. In the case of an R&R flight and the troop flights to and from the states, this meant that one of the passengers, generally one of the highest ranking officers, would be told as he boarded, "And oh, by the way, you're the troop commander." I was given the honor for the R&R flight to Bangkok. It wasn't the first time I had been an aircraft troop commander, so I didn't think much of it. The main duty seemed to be to deliver a roster packet to the R&R people in Bangkok.

The plane had just reached cruising altitude for the two-hour flight when one of the stewardesses tapped me on the soldier. I was sitting in an aisle seat. She squatted down and asked in a very low voice, "Are you the aircraft troop commander?"

"Yes," I answered a little hesitantly.

"We have a problem in the rear of the plane." Her voice was breaking, and she was obviously pretty upset.

Hey, this was her plane! What the hell kind of problem could it be that I could handle better than her? "What is it?"

"There's a guy who's acting real strange."

Well, we were all kinda strange. "What's he doin'?"

"He's talking funny and making funny gestures."

"Has he got any kind of weapon, a knife or somethin'?"

"Not that I can see."

"Well, what danger is he presentin'?" I really didn't want to get involved in this.

"He's just really strange. He's scaring us." She looked at me expectantly, like I had a solution that was just about to pop out. Other than suffering the usual panic that possessed me whenever I was in the air, I wasn't particularly afraid. We had been searched pretty thoroughly before boarding, so I thought it unlikely he had a weapon. I would have been content to do nothing except that from the look on the stewardess' face, the nothing course of action was not something she would settle for. She said helpfully, "There's an empty seat beside him."

Yeah, I said to myself, the empty seat you're supposed to be in. "Okay, I'll come back in just a minute. Make like nothin's goin' on, and I'll be back shortly." I didn't want this guy, if he was a nut, to get the impression that I was taking formal control of him.

She left, and after a minute or so, I wandered toward the rear. He was sitting in the last row, by the window. It was a short row, with just two seats. I went by and into the lavatory. when I came out, I sat down in the empty seat. "Too crowded up there for me. Think I'll sit here." I was trying to be nonchalant. He was looking out the window. It seemed to take a couple of seconds for him to focus on the fact that someone was speaking to him. He swung his head around, and I got a full view of what had disturbed the stewardess. This guy had the original wild-eyed stare. Based on his eyes alone, any reasonable individual would conclude he was goofy in the extreme.

He had a 173rd patch on the pocket of his khaki shirt, and I said, "So you're in the 173rd. I am to. In headquarters now, but I was in 1st Bat. What battalion you in?"

The question was a puzzle. He lowered his eyes as if he was concentrating and began moving his hands in little jerks. His fingers were also in motion. They seemed to want to go in directions different than his hands, however. The effect was definitely disconcerting. I was willing to concede that the stewardess' concern might not have been an overreaction. Finally, he stammered something about the 4th Battalion.

"Oh, 4th Bat, huh? Whose your company commander? I know some of those guys."

This question was beyond the pale. After a lengthy pause during which his hands and fingers waged a number of small struggles, he said, "I don't know."

"Well, what company are ya in?" For a trooper, even a crazy one, not to know his company commander's name was a shock to me.

Company commanders defined a grunt's world. This guy, however, was obviously in his own world.

Finally, he recalled that he was in Charlie Company. I said, "Oh, that's Jackson, Captain Jackson. Good man." Jackson had been the CO for a number of months.

"I don't know," Loony said.

I spent the rest of the flight trying to keep a conversation going. I figured the energy he was putting into his answers might prevent him from paying heed to any dangerous ideas the voices in his head came up with. Several bits of information he divulged were that he had been in Vietnam 18 months, had been in the field most of that time, and was a permanent point-walker. That didn't sound quite right as most companies would not want a mental case walking point unless they were headed through a mine field. But I decided not to argue. I was damned happy when we landed in Bangkok, so happy that the stewardess' failure to express her thanks didn't even bother me.

Bangkok in 1968 was sex, pure and simple. Bars, dance halls, massage parlors—all had girls, most not much more than teenagers, at dirt cheap prices, and at least a few of whom seemed to enjoy their work. And more than a few of them were downright Oriental gorgeous, with long shining jet-black hair, deep luminous eyes, tiny waists, and perky breasts. They came in a variety of skin colors, from a creamy off-white to a rich deep brown. Forty years later, in a time of deadly sexual diseases, high moral codes, overbearing religious pontificators, and empowered women, describing in detail what one did as a young oversexed male with money to burn in the sin capital of the world would not be politically correct. I will say the vices I sampled did not include drugs. Indeed, I did not even see any evidence of drugs. As was the case with my entire Southeast Asia experience, in Bangkok I was either one step ahead of the drug epidemic or horribly naive.

The girls in the dance halls and massage parlors wore big buttons with numbers. In the dance halls, the girls danced with each other on the dance floor while the customers eyed the merchandise. If a customer saw something that caught his fancy, he would ask one of the older hostesses to bring him number 7, or whatever. At the massage parlors, the girls sat in a small amphitheater, usually looking at a television mounted above a large picture window. The customers would gaze upon the merchandise through the window. Again, once a selection was made, the choice would be communicated by indicating the young lady's number. For a young soldier whose sex life had been inadequate or largely non-existent prior to a visit to Bangkok, the system was a sure-fire way to make up for lost time.

I did have one legitimate platonic date during my five-day stay. The desk at the hotel was run by two giggling girls, probably in their late teens, one of them Chinese. They seemed to enjoy watching and commenting on the steady parade of women of lesser scruples accompanying the troopers up to the rooms. Maybe they were even a bit envious. Through a complex set of circumstances, I ended up taking the Chinese girl out one night. A couple of guys from the 173rd AG Company were in town. They were going out to eat at a fancy restaurant and asked me to come along. Each of them had latched onto a girl for his whole stay. I, on the other hand, was "beaucoup butterfly," seeking a different partner every night, with still a further diversion each afternoon—remember, I was young.

When they asked me to accompany them, it was too late to find a friendly whore who I would be willing to put up with for the whole evening, and in addition feed. So I asked the Chinese girl, and she assented. It was probably a mistake. We had an enjoyable evening, but I knew the next night I would be leading some professional past the desk up to my room. If by some fluke the Chinese girl liked me, my subsequent actions would be a slap in the face. But sensitivity has never been my strong suit. Some weeks hence, however, the Chinese girl was to even the score. That story comes later.

Bangkok's attractions included several things besides girls. One was Singha beer. The stuff came in big bottles and went down like water.

Another was a decent pizza place, at least by standards of the late 1960s. And a third was snakes. Bangkok had a big snake farm where cobras and king cobras were milked. Snakes have always fascinated and semi-terrorized me, so I was enthralled by the snake milkers running around as blithely as you please among all the slithery varmints.

In addition to the government snake place, a number of smaller private snake houses competed for the tourist dollar. Most had a handful of snakes in cages and one or two big boa constrictors or pythons that handlers would drape over your shoulders so you could have your picture taken.

Which reminds me of a story I heard from a Vietnam vet friend several years later, after I had returned to the states. He was a lieutenant in the Marine Corps, in Marine artillery. He and a small group of hard-drinking Marine lieutenants and NCOs went to Bangkok. They visited a snake farm one morning, already well into the day's drinking. One of the lieutenants had an eight-to-ten foot snake placed around his neck, the snake's body as thick as the guy's thigh. The lieutenant stood facing the camera. His right hand gripped the snake's neck just behind its triangular evil-looking head, which was about the size of a large man's fist, a very large man.

Actually, a very large man, a bleary eyed gunny sergeant, was standing a couple of feet away. As the Thai picture taker was fumbling with his camera and the lieutenant was saying through a forced grin, "Hurry the fuck up," the gunny and the snake were glaring intently at each other. The snake was touching some primeval Marine instinct in the gunny, and he reacted primevally. With a curt "I hate fuckin' snakes," the gunny drew back and launched one of his huge appendages. It slammed into the snake's head. The snake immediately went into constriction mode. The lieutenant felt those thigh-size coils on each side of his neck begin moving rapidly toward each other. He quickly threw his arms up and jumped forward, sending the snake crashing to the ground. The Thais were jabbering angrily, the marines, except for the lieutenant and the gunny, were guffawing drunkenly, and the snake was ponderously trying to pull itself together. The lieutenant, white as a sheet, was cursing the gunny, who seemed immensely satisfied with the morning's work. Someone threw 20 bhat—bhat was Thai currency, with one bhat being worth about twenty cents—at the Thais, and the group departed for more adventures, the lieutenant still hurling obscenities at the gunny.

The U.S. military's support of sin in Bangkok was covert but extensive. The incoming R&R flights were met by military chartered buses, which took the troops to a reception center. Some perfunctory remarks about the dangers of alcohol, drugs, and unprotected sex were rattled off, and then the buses took the troops to different hotels, all of which either had girls on the premises or had no restrictions on bringing girls in. Drivers at the hotels tried to get a trooper to contract with them for his full five-day stay. A contracted driver would chauffeur the individual to the dens of iniquity, the shopping places, and the restaurants, and be on call pretty much the whole time. A driver would also likely try to get the trooper to make a PX and commissary run. If he was successful in this con job, the driver would have some material for the black market. Many troops developed what they thought were close friendships with the drivers, not focusing on what a mercenary group of thieves the latter were. And behind this whole system of sin and corruption was Uncle Sam, God bless 'im.

I returned from R&R near the end of July. My tour in the S-1 shop was coming down the stretch. My request for another six-month extension in Vietnam had come through several weeks before, and the question of where I was to spend the six months began pressing. I would have liked a company commander's slot in the 173rd, but something told me I would be pursuing an unobtainable goal. Those competing for companies in the elite 173rd included lifers with West Point rings and ranger taps. With a few exceptions such as Wolfowitz, they were the cream of the crop. Moreover, most were impressive physical specimens with outgoing personalities who made great initial impressions. I wasn't a runt, but over the years not many people have given me second looks. In addition, being laid back and cynical, I had a great deal of difficulty ginning up the effort to grab someone's attention on first meeting.

Thus I didn't see much possibility of getting a company in the 173rd. If I truly wanted to be a company commander, I should have attempted some contacts with battalion commanders, but I didn't make the attempts. Maybe in truth I didn't want the job. I was concerned about my lack of formal infantry training. But I think the main thing was that aggressively lobbying for a job was not something I've ever been comfortable with.

Therefore, I developed the notion of taking a week or so to travel around Vietnam looking for a home. Special Forces, the Green Berets, were my preference. I envisioned myself leading a Mike Force on a Sneaky Pete operation into Cambodia or Laos. That would be the life. The fact that I had no Special Forces training didn't phase me. After all, I had no infantry training and yet had ended up a platoon leader in the 173rd.

Major Tree was amenable to the idea of my taking off for a few days. In fact, he probably welcomed it. So I had some travel orders put together authorizing travel to a number of places from the Central Highlands south to the Mekong Delta. The extreme north, I Corps, held no interest as I envisioned it overrun with Marines, the 1st Cav, the 101st, and the Americal Division. With all those units, what room was there for real Sneaky Pete operations?

If truth be told, however, my main destination was the Pearl of the Orient, Saigon, and my main purpose was to see the old stomping grounds. It had been a year since I had left. Both Saigon and I had been bloodied—me at Tuy Hoa and Dak To, Saigon during Tet. I might do a little job hunting, but mostly I wanted to stroll down Tu Do Street and wander through Cholon. Saigon was off-limits to anyone not on official business. With my travel orders, however, I was on official business. Consequently, toward the latter part of August I departed LZ English. I would be back for a brief stay following my wanderings and before the 30-day leave to which I was entitled for the six-month extension—after my sybaritic excursion to Bangkok, that is where I intended to take the 30 days—but for all practical purposes I had stacked arms in the S-1 shop.

A C-130 flight went directly from An Khe to Saigon several times a week. I was getting to be an old hand at hopping C-130 flights. Air time to Saigon was a little over an hour. We arrived about nine in the evening. Tan Son Nhut was the same bustling amalgamation of U.S. efficiency and Vietnamese seediness. I didn't know what the curfews or travel restrictions might be now, but I chanced it and caught a ride to the Victoria Hotel, just across the street from the New Prince, my old BOQ. The room was air-conditioned much too cold, the beer was adequate, and the girl was lackadaisical. Same old Saigon.

But not quite. The next morning I put on civilian clothes and made my way to the PX in Cholon. The smell of rotting garbage, defecation, urine, and nuc mam was certainly familiar. But at the PX gate, the MP said as I flashed my ID card, "Sir, you're supposed to be in uniform."

"Really? I worked here a year ago. Then, you were only in uniform if you were workin'."

"New rules after Tet, Sir. Everybody has to be in uniform all the time."

"Even in the bars?"

"That's right, Sir. Even in the bars."

He was friendly and didn't seem intent on writing me up, so I said, "Okay, I'm on my way back to get dressed. Thanks a lot."

"Right, Sir."

Uniforms in the bars. Somehow the idea appealed to me. There had seemed something ridiculous about trying to deny the huge American presence in Saigon by keeping uniforms out of bars and restaurants, so maybe Tet had produced something beneficial. I went back to the hotel, put on my jungle fatigues, and reemerged.

Except for the uniform situation, Saigon was much the same. The pizza place still existed at the north end of Tu Do street. The bar girls still hustled Saigon Tea with a passion. The contrast with Bangkok was dramatic. The girls in Bangkok sold sex. The girls in Saigon sold tea. After several days, I had enough remembrances and was ready to get to Bangkok for my thirty days of debauchery. The hell with job-hunting, the hell with Saigon Tea, the hell with anything but those Bangkok babes. I beat a quick retreat to An Khe and LZ English and spent my last week trying to avoid any meaningful work—much to John B. Sweat's delight. Even though I didn't find a job, I put in a request for a transfer to Special Forces. The paperwork would be processed while I was on leave, and if it were approved I would at least have something new when I returned. I also wrote a letter home telling my parents I would be staying in Vietnam for my final six months in the Army. "And oh by the way, I'll be taking 30 days leave in Bangkok. If there is an emergency, the Army will probably be able to find me."

I had to give the evening briefing for several days when Major Tree was away. He had severe back problems and went to Quin Nhon for a going over by the medical quacks. At the first briefing, I nervously finished my short spiel that "the brigade strength is on the board" and glanced at BG Allard. He was intently scowling at me from his padded, over-stuffed easy chair. The look seemed to be asking, "What is with this guy? Two years here and he wants more? Something's not right." Maybe so, General, maybe so.

A day or so before I departed, my replacement arrived. He was a wizened little captain, new in country. I seemed to be making a habit of being followed by wizened little replacements. The lieutenant who had taken over Alpha Company's 3rd Platoon from me back in January had been in the wizened-little category. Major Tree seemed happy to have me on the way. Shortly before my trip to Saigon, he had asked what I thought about expanding the S-1 shop with several assistant S-1s. I had said I didn't think it was necessary, implying not very tactfully that such an expansion was empire-building. Consequently, Major Tree undoubtedly viewed me as an obstacle to progress. And indeed, once me and my backward attitude were gone, the S-1 shop quickly grew to be a one major, four-captain operation.

Back at An Khe, an incident occurred that was indicative of the deterioration of discipline in the U.S. Army, even in the 173rd. I went to the 173rd's finance office to make a substantial withdrawal, $2,000, for my trip. After all, 30 days of whoring was not going to be inexpensive. The cash-dispensing clerk was a black guy with an attitude. Something about a youngish looking captain withdrawing a huge hunk of money for a trip to an R&R paradise roused his sense of injustice. Why should this honky be so blessed? He made a comment that approached insubordination, a comment that in the Army of two years before would have been inconceivable. But this was late 1968, in a rear area, and mutiny was in the air. The comment was something like, "What the hell you gonna do with all this goddamn money, Captain? Goddamn officers shouldn't have this kinda dough."

A number of enlisted troopers were in line behind me, most of whom had heard the comment. Was this the way things were now at An Khe? I managed to stammer, "You're out of line soldier," but I wasn't thinking quick enough to say anything more. Two courses of action would have been preferable. One was to close the window down, get the guy's supervisor, and raise hell. The other was to come up with a response that would have put the insubordinate asshole in his place, maybe just: "I need the money to screw myself silly, Soldier. What's it to ya?" What I did do was to report the incident to the finance officer, a major. Since the S-1 had staff responsibility for finance, the major answered to Major Tree, who I also called about the incident. Perhaps someone jumped on the mouthy shithead's butt.

Debauchery Again

This time, my trip to Bangkok was not on an R&R Boeing 707 cattle car. Once or twice a week, a C-130 made a trip from Cam Ranh Bay to Bangkok by way of Saigon. By taking this flight, I would stay away from the R&R crowd and the R&R in-processing, and could wear jungle fatigues instead of the R&R uniform of khakis. In other words, I would not be subject to much in the way of bureaucratic scrutiny.

While overnight at Cam Ranh Bay, I ran into Ricketts, the Australian-born sergeant who had been a squad leader in the 3rd Platoon of Alpha Company—November. He had wangled a job at the troop transient facility, and the living was obviously good. He had put on about 20 pounds. A load of lard and pressed uniforms sure could destroy a "cold hard-charging" image.

I also ran into Ditmar Jack, the lieutenant who had joined the 173rd at the same time I had almost a year before and who had been with Bravo Company. He was DEROSing. He was also full of himself, having picked up a Silver Star somewhere along the line. He, I, and a couple of other 173rd junior officers had a few beers at the transient Officers Club. Under the cover of how hard it was to lead men in combat, Jack went into his heroics in considerable detail. He also took a few snide swipes at Alpha Company for not rushing to the rescue of Charlie and Delta that fateful day at Dak To. Apparently as a sop to me, he did say Alpha had been through a bad time on Hill 882. "A few guys I respect told me it was rough." Well, thanks shithead. I hope your political career, the reason you came to Vietnam, turned out well, although in the intervening decades I don't recall running across your name among the movers and shakers.

Waiting around airfields was a part of the Vietnam experience, particularly for people like me who had embarked on careers in the war zone. The wait at the Cam Ranh Bay field for the flight to Bangkok was especially long that late August day in 1968. I arrived at the airfield early in the morning, but the flight turned out to be hours late. The Cam Ranh Bay field was an extremely active place. Boeing 707s were arriving from and departing for the states. C-130s were taking troops, supplies, and equipment up-country. Jet fighter-bombers left to pound various remote patches of jungle. Choppers kept the air in turmoil. Passengers waited in a large hanger with some seating and much controlled confusion. The place was the proverbial beehive of activity, a crossroads of a thousand stories. The wait was long, but the ceaseless activity provided ample entertainment.

Eventually, the run to Bangkok departed. The passengers, who weren't many in number, were not representative of U.S. forces in Vietnam. They were mostly in the Old Asia Hand category—Special Forces types who measured their tours in terms of years rather than months and who divided their time between Vietnam and clandestine bases in northern Thailand, insiders who knew enough about tweaking the system to wrangle an unofficial R&R, Air Force wheelers and dealers on semi-authorized procurement missions. We stopped in Saigon where a few more war professionals boarded, and then made Bangkok about 10 in the evening. I took a taxi to the hotel where I had stayed on R&R, the one with the Chinese girl I had taken out.

So how to summarize the 30 days in Sin City? Well, to hit the highlights, I met a semi-working girl, moved in with her, bought her a house full of furniture, endured her increasing disinterestedness in sex, read a lot of books, and got revenged on by the Chinese desk clerk.

I met Trachit Pangbon in one of the city's dance hall-meat markets, but the exact circumstances are lost in a cloud of Singha beer. I have this vague recollection that she was not a full-time number-wearing employee, just a friend of one of them, perhaps in need of some end-of-the-month rent money. She was short, dark, cute, and serious. When she discovered that I was in Bangkok for not just five days but a full month, presumably with a hefty wad of cash, she set her sights. I never had a chance.

She had just rented waterfront property in the suburbs, meaning a house built on stilts in one of the swamps and marshes that made up a good part of Bangkok and its environs. The house had three rooms and a bath and was set in the middle of a row of about ten similar dwellings. A facing row of houses was on the other side of a wooden sidewalk that provided access to dry land. The houses in the rows were about three feet apart. The inhabitants of the little community appeared to be mostly families, with a few single girls mixed in. One of the next door neighbors was an ex-working girl with a live-in U.S. Army boyfriend. He was a sergeant in the Army's headquarters complex in Bangkok, a fat happy guy who seemed to have found his personal paradise.

The swamp over which the houses were built served as garbage and trash disposal. Cooking scrapes, newspapers, bags, old clothes, all ended up in the two feet of black, evil-looking water. The toilet facilities, a porcelain-surrounded hole in the floor, emptied into a large pipe that extended down into the muck. Maybe it connected to a city sewer pipe; maybe it just added the urine and defecation to the other garbage and trash.

So this was my home for almost four weeks. I spent considerable time reading. Among the books were several by Bernard Fall, who wrote about the French debacle in Vietnam. *Dien Bien Phu* and *Street Without Joy* described what the United States was trying to avoid. Despite my two years in Vietnam, I hadn't given much thought to where the war was going, to who would eventually "win," to whether the cause was worth the sacrifice. For me, Vietnam was still an experience, part of my growing up. The larger issues were immaterial. But I was a history buff, someone who enjoyed reading of the trials and tribulations of the past. Thus I read Fall's works as one interested in the subject, one who actually had some first-hand knowledge of the matter, but one who really didn't care about the big picture.

Once I had sprung for about 600 bucks to furnish her new quarters, Trachit Pangbon quickly settled into domestic life. We went out a few times, and spent several days at Patya Beach on the Bay of Thailand, but mostly it was evenings over the klong, a Thai word for "canal" that seemed to encompass pretty much any putrid patch of water. During the days, we did some shopping, and I often went off on my own, searching for bookstores and, as Trachit's interest in sex waned, massage parlors. I wanted to do some running but couldn't find a field to circle. I saw the movie *The Graduate*, and the music left a distinct impression. Simon and Garfunkle's songs captured a mood, a melancholy, of the times. It was not a lethargic-inducing melancholy but one that fed an unease, a restlessness.

I was not Trachit Pangbon's first love. She had enjoyed a relationship of several years with an Air Force lieutenant stationed at a U.S. air base near Patya Beach. She might even have expected to go to the states with him. But as with most such relationships between GIs and local honeys, his "I'll send for you" marked a permanent goodbye. He ended up with fond memories to counter his future humdrum existence in middle class America. She learned that GIs were a bunch of silver-tongue devils. But he was still much on her mind as she mentioned him often. Maybe his memory was the cause of her declining interest in sex, that plus the fact that I had made the mistake of paying up front.

The Army sergeant next door to us over the klong may have found his personal paradise, but his girl seemed to have also. She was content to spend hours on her porch chattering amiably with any and all who happened by. Towards evening she would fix herself up a bit for the sergeant's return home. She was more Chinese than Trachit Pangbon, but evidently she wasn't from the industrious branch of the Chinese people.

She and the sergeant had a dog named Laddie. In Western fashion, the sergeant treated it kindly and gently, like one of the family. When the sergeant was around, the girl was equally mannered. When he was away, however, she reverted to the oriental approach to dog care: kick and beat the muthafucker to kingdom come. One day, I thought she might have gone too far. I awoke about 9 in the morning to the sound of the dog howling in pain. The howls were punctuated by her screams and curses and sounds of impacts. The noises continued for close to 30 minutes. Eventually they subsided, to be replaced by an intermittent whimpering. When I finally emerged, ready for the late morning smells wafting up from the klong, she was sitting on her porch, the picture of demureness. I asked, "What was wrong with Laddie?"

"I show him God."

"Yeah? What did he do?"

"He grabbed meat off table."

Maybe the sergeant's paradise had a flaw or two in it.

Shortly after my arrival in Bangkok, I wrote to Sgt. Brotzman back in An Khe to attempt to stop my paperwork requesting a transfer to Special Forces. I was fearful that if the transfer did go through, I would end up with no more than a desk job at Special Forces headquarters in Nha Trang. Although my chances for a company in the 173rd were slim, they were probably better than my chances for command of a Special Forces A Team. As my return address for Sgt. Brotzman, I gave the address of the R&R hotel.

I was dropping by the hotel every few days to kid with the desk clerks, one of them being my little Chinese platonic date. How she had felt when I turned up again and then left to set up house was something that didn't push its way into my consciousness. If I had given the matter any thought at all, which I didn't, I would have assumed she understood that my "needs" required more than a platonic relationship. And she did not strike me as anything more than platonic relationship material.

But if my cavalier attitude hurt her, she got revenge. What she did was to infuriate me almost to the point of violence, leaving me wanting to commit mayhem. And all over $5.

One day when I went by the hotel, she showed me a letter from Sgt. Brotzman. It was undoubtedly a reply to my request about the Special Forces transfer. I reached for it, but she pulled back. "Twenty baht," she said. At first, I thought she was joking. I just grinned and kept my hand out across the desk. She placed the letter beyond my reach and went back to writing in her ledgers. Her co-worker was also studiously engaged in activity.

"Hey, c'mon. Gimme my letter."

"Twenty baht," she said, without looking up.

"What d'ya mean? That's mine. You can't keep it. Give it to me."

"Twenty baht."

"Look. Stop joking around. That's an important letter."

"Twenty baht."

"Now I mean it, dammit. I'll report this hotel to the R&R people. They'll have MPs here, maybe close you down."

"Twenty baht."

This continued for some time. I was becoming enraged. This little no-count homely girl who I had deigned to take out for an evening was trying to extort money from me, a goddamn Captain in the elite 173rd Airborne Brigade. Who the fuck did she think she was?

I went over to the bar and had a beer to try to calm down. The courses of action were not appealing. I could jump the desk and physically take the thing, in which case the Thai police and I might have a set-to. I could continue to plead, which was obviously delighting the girl and her co-worker and was just as obviously getting me nowhere. Or I could pay the twenty baht.

There was no way in hell I was going to fork over five whole dollars to get my own damn letter. And as mad as I was, I was in enough control to keep from the physical approach. So I attempted one more round of pleading, being close to positive that it would be futile. It was.

My attempt only titillated them more. So before I throttled someone, I turned and left, figuratively kissing my letter goodbye. If there was ever a time in my life when I truly "trembled with rage," it was during this little incident.

What's the moral of the story? There probably are several, but the one I came away with is, it don't pay to be nice to homely Chinese girls.

My 30-day leave in Sin City was coming to an end. Even though it hadn't been perfect, I was reluctant to depart. I said goodbye to the neighboring Army sergeant and his lady. I promised to write Trachit Pangbon and to return within a few months on R&R. On a rainy depressing evening, we took a taxi to the airport, and I caught the C-130 back to the 'Nam. My last six months were coming up, I was returning to an unknown assignment, and I wasn't a happy cowboy.

Sgt. Brotzman greeted my arrival back in An Khe with the news that he had succeeded in stopping my request for a transfer to Special Forces. This was the news that was in the letter now possessed by the homely Chinese girl. Maybe she's still got it. I was a little disappointed. I needed a change of pace. The thought of another six months in the 173rd was depressing.

John B. Sweat was also in An Khe. He was on his way home, DEROSing. He had that attitude of condescending superiority many short-timers acquired. He reported that in the short month since my departure Major Tree had made substantial progress on his empire-building. I had been replaced by four captains, and two clerks were now handling John B. Sweat's duties. The S-4 must have been gnashing his teeth at the rapid growth in the webtoc across the way.

We celebrated my return, John B. Sweat's departure, and Sgt. Brotzman's existence with an afternoon at the Fortress just outside An Khe. I did most of the drinking and all of the wenching. John B. Sweat and Sgt. Brotzman spent much of their time explaining to the other patrons, most of them young enlisted troopers, the conduct of their drunken leader.

Major Tree bent over backwards to accommodate my desires regarding an assignment. The trouble was, I didn't know what I desired. I wanted to be in one of the battalions, one where I would have the best shot at a company command slot, but I didn't realistically think I actually had such a shot. I was too junior a captain and had not been to the career course. And I had not buttered up any of the battalion commanders. Two of the battalions needed captains—the 2nd and the 4th—and after a couple of days of hemming and hawing I asked Major Tree to send me to the 4th.

The 4th of the 503rd, 173rd Airborne Brigade, was still headquartered at Tuy Hoa. For about a month, however, it had been involved in an operation on the other side of Vietnam. Along with several battalions of the 4th Infantry Division, the 4th Battalion was screening a Special Forces camp southwest of Pleiku, on the Cambodian border. The camp had been attacked and laid siege to by a sizeable NVA force. For a week or so until the relief task force arrived, the camp's existence had been in jeopardy. The NVA had now faded back across the border, probing just enough to keep the U.S. forces in the area.

I caught a C-130 flight to Pleiku and a chopper to the 4th Battalion's forward area. Also on the chopper flight was a 4th Battalion captain I vaguely knew. He had already been a company commander and most recently was on the battalion staff. Although very close to his DEROS, he was coming out, somewhat reluctantly, to take over one of the companies for a week or so. The company commander had been wounded, and the battalion commander had not decided on a permanent replacement. I thought this might be an opening for me. Consequently, I viewed the upcoming introduction to the battalion commander as a time when I needed to avoid my usual unimpressive first impression.

Thirty seconds into the meeting, however, I knew it was hopeless. LTC Sandy Wayan was a tall photogenic officer who was to go on to several stars. He was also one of those physically imposing individuals who are much taken with themselves and, in judging others, are prone to attach considerable, indeed inordinate, importance to appearance. After all, when you are great yourself and physically good-looking, you tend to draw a correlation between the two characteristics, even believing that the absence of one means the absence of the other. Thus if appearance-wise someone happens to be below par, he or she is below par in other respects as well.

So LTC Wayan took one look at me, listened to my nasal backwoods Virginia draw for several seconds, and made his judgment. Of course, I made an equally quick judgment about him. In my frame of reference, a physically imposing guy was usually an A Numbah One Asshole, never mind that he might actually have some talent. Thus my new commander and I acquired instant unfavorable impressions of each other. He said that I would be the battalion's S-3 Air. He feigned interest in me for a few minutes and then passed me off to the S-3, who would be my immediate boss. During my almost month with the 4th battalion, I was to have only one other conversation of any length with his highness, my departure conversation. The S-3 was a major and new to his duties. He seemed like an okay sort but was scrambling to get the job under control and to understand what his boss expected. Complicating his indoctrination was that he was also new to Vietnam, on his first tour.

The fire support base where the battalion was located was on a small hill. Several artillery batteries and a number of logistical elements were part of the ensemble, making for a crowded situation. After my introductions, I looked for a place to call home. It was the dry season, so a hooch wasn't necessary. I decided just to plop right beside the headquarters tent. In fact, the thigh-high sandbag wall encircling the tent was wide enough for an air mattress. Therefore, when I turned in for the evening I laid my carcass on the sandbags. This was home for two nights. Following the second night, the major told me LTC Wayan didn't approve of my sleeping arrangements. I had to find more standard quarters.

Undoubtedly contributing to the colonel's unhappiness was that I had not participated in a late night planning session that second night. The session was to work out the details for the battalion's move back to Tuy Hoa. We were to go by chopper to the Pleiku airfield and then by C-130 to Tuy Hoa. The colonel wanted to plan the thing by the book, organizing loads by aircraft, determining the number of aircraft required, and so forth. Being totally ignorant of such things, I thought such extensive planning was unnecessary. Why couldn't we just shove everything on planes until we were done? Besides, an E-8 operations sergeant was in immediate charge of the planning, and he was an asshole. (It seemed a goodly proportion of the battalion hierarchy were assholes.) So while he and the colonel played with planning charts, tables, and templates, I went to bed.

If truth be told, the main problem was the same one I had experienced when I returned from home leave six months earlier. My mind and body were still on civilian time. To get them off civilian time, I needed a real job, a demanding job, a challenging job, one that filled the hours. Anything less, and I folded up. And being S-3 Air was considerably less. The lack of something meaningful to do was to make my sojourn in the 4th Battalion an unproductive one. Fortunately, the sojourn was to be brief.

With the arrival of the U.S. task force and the departure of the main body of the NVA attackers, the defense of the Special Forces camp had deteriorated into a long picket line facing west. The line companies were broken all the way down into five- and six-men fire teams. These were positioned along possible avenues of approach—ridgelines, valleys, streams, trails. The positions were as much as a quarter mile apart. The theory was that an attacking NVA force would be discovered when it stumbled across one of the outposts. The other outposts would then be called in, and the platoons and companies reconstituted to meet the threat. Whether there would have been enough time to do this seemed to me to be an uncertainty, but hey, I was only an observer. In any case, the possibility that the theory would be tested was fading. The NVA gave no sign they were thinking of returning, and hence planning for the task force's breakup and departure was underway.

The departure was to come less than a week after my arrival. That was a short period but long enough for me to seal my second-tier position among the battalion's captains. There would be no company for this child in Wayan's unit. Indeed, I was behind even a lieutenant. One of the company commanders was a senior lieutenant, Charlie Jones. This individual, not the same as the 1st Battalion's Charlie Jones, was in Wayan's mode—tall and impressive looking. He also certainly seemed to be more than competent. He had been with the battalion since way before Dak To and had only a few weeks to go before DEROSing. Consequently, his company would be available, but with Wayan's negative opinion of me apparent and growing, it was obvious I would not be in the running.

There was one unique thing about Charlie Jones. He was the only company commander or platoon leader I encountered who wasn't armed to the teeth. He didn't carry an M-16, a CAR-15, or a shotgun. He only had a pistol, the standard Army Colt-45. Apparently he took seriously the principle that leaders were to lead and not play Cowboys and Indians by getting involved in firefights themselves. Me? Half my motivation in becoming a Vietnam lifer was the hope of having an opportunity to go one-on-one with Charlie.

Incidentally, shotguns had become something of a fad among officers in the 173rd, and with deadly consequences. A 4th Battalion platoon leader was to be killed shortly after my departure from the battalion because his shotgun was no match for an NVA's AK-47. The two came across each other on a trail—the platoon leader was playing point-man. With about 40 meters separating the weapons, the single-shot shotgun came off second best to the 30-round banana clip of the

AK. The platoon leader left behind an in-country fiancée—an Air Force nurse at the hospital at Tuy Hoa Airfield.

I sunk further down on Wayan's shitlist the day the battalion left for Tuy Hoa. The firebase had been broken down, and the equipment and troops were in the process of being moved. The headquarters group was waiting by a road for a Chinook. I was chewing bubble gum and absent-mindedly blowing bubbles. The S-3 pulled me aside and said: "I know this sounds stupid, but Colonel Wayan just told me to tell you to stop blowing bubbles. He doesn't think it's professional."

"You're kidding."

"Nope. Bubbles are out."

Some people are better able to adjust to their surroundings than others. One of my life's faults has been a paucity of adjustment ability. The adjusters in this world would not have been much bothered by this incident. They would have told themselves, "Well, that's the kind of guy I'm working for," altered their conduct accordingly, and not thought further about it. But I take such reprimands deeply and personally, dwell on them extensively, and don't forget. Such small incidents can forever thereafter color my views of and attitude toward the perpetrator. Any lingering possibility that LTC Wayan and I could develop a tolerable relationship was dashed on that dusty road near the Cambodian border. Bazooka Bubble Gum did the deed.

The battalion arrived back in Tuy Hoa for a three- to five-day stand down, another indication of the changing nature of the war and the 173rd's method of operation. A year previously when I had joined the brigade, five-day stand downs weren't part of the program. And inconceivable a year earlier would have been the situation of the deputy brigade commander and his rehabilitation squad.

By the fall of 1968, the 1960s were catching up with the 173rd Airborne Brigade. Rebellion, mostly muted but occasionally overt, was breaking out in the ranks. Discipline was giving way to something soft and mushy. The grandfatherly old fart who was the deputy brigade commander and who I had accompanied on the chopper ride from hell several months previously had been sent, or maybe banished, to Tuy Hoa. Ostensibly, he was the senior 173rd officer at Tuy Hoa and the commander of a task force the major component of which was the 4th Battalion. The reality concerning military operations was that His Highness Sandy Wayan was the real power and the grandfatherly old colonel was no more than a figurehead.

The grandfatherly old colonel was not a nonentity, however. His presence was felt in other areas. In fact, his efforts at rehabilitating certain dregs had made him a disruptive force. What the colonel had done was to create a rehabilitation squad of about five or six black guys who were troublemakers of one sort or another. Rather than being thrown in the slammer for their infractions, and for the most part their infractions—fighting, insubordination, drug use, and the like—were sufficient to warrant slammer time, these dregs were embraced by the colonel. Apparently, his theory was that they didn't need punishment or discipline but tender loving care. He kept them halfway occupied raking the sand around his tent, policing up a bit, and following him in his meanderings. He and his entourage made quite a sight: a fat old fart in a baggy uniform—incidentally without jump wings as he was a leg, that is, not airborne qualified—trailed by a laughing, jiving group with Afro-hairdos, unbuttoned shirts, trousers rolled up rather then bloused, and lots of beads.

Naturally, the privileged position and antics of these young troopers were bitterly resented by the law-biding members, the vast majority, of the 4th Battalion. The resentment occasionally boiled over in the mess hall when one or more of the group would sashay through, loud and arrogant. The fact that more scuffles didn't arise from these encounters was a wonder.

For me, the next two weeks were one of my drunker periods. Without a meaningful job, with a bad attitude, with a handy officers-NCO club, I headed in only one direction—down. An E-6 staff sergeant was the proprietor of the club, and he just happened to have been one of

Captain Jerome's radio operators back in Alpha of the 1st Battalion. He had extended his time in Vietnam for a promotion opportunity and the cushy job of running a bar. He, I, and several others got drunker than nine skunks the night of the 4th Battalion's return and then went carousing in a fishing village adjacent to the 173rd's area.

The situation of the fishing village was unusual. It was completely surrounded by American installations—the 173rd to the south, Tuy Hoa Airfield to the north, and an Army aviation outfit to the west. The village was separated from these installations by several strands of fencing, a couple hundred meters of open field, and more fencing. A vehicle trail through the fences and across the open space was the only official route of ingress and egress. The trail itself was surrounded on both sides by fences, and access was through an MP checkpoint. In theory, the village was off-limits. In practice, it had become, as had all villages near U.S. bases, a place for entertaining young guys with active hormones. The fences contained a number of holes, and each night individuals and small groups would make their furtive way to the attractions. I could have done without being introduced to this diversion.

I awoke late the next morning and found myself alone in my quarters, which was a large room I was to share with five or six other junior officers and NCOs. The hangover was a real pounder, throbbing behind my eyes and down my neck. My mouth was the dryness and fuzziness of cotton. I made my unsteady way to the headquarters buildings. Other staff members were hard at work and had obviously been so for some hours. The S-3 pulled me aside, "Where've you been?"

"Well, uh, I didn't know things would get goin' so early today."

"You're not makin' a very good impression 'round here. My advice to you is to do some shapin' up. I hope I don't have to say anything more about this. Now on another thing, the CO is making you the S-2. You need to get with Sergeant Williams, the battalion intelligence sergeant."

Shit. Chewed out and made the S-2 to boot. A worse non-job than S-3 Air. My last six months in the 'Nam were shaping up as a real downer. I found Sergeant Williams, an E-7, and ascertained that the first priorities were to inventory and sign for the battalion's collection of secret documents, and to ensure that we were in compliance with all document storage regulations. "Sir," he said, "I gotta tell ya that the battalion's secret documents are a mess."

"Well, who's signed for 'em now?"

"That's not real clear, Sir. Captain Johnson, the previous S-2, has been gone for over a month. I suppose he's still responsible."

"Look, I just ain't motivated to get involved in this crap. You get everything up-to-date, make sure where everything is, and then I'll be ready to sign."

"That's gonna take some time, Sir."

"No problem. Maybe I'll be gone by then."

"You got plans, Sir?"

"Not really, but ya can always hope."

So I left Sgt. Williams with the task of inventorying the battalion's collection of secret documents. I had no desire at all to get involved in anything having to do with pushing paper. Five months as assistant brigade S-1 had given me enough frigging paper for a lifetime. If I couldn't be in the boonies, I didn't want to be doing anything. Drinking was my only solace, drinking and writing Trachit Pangbon. I hadn't received any letters from her, although I didn't really expect any. Still, as down as I was, I could have used evidence that someone, even a money-grubbing Thai working girl, gave a crap about me.

The weather wasn't helping my mood. Several days after we arrived at Tuy Hoa, and just prior to the line companies' scheduled insertion into the surrounding mountains, a typhoon-like storm blew in from the South China Sea. It blew in and settled down. For almost a week, the wind howled at gale force and the rain came down in sheets. The temperature was almost chilly. The battalion hunkered down to wait it out. There were desultory staff meetings and efforts at bringing paperwork and equipment maintenance up to date. Mainly, however, the time was spent watching the fury of nature on a rampage and being thankful that we weren't in the mountains.

One of the meetings—one of the few I didn't find a way to avoid—brought home how out-of-touch I was with the battalion leadership. The meeting was actually a briefing by one of the company commanders, a Captain Wynsack. He had been a company CO for only a few weeks, but this was his second tour in the 'Nam. His first had been with the 101st Airborne, where he had spent considerable time as an infantry platoon leader. He was a senior captain and had been through the infantry career course at Ft. Benning.

I had already had considerable experience with the good Captain Wynsack. One of the brigade S-1's functions had been to assign all new lieutenants and captains. The AG personnel people at An Khe provided recommendations, and the general gave final approval, but Major Tree was the primary decision-maker. Until a decision was made, a new lieutenant or captain would park his carcass at An Khe, just as I had parked my carcass at Bien Hoa over a year previously while I waited for an assignment. Most took the few days wait in stride, unhappy but not causing Sgt. Brotzman too much trouble. But Wynsack had been different. He had commandeered Brotzman's phone and proceeded to pester Major Tree and I personally between calls to various friends in the far corners of the Republic and to his wife, who was an Army nurse stationed in Thailand. He was actually a likeable guy, just burdened with a type A-triple plus personality.

Wynsack also had a serious unrealistic streak, as this particular meeting was to show. The purpose of the meeting was to describe innovations he was instituting in his defensive positions. Instead of a rectangular trench covered with a few sandbags on small logs to accommodate three to five troopers, Wynsack envisioned a Y-shaped arrangement. The bottom leg of the Y would be a small two-person hole. Each of the upper arms of the Y would be in essence a tunnel. A shallow trench would be covered on the sides and top with sandbags. A small opening in the front would allow the trooper to aim his weapon. The idea was that when the shit hit the fan a trooper would crawl into the tunnel. He would be pretty much forced to fire his weapon in the direction the tunnel pointed. Because the tunnels would be on diagonal angles to the company perimeter, firing along the axes of the tunnels would result in intersecting and overlapping fields of fire—the school solution.

As Wynsack preceded with his presentation, my reaction moved from alcoholic disinterest to quizzicalness to incredulity. What the hell had he been doing during all his time in the field with the 101st? I could almost understand this blarney from an FNG, but Wynsack had beaucoup months in the boonies. Yet his plan was divorced from reality.

For one thing, constructing cute little Y-shaped bunkers presupposed the availability of abundant time, compliant soil, and adequate tools. At the end of a hard day of humping, a grunt was lucky to wrestle a basic hole from the reluctant, often rocky, ground. For another thing, Wynsack's tunnels would be claustrophobic. Cover was one thing. Cramming oneself into a mole-like environment was something else. Most grunts liked to feel they knew what was going on around them. Wynsack's tunnels limited a grunt's view of the surrounding world to a little aperture directly to the front. Not one grunt in 20 would stay in such a confined space in a firefight.

As Wynsack neared the conclusion of his presentation, I glanced around the room. No one showed any sign of skepticism. Indeed, when the presentation was over, several individuals asked technical questions, indicating they accepted the basic viability of Wynsack's Y-shaped bunkers. LTC Wayan in particular seemed enthralled. He obviously respected Wynsack, so any idea Wynsack had necessarily deserved a serious look. I was sorely tempted to raise my hand and say: "You've got to be kidding. This is the most unrealistic crap I've heard in a month of Sundays. There ain't no way you're gonna get grunts to construct and use these frigging things."

But I didn't. I was too much out of favor to have anybody take my skepticism seriously. Let's just see how many Y-shaped mole-holes ever get built, was my silent thought.

In addition to the battalion staff, one other individual listened to Wynsack's presentation. He sat by himself at the back of the room, looking mean, arrogant, and contemptuous. He was currently the brigade Inspector General, but he was obviously at heart no rear echelon flunky. He wore the infantryman's combat web gear, something few others in the rear did. And his headgear was a beat up ranger cap rather than the standard issue sissified baseball cap of the 1960s. He was to become a major embarrassment to the 173rd Airborne Brigade.

LTC Anthony C. Herbert was by most accounts, including his own, the most highly decorated soldier of the Korean War. The warrior's fierceness he exuded certainly didn't contradict the reputation. Still, I wondered at the time about his waiting until mid-1968 to appear in Vietnam. This had been the only war around for a bunch of years, and most bona fide warriors in the U.S. Army had long since sampled the waters. But this seemed only a minor point.

The IG job was merely supposed to be a pause for LTC Herbert. His ticket as an infantry battalion commander was due for punching, and he was just biding his time until a battalion became available. Unfortunately for him and the reputation of the 173rd, he was not a good time-bider. He had an office at An Khe, but the IG job—investigating complaints—took him throughout the brigade. He saw General Allard's air-conditioned flower-surrounded trailer at LZ English. He saw the old colonel's protected entourage of bad-asses at Tuy Hoa. He saw the rear echelon excesses at An Khe. This stuff was disturbing to most bona fide soldiers. In Herbert, however, it apparently aroused an uncontrollably urge to rebel.

Herbert got his battalion sometime after I left the brigade. His version of what transpired, of his rebellion, was set forth in his book, *A Soldier's Story*. The bare facts are that after two months in command,

Herbert was relieved and given a career-killing efficiency report. He fought back, appealing first within the Army and then taking his case to the media. He even made CBS's *60 Minutes*. His defense consisted in large measure of attacking the actions and integrity of General Allard's successor and the successor's deputy. Initially, Herbert garnered a fair amount of support. As time went on, however, the support eroded under questions about his own integrity.

This public airing of the 173rd's dirty linen occurred after I had returned to the Land of the Big PX. I was sympathetic to the assertions Herbert was making about the decadence into which the brigade's leadership and rear had fallen. But I was suspicious of the man. He was obviously a self-promoter. And some of his story just did not ring right. For instance, during his two short months in command, his battalion staff put him in for several Silver Stars. That was too much self-aggrandizing for me—battalion staffs don't do things like that without at least the implicit encouragement of the commander. Moreover, if battalion commanders want to get in on the action, and I sympathize with the desire, they ought to do so without seeming to have as the main purpose an increase in their chest hardware. The whole truth of the Herbert affair is by now permanently obscured in the murky depths of history.

The rain continued. The battalion waited. My drinking increased. I was struggling out of the sack around 9 or 10 in the morning. The days were spent trying to stay out of sight. The evenings were spent boozing. The officers-NCO club run by my old Alpha Company buddy was the usual watering hole. Some nights I was the only one there. One night I tried to get him to take me on a return trip to the fishing village. He was procrastinating, so I grabbed the only other patron, an E-5 from some headquarters section, and we made our drunken way through the wire and across the field to the ladies. As I dozed on a bed, a hand came through the thatched side of the hut and roughly removed my watch. I was aware of what was happening but too drunk to do anything about it.

Another night a group of us went to an officers club at the Tuy Hoa Air Force base. It was an elaborate building with, of all things, a large stone fireplace. Powerful air-conditioning made the roaring blaze welcome. The club was patronized by nurses from the base hospital, but the ratio of horny men to available women was much too great to give a drunk like me any real chance. Several of us checked out the nearby nurses' barracks. It was guarded by MPs. A desk clerk relayed our invitation for a drink but there were no takers. These gals could have the pick of the litter, and that weren't us.

Finally, the weather broke and the 4th Battalion was off to the mountains. I was given some sort of nebulous responsibility concerning the lifting of the supplies and equipment. The upshot was that I spent most of a day at a chopper pad at the nearby Army aviation outfit, watching the Chinooks pick up the sling loads of 105 howitzers, ammunition, field tents, and whatever. Even "Big Windy" put in an appearance for a few trips. "Big Windy" was the call sign for a Sky Crane crew. Sky Cranes were the largest helicopters in the Army's inventory. They looked like giant spiders. A Sky Crane consisted of a cab for the pilot and copilot, a humongous rotor, and a thin shaft extending to the smaller rear rotor. Loads were slung from the shaft, big loads. In spite of my pounding hangover, that one day was an education in airlift operations.

Within a day or so of the 4th Battalion's reinsertion into the boonies, the old colonel's entourage took a hit. A couple of his bad asses got in a fight in the mess hall. Even the colonel realized that they might be incorrigible, beyond the pall. They were thrown into a conex container, and the 173rd's Provost Marshall called. He was the former headquarters commandant, the MP major who Major Tree had enjoyed harassing. He was now in his element. He appeared from LZ English with a squad of MPs in two Hueys. The cops trussed up the culprits, threw them on the choppers, and headed for An Khe. The colonel's handiwork probably ended up walking free back in the Land of the Big PX well before any of the onlookers.

What became of the remainder of the colonel's boys, and what adventures lay ahead for the 4th Battalion, were about to fall off my scope. Shortly after the battalion's move to the field and the Provost Marshall's visit, and just after I had reluctantly signed for the battalion's secret documents, the battalion executive officer located me: "Holland, we've gotten one of those MACV levies for MAT teams. Looks like you're it."

A wave of relief swept over me. I was to get out of this place. I would be leaving the airborne, the elite, but my current usefulness was about zero. I tried to hide the eagerness, probably unsuccessfully: "When do I leave, Sir?"

"Well, it's not definite yet. We're trying to fight it. The colonel is personally gettin' involved."

I wasn't worried. I couldn't envision LTC Wayan or anyone else being unhappy about my departure. And unless the brigade S-1 shop had changed, there was no appealing one of these levies. I noted to the XO that someone would have to sign for the secret documents I had just signed for myself.

LTC Wayan called me out to the field the next day. I didn't think the trip was necessary, but Wayan was a great one for appearances and procedures. As the chopper flew in, I realized that the fire support base was set smack dab on the hillside where a year before Lima had ambushed the point of a VC unit and spent the night trading grenades and small arms fire. The 4th Battalion was conducting company-size operations, which struck me as concentrating too much for the amount of opposition in the area. The 1st Battalion and Alpha Company a year earlier had been successful with the platoon bushwhacker approach. But this was a war where the lessons of experience were sacrificed to personnel turnover and the one-year tour rotation.

As I waited for the interview with Wayan, I noted that many of the members of the company guarding the fire support base were assembled for PT. This was something else different. During my time with Alpha Company, PT would have been more than unnecessary. It would have been destructive. We were too damn physically beat to benefit from jumping jacks. During the periods when we drew fire support base duty, the time was spent in rejuvenating. But again, times were different.

Finally, I was ushered into LTC Wayan's presence. He made like he was sorry to lose me. He even went through a little charade of placing a call to Major Tree at LZ English: "Tree, you're taking another one from me. You sure that's unavoidable?"

After an alleged answer, he said, "Well, I hope this is the last for awhile. Holland's a good man. I hate to see him go."

Whether Major Tree was actually on the other end of the line was uncertain. With all the trouble I had experienced with making calls, I couldn't image being able to talk directly from a fire support base in the mountains around Tuy Hoa to LZ English. Even money said Wayan was just putting on a show. "I tried, Captain Holland. You know about this stuff, so I'm sure you understand. These levies are really hitting us hard. I hope this stops soon. I wish you could have stayed as part of the team."

Yeah, right, I thought. I said, "I wish I could have stayed too, Sir. But these things happen."

"Well, good luck to you. When are you leaving?"

"I'm supposed to be in An Khe tomorrow. By the way, Sir, I'll just pass on a thought. I was up here, in this very field in fact, last year with the 1st Battalion. We had a lotta success with platoon-size ambushes and bushwhacker operations. The VC were in small groups, and we snuck around and played their game. And got not too bad at it."

"Hmmm, that's interesting. That's something to think about." He did indeed sound genuinely interested. Finally, just as we were about to part company, we had found a little common ground. Still, I would always remember LTC Wayan, future General Wayan, as the guy who called me down for blowing bubbles.

The next morning, leaving the battalion's secret documents to be signed for by some other poor sap, I caught a chopper to An Khe. Leaving before someone has taken responsibility for stuff with your name on it is not particularly smart, but I was anxious to get the hell on my way. In An Khe, Sgt. Brotzman was still around and let me bunk in his spare office. I processed out that afternoon and the next morning. The reporting date to Di An, the base camp of the 1st Infantry Division—the Big Red One—and the location of the training camp for the Mobile Advisory Teams, was several days away. I could catch a flight to Saigon that evening and have a few days on Tu Do Street. So I said goodbye to Sgt. Brotzman, An Khe, and the 173rd Airborne, and departed for the unknown. For the first time since I had returned to Vietnam from home leave in early March, seven long months previously, I was feeling good. A MAT team was no company command, but it was a combat assignment. No more frigging paperwork for this boy. I was back in the war.

PART II
CO VAN MY

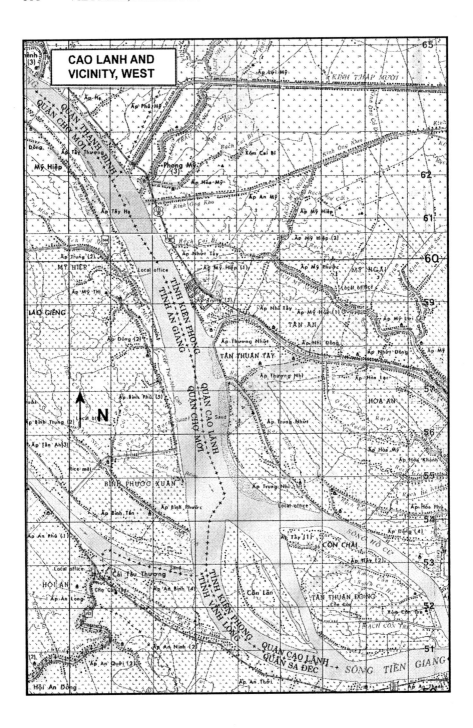

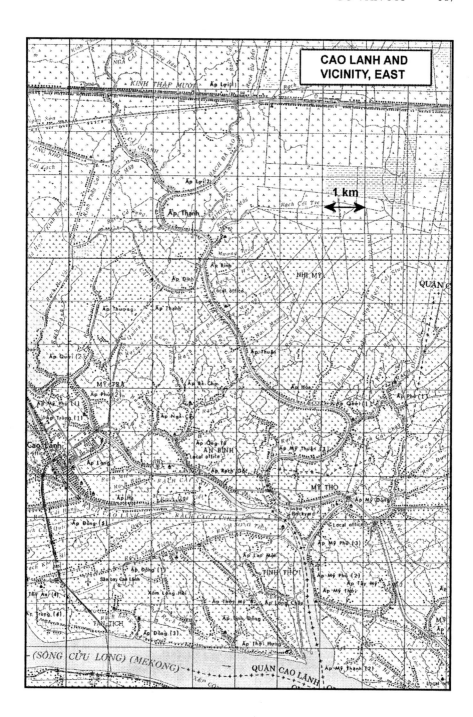

CAO LANH AND VICINITY, EAST

To The Mekong

In Saigon, I found what a tourist brochure for a country at peace would have called a "quaint" hotel. It was on Nguyen Hue, the next street over from Tu Do. The upper floor, about the 4th, had a courtyard in the center. The floor was made with large ceramic tiles, and a number of large plants in pots were scattered about. The rooms opened onto the courtyard. They were large and not air-conditioned but cooled with ceiling fans. I spent a couple of enjoyable days visiting my old haunts, buying Saigon tea, eating Chinese dinners in Cholon, and reading.

The reporting day for the MAT school was a Friday. The reporting place was Long Binh. I took a taxi to the Bien Hoa highway and hitched a ride on a U.S. truck for the 10-mile trip to Long Binh. Upon reporting, I learned that the training wasn't supposed to start until Monday. After taking one look at where we were to spend the weekend, a barracks with bunk beds, I went AWOL. It was back to Saigon for two more days of fun and frolic. I barely made the last bus Monday morning carrying the group from Long Binh to Di An.

On the 45-minute bus ride and during the in-processing at the Mobile Advisory Team training center, I took the measure of my comrades. For the most part, they were a disgruntled lot. Being yanked from a U.S. unit for service with a Vietnamese unit was not what most of these guys had in mind for the last part of their year in Vietnam. Out of the class of approximately 40, I might have been the only one looking forward to what was ahead. Certainly, I was the only one doing so on my team. One of the first orders of business after arriving at Di An was to receive our team assignments and to meet our mates. My first impression of my group reinforced my view that a MACV

MAT-team levy wasn't designed to produce a group of happy campers. Staff Sergeant E-6 Mitchell sullenly announced right off the bat that he thought this was ridiculous and was writing his congressman. Mitchell was a short heavy-set balding guy whose eyes and face showed alcohol damage. He had been a squad leader in a mechanized infantry company in the 9th Infantry Division in the northern portion of the Mekong Delta.

The ranking NCO was an E-7 named Roca. He had been with the 25th Infantry Division to the northwest of Saigon. He was an intelligence specialist and had apparently spent his first seven months in Vietnam sitting in a command track vehicle, drinking coffee. He obviously resented being ejected into the unknown. Physically, he was on the over-weight side and looked like he had been avoiding any form of exertion for a number of years. At least he didn't show signs of advanced alcoholism. The third NCO was an E-5 medic on his second Vietnam tour, Sgt. Blane. The first tour had been with the 25th. He had been back in Vietnam for only a few months and had some cushy job at Nha Be, the port facility to the south of Saigon. Medium height, lean to the point of gauntness, he appeared much less perturbed about his new assignment than the other two did.

Finally, there was the other officer, my second-in-command. First Lieutenant Silver was an artillery officer and had been with a 155-mm battery in II Corps. He seemed innocuous enough, but a little finicky. If you were selecting someone to accompany you into a bad-ass bar, it wouldn't have been Silver.

Of course, they probably had as many doubts about me as I did about them. The doubts likely started with the fact that I had been in the 'Nam two years and counting. What's the story with the Captain, is he some kinda nut?

One question on all our minds concerned where we would be sent. The team destinations weren't to be announced until near the end of the three-week course. The possibilities extended over the whole country. I definitely didn't want II or III Corps—I had already been there. I

Corps in the north didn't appeal to me either. I had the impression it was too crowded, what with the Marines and now the 1st Cav, the 101st Airborne, and the Americal Division. Maybe there was room for a five-man advisory team, but I was doubtful. That left IV Corps, and the Mekong Delta. Geographically, it was a large place. And the American presence was minimal. Of the large U.S. units, only the 9th Division operated there regularly, and then mostly in the northern part. The rest of the U.S. combat effort consisted of aviation units, Navy gunboats, Special Forces teams, and advisors. IV Corps might be fun, a place with some elbow room and an assortment of non-standard gunslingers.

MAT school was located in a corner of Di An. The buildings were permanent wooden structures. We were housed in open-bay barracks, officers and NCOs all mixed together. We were told this was to enable us to get to know each other better. By late 1968, Di An had been a U.S. base for three years. It had taken on the appearance of an established Army facility in the American south. The grass was cut, the bushes were trimmed, and the buildings were painted.

The course wasn't half bad. The classes ran the gamut—weapons, first aid, unit structure, customs, and even language. Concerning the last, about ten hours of Vietnamese were foisted on us. Mostly, it was just vocabulary—military terms, food, and the like. Sgt. Mitchell didn't take to the language instruction very well. During one class, the instructor was going around the room having people pronounce various words. Learning Vietnamese was obviously not Sgt. Mitchell's idea of fun. Pronunciation of the sing-song oriental phrases was incompatible with his guttural Alabama draw. Remembering those phrases was incompatible with his pickled brain. When his turn came to perform during this particular class, he went into a slow tirade. "I ain't gonna do this. This is crap. I ain't goin' out to no gook unit anyway. My damn congressman's gonna get me outta this."

He looked defiantly at the instructor, a short fat mild-mannered captain who was a graduate of the Army's language school. The captain gave the impression of being a misplaced intellectual. He certainly wasn't prepared for the anti-intellectualism of an Alabama redneck. He tried to mollify Mitchell: "You ought to try to learn this, Sergeant. It might be useful."

"I ain't gonna be out there. My congressman's gonna get me back to the 9th Division. I'm an American. I should be with an American unit."

The captain let it drop and went on to the next person. I sat there contemplating the future, which at the moment was not boding well. Sgt. Mitchell was not a guy I wanted accompanying me to some far corner of Vietnam where the nearest other Americans were a helicopter ride away. Being an adviser to foreign troops required certain skills and attitudes, and Mitchell didn't seem to have an abundance of the necessary qualities.

Most of the instruction was in the classroom. One day, however, was spent at a firing range, familiarizing ourselves with weapons we would likely find in the Ruff-Puffs. Some of the weapons were those currently standard in the U.S. Army—the M-16 rifle, the M-60 machine gun, the M-79 grenade launcher. The Ruff-Puffs were at the bottom of the totem pole, however, and they also possessed some items that had long since departed the U.S. inventory. These included the M-1 carbine, the M-1 and M-14 rifles, the Browning Automatic Rifle (BAR), and the .30 caliber machine gun. I had a memorable moment with the .30 caliber. We were firing at a little mound of dirt a hundred or so meters away. My first shots kicked up earth about three-fourths of the way to the mound. Just like the books say to do, I adjusted the elevation just a tad, putting the next rounds at the mound's base. A hair's further adjustment and I was obliterating the mound—fire a burst of six, fire a burst of six, fire a burst of six. The range instructor, a standoffish E-7 who had shown considerable contempt for us over the week we had been in the course, seemed impressed, even managing a compliment. It was a small moment but one of those that stick with you.

The three weeks went quickly. The school had a small officers-NCO club where we soaked up suds in the evening. There was even a basketball court. I discovered my jump shot was long gone. Finally, a few days before the course ended, we received our assignments. Wonder of wonders, our team, MAT-104, was going to the Delta! Just what I had hoped for. We were to be in Kien Phong Province, which was bordered on the south by the Mekong River and on the west by Cambodia.

For our last night at Di An we were moved to another barracks to make way for the next incoming class. Sgt. Mitchell was beginning to worry me more and more. He went on a bender that final evening, becoming antagonistic and belligerent. His mood was exacerbated by an event back in the World. The 1968 election had just taken place, and Mitchell's candidate, although putting in a good showing, had come up short. That candidate was George Wallace, whose state's rights, segregationist effort struck a cord in Sgt. Mitchell's redneck Alabama heart. His post-election bender was a dilly and showed that he had the potential for being a disruptive force of the first magnitude.

MAT-104 and several other teams bound for the Delta were to catch a C-130 from Di An to Can Tho, the major city in the south of the country. The junior officers—the executive officers—in each team went on a separate journey. Their destination was Nha Trang, on the coast, and their mission was to shepherd to their teams a conex container with equipment including, among other things, a five-man tent, a table, a few chairs, lockers, an M-60 machine gun, and radios. We were told not to expect the XOs and their goodies for at least two weeks.

On the morning of our departure, we did the standard Army hurry up and wait routine. We got to the airfield at 0600 and then napped on the runway before our plane arrived in early afternoon. We finally landed in Can Tho around 1700. After the usual delay, a bus showed up to take us to a transient facility, an old thick masonry building with no air-conditioning and an inadequate number of fans. It was stifling, sufficient reason for most to leave for nearby bars and some heavy drinking.

The next morning it was back to the Can Tho airfield for the last stage of the journey. We were to catch a Mohawk, a twelve-passenger or so two-engine Army plane, to Kien Phong Province. A Special Forces club was in the airfield complex, so we worked on the previous evening's hangover as we waited on another afternoon flight. Eventually we were off, flying up the Mekong toward Cambodia. From the Mohawk's windows, I had my first good look at the terrain of the Delta. It was flat and wet, with vast areas of cultivation, mostly rice paddies. The time was near the end of the rainy season, and the paddies were covered by sheets of water. Small dikes interrupted the sheets in rectangular patterns.

After an hour's flight, a steep descent, and a gut-wrenching full-brake stop on an extremely short runway, we were on the ground, and pretty much alone. The airfield complex consisted of the PCP runway and a small hanger. A couple of Vietnamese guards lounged near the hanger, but no Americans were around. Nor was there anything resembling a town. To the north and east of the airfield, a hundred or so meters away, were tree lines. The Mekong was on the other side of a few huts to the south. A road passed on the west. Immediately after dropping us off, the Mohawk departed, leaving us feeling very much lost and forlorn. I would not have been surprised to see a Viet Cong battalion trampling in our direction.

The Vietnamese guards looked at us disinterestedly. I walked over to them and tried to ask directions, but they knew less English than I knew Vietnamese. One pointed to a field phone on an otherwise empty desk in a corner of the hanger. A sign was taped to the desk beside the phone: "FOR TRANSPORTATION, CALL PROVINCE ADVISOR ADMIN." I cranked the phone, got an American sounding operator, and asked for "Province Advisor Admin." After a few rings, someone answered: "Admin."

"Yeah. This is Captain Holland. I'm down at the airfield with a MAT Team. Could somebody come get us?"

"Who is this?" The tone of the question indicated incredulity in the extreme from someone who didn't want to be bothered late in the day.

"I said, this is Captain Holland. I'm at the airfield with a new MAT Team. This place is the middle of nowhere. We need transportation to somewhere."

"Just a minute." The phone at the other end must have been a regular phone that didn't require a button to be depressed in order to talk because I overhead the exchange. "Sez he's some Captain. With a MAT Team, whatever that is. Sez he needs transportation from the airfield."

"Damn, I thought they weren't coming for a few days." There was a pause, then, "Tell'em someone'll be there shortly."

"You guys just relax. Someone'll be there shortly, or at least before it gets dark. You don't want to be there after dark."

"Great," I said sarcastically. "We'll be waiting."

I turned to Mitchell, Roca, and Blane. "Someone'll be here sometime."

"Didn't sound like they was expectin' us," Sgt. Mitchell said. His scowl indicated his irritation.

"Shit, Mitch. What'd you expect? A fuckin' red carpet? I'm just glad I'm short. When this shit's done, I'm retirin'." It was Sgt. Roca speaking. He had four months till DEROS. They continued grumbling, so I walked off aways. There had been constant moaning since we had left Di An, and I was fed up with it. On the other hand, our reception thus far in Kien Phong Province wasn't the greatest morale builder. I was close to a little griping myself. The thing that kept me from joining my NCOs in their malcontentness was the thought of soon being back in the war. I hoped the unpromising start was not a prelude to disappointment.

Eventually, a three-quarter ton appeared on the road and turned into the airfield. It pulled up to us, and a young sergeant hopped out:

"Welcome to Kien Phong Province. Sorry we didn't know you were comin'. We would'a been more prepared." At least he was friendly. We threw our stuff aboard. Mitchell, Roca, and Blane piled in the open back. I got in the cab, intending to pick up what information I could from someone who wasn't openly hostile. The ride to town and the province compound didn't produce a whole lot, but I did get a few basics.

The Kien Phong Province advisory mission was not the normal MACV structure. It was a Special Forces operation, although it was scheduled to convert to MACV control in a few weeks or months, the timing was unclear. But for the moment, the province advisor was a Special Forces lieutenant colonel. "What's he like?" I asked.

"Sir, Colonel Steintz is somethin' else," the sergeant said with a laugh. "Just between you and me, I'd stay the hell away from him as much as I could." He turned and looked at me intently for a few long seconds. Then after seeming to make a decision, he said a little more seriously: "Really, Sir. The colonel is a little strange at times." Despite some prodding on my part, the sergeant wouldn't say anything more on the topic.

Great. What the hell kind of situation was I getting myself into? To make up for the aggravation, there damn well better be some combat in this for me.

The road took us from the airfield to the town of Cao Lanh, the province capitol. The distance was about two and a half miles. Cultivated fields, huts, bushes, and isolated stands of trees bordered the road. The sergeant said that in the other direction, just beyond the airfield, the road met the Mekong River at a group of huts called Tan Tich (pronounced Tick). The Mekong was about a half mile wide at that point. A ferry provided transportation to the other side. From there, one could drive all the way to Can Tho, about 40 miles. Indeed, the sergeant said that regular supply convoys traveled the Can Tho-Tan Tich ferry-Cao Lanh route.

Moreover, this was the only ground route into and out of the province. A road had paralleled the north bank of the Mekong, intersecting some miles to the east the main north-south highway connecting Saigon and Can Tho. It had crossed a number of canals and Mekong tributaries, however, and many of the bridges had been destroyed during the Tet fighting ten months previously. So for the time being the province was in an advanced state of isolation.

The metropolis of Cao Lanh interrupted my informal background briefing. First we crossed a narrow one-lane steel girder bridge over a muddy canal. This was followed by a 250-meter section of road with a large pagoda on the right and huts and a few masonry structures on the left. Then a concrete arched bridge crossed a deep-looking canal about 15 meters wide. On the far side of this bridge was the town proper. Dreary unpainted wooden buildings interspersed with a few two- and three-story masonry efforts hugged the road for about 100 meters to an intersection. More of the town lay to the right, or east. We turned west, toward the U.S. and Vietnamese military compounds.

Immediately after the turn, on the right, was the compound of the 44th Special Zone. This was a headquarters whose bailiwick spread over several provinces on the Cambodian border. Sometime after my tour it was commanded by the famous—or infamous, depending on your point of view—Colonel David Hackworth, the well-decorated iconoclast who after lambasting the Army on CBS's *60 Minutes* in 1970 or thereabouts retired to a self-imposed exile in Australia. He make a million farming, and then decided the U.S. needed the benefit of his late-blooming anti-war views. So he wrote his autobiography and then ended up back in the U.S., writing a column for *Newsweek*.

Just past the 44th's compound on the left was an ARVN supply outfit. On the right was the province headquarters. It was an old masonry building left over from French times. It was in the middle of a large area of rice paddies, standing with a few trees as a feeble embodiment of the Vietnamese Government.

Finally came two Special Forces compounds. On the left, bordering a canal, was one of the oddities of the war—a Mike Force with air boats. The Mike Force was made up largely of Cambodian mercenaries. The U.S. cadre was comprised of ten to twelve Special Forces types. The air boats were the Everglades style machines with huge propellers enclosed in wire cages and powered by something resembling aircraft engines. The boats were apparently ideal for zipping during the wet season over the vast flooded plains of the Delta.

On the right was the Special Forces headquarters for the province. Since the Special Forces commander was also for the moment the province advisor, the headquarters was also the province advisor's compound. The facility was set back from the road about 100 meters. Bordering the main road, just at the turn-off to the compound, was a bar. It was a favorite haunt of the Special Forces boat NCOs. I was to spend more than a few hours there.

The Special Forces province advisor's compound was standard issue. The berm was two rows of upright steel landing mats filled with earth. The resulting wall was about eight to ten feet thick. Fortified positions were on top. Just inside the berm was open space, much of it for parking or storage. Then a more or less continuous four-sided structure paralleled the outer wall. The structure contained offices, sleeping quarters, supply sheds, and the ubiquitous bar. The center of the structure was an open court yard, which also contained a mess hall. On the walls of the offices and public areas were plaques with quotes from the works of Kipling. The compound as a whole probably measured 75 meters by 75 meters.

We pulled into the compound, and the sergeant took me to the admin officer, a captain. He in turn introduced me to the executive officer, a non-Special Forces major, and the combination Province Advisor-Special Forces area commander, the lieutenant colonel the sergeant had warned me about. The colonel's appearance alone certainly created wariness. He must have been a football player in college, probably an offensive lineman. He was close to 6 feet 5 inches and pushing

275 pounds. As with many football players, his head sat directly on his shoulders, obviating the need for a neck. The top portion of his head was disproportionately small, but by the time the chin was reached, things had regained perspective. A tiny little flattop adorned the point between his ears. He might have been the only U.S. citizen in late 1968 with a flattop, within or without the military. He spent only a few minutes with me, making it clear he had more important matters on his agenda. That was fine with me. The less contact I had with this Neanderthal, the better I was going to like it.

From the admin officer and the XO, we received briefings that began to answer our questions about our status and immediate future. MAT 104—us—was to be the advisory team for the 64th Regional Forces Battalion, which was a new outfit that had recently finished training. Many of its members were Hao Hoas—pronounced Wha Hows—a Buddhist sect. In fact, the pagoda that we had passed coming into town was a Hao Hoa pagoda, and the battalion was to be head-quartered on its grounds. When Lt. Silver and our conex arrived, we would establish our quarters with the battalion. In the meantime, we would find what places we could in the Special Forces compound.

The living quarters at the compound consisted of rooms housing six to eight persons each. I found an empty upper bunk in one of the rooms. The other occupants were lieutenants—some Special Forces, some MACV. Four or five of them were combat arms types part of whose jobs was to accompany Vietnamese units on their operations. From them I got a clearer idea of what the team's job was to be. Although we were called advisors, in reality we were to be air support coordinators. We would be providing the communications to trans-portation choppers, medevacs, chopper gunships, and Air Force fighter-bombers. Our Vietnamese charges would also expect us to be a spigot to the U.S. supply pipeline. We had been warned about this at the Di An school. What was available to U.S. units in 1968 was far and away more than what was available to Vietnamese units. Indeed, the 64th was not yet armed with M-16s.

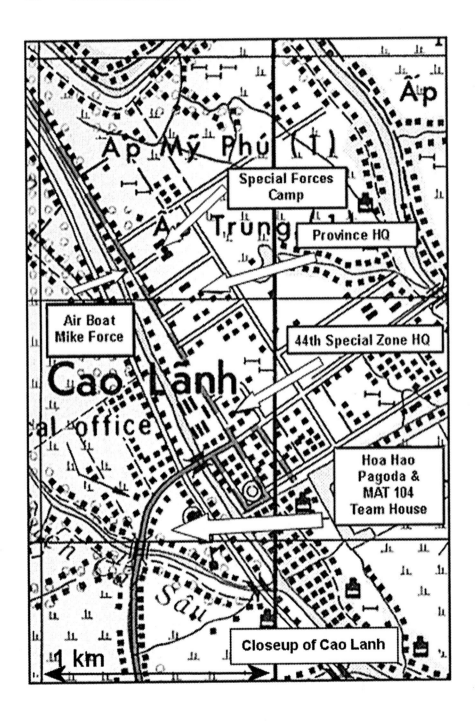

Special Forces Camp

Province HQ

Air Boat Mike Force

44th Special Zone HQ

Hoa Hao Pagoda & MAT 104 Team House

Closeup of Cao Lanh

1 km

So "advisors" was apparently a misnomer. According to the more cynical of the lieutenants, precious little advising was being done. The "advisors" traipsed along with the headquarters group of the battalion on operations, doing nothing unless something from the sky was called for. The lieutenants didn't think our MAT team would have any more to do even though we were to be living with the battalion. A couple of the more gung-ho lieutenants were not happy with their fate, desiring greater participation in combat decision-making. They appeared surreptitiously envious of the 173rd combat patch on my right shoulder.

As for the operations themselves, for the most part they were daytime only. The battalion would depart before dawn on a mission, and return before dark. At night, the unit had defensive responsibilities around Cao Lanh. If the unit was overnight in the field, the town was open to Charlie. Normally, only two advisors went on an operation. Since there were only two to four operations per week, members of a five-man team could end up going to the boonies just once a week.

I determined right off to go on every operation. There was no way I was going to sit around when I could be chasing Charlie, even if I was nothing more than a glorified RTO. An alternative would be to take two advisory teams on an operation, having one team with the point and one with the headquarters group. Giving the disgruntlement of my team, however, trying to force them to the field any more then absolutely necessary would likely provoke a revolt.

And the disgruntlement was quickly increasing. The fuel for the increase was provided by the bar in the compound. It was open pretty close to 14 hours a day, from before noon to after midnight. My NCOs, particularly Sgt. Mitchell, latched onto the bar our first evening, satisfying both their copious thirst and their desire to have their unhappiness fed. They heard from other NCOs of the travails of being an advisor. The other NCOs were mostly experienced, and comfortable, in the fuzzy world of the MACV advisor, and their griping was the griping of the contented. My guys needed certainty. Flexibility was near the bottom of their attributes. They came from the world of TO&E, or standard, units. Their griping was serious.

I joined Mitchell, Roca, and Blane in the bar about mid-way through the first evening. Mitchell was already well snockered, and getting louder and more belligerent. "Goddamit, Sir, this shit is rotten. We ain't gonna have no support out there. Why the hell we got to do this? This is the worst crap I ever been in!"

"Now Mitch. You're in the Army. You do what they say. Besides, it ain't gonna be that bad. We'll get through it." Sgt. Blane was talking. He was also snockered, but he was the more laid back of the bunch. In an unenthusiastic way, he was trying to take the edge off Mitchell's growing anger.

I tried to calm Mitchell down a bit, but the alcohol was controlling him. I was beginning to develop real concerns about the situation. If Mitchell was a belligerent drunk—as he apparently was—and if we were to be in proximity to this bar for the foreseeable future, it was not going to be a pleasant experience. After a bit I left them to their drinking and complaining. By now the bar was pretty well filled. Half the compound was in attendance, and this was a week night. If there was this much activity in the middle of the week, these people were heavier drinkers than even I was.

The next morning I was informed that the 64th would be going on an operation the following day. Since completing training a few weeks before, the unit had been on several operations. One of the Special Forces lieutenants had been accompanying them. He would go out the following day, show me what a glorified RTO did, and introduce me to my counterpart, the 64th Dia Phon Quan's commander. Dia Phon Quan was the Vietnamese term for Regional Forces Battalion, as I recall. I relayed the news to my hungover NCOs and asked if any of them wanted to accompany us. There were no takers. Just as well because by mid-afternoon they had re-established residence in the bar, with Sgt. Mitchell working himself into another alcoholic temper tantrum.

Early and before bright the next morning, the lieutenant and I drove to the Hao Hoa Pagoda. The lieutenant was outfitted in standard web gear and armed with an M-16. The only indication, but a pronounced one, that he belonged to the idiosyncratic, iconoclastic sneaky petes was a large-brimmed floppy camouflaged hat. The boys back in Alpha Company of the 1st of the 503rd would not have been able to contain their mirth. I went completely standard—web gear in the proper configuration, M-16, helmet. With a new start I thought I would try dressing the right way for a change. Besides, since humping with a rucksack wasn't on the agenda, the shoulder harness and belt of the web gear wouldn't be competing with a 50-pound load.

Trucks—deuce and a halfs—were beginning to fill with members of the 64th Dia Phon Quan. The lieutenant introduced me to Dai Uy—Captain—Than, the battalion commander. He was an older man, probably in his forties, and with about as much proficiency in English as I had in Vietnamese. He had a helmet with a U.S. camouflaged cover, jungle fatigues, a flak jacket, and a .45 caliber pistol. Most of his men wore steel helmets without camouflage covers and regular fatigues. They hadn't yet received M-16s.

The operation was to the southwest of Cao Lanh. The trucks took us back past the Special Forces compound for about five or six kilometers. We off-loaded, walked across a small arched bridge, and began a wide swing to the south and then the east that was designed to bring us back to Cao Lanh on foot. The area was fairly heavily populated, almost one long town. Many of the structures were substantial wooden buildings with porches and sufficient size for multiple rooms. The route was a heavily used, packed, wide dirt path. Masonry arched bridges crossed the many streams. There were no vehicles. The people did not seem unfriendly, although for the most part they acted as if they were ignoring us.

I was exposed to several things on this first operation. One was that the Vietnamese military, at least in Kien Phong Province, had latched with a vengeance onto certain procedural aspects of the training provided by Americans. The use of map overlays fell into this category. Tracing paper overlays showing the route of an operation were distributed down to company level. The overlays also had various reporting points and other control measures. This was a much more formal way of operating than had been my experience. I was used to verbal stuff only: "Go to the blue line"; "Climb that hill"; "Head for grid coordinates" thus and so. During my tenure with the 173rd, somebody at the battalion level or higher was preparing or relaying written operating plans, but by the time instructions reached the company and platoon level, they were oral.

The overlays had to be mounted on a map, which then had to be folded so that the information could be seen. The map was then placed in the plastic bag being used as a map protector. All this was somewhat cumbersome and was to cause me a few problems until I got the hang of it, which took several weeks.

Co Van My radio use was another new world. Co Van My, with the "My" pronounced "Me", was Vietnamese for "American advisor." The advisory net paralleled the Vietnamese net. If the operation was a large one that involved the use of a tactical CP, our point of contact was the advisor in the CP. If there was no tactical CP, we communicated directly with the province headquarters operations room, where an advisor's radio was manned. If we had air support, be it transportation choppers, gun ships, or Air Force fighter bombers, we communicated directly with them, or with an air controller who in turn was in direct communication with the air assets. As with American units, much of the communications was simply giving location, or supposed location.

A third new world was the interpreter situation. The lieutenant and I were provided an alleged interpreter by the Dai Uy. He was a young soldier who picked his way very carefully from English word to English word. The lieutenant said this was typical and that we should not expect anything better. We had been warned at Di An that interpreting would be a problem. I suspected one of the many things bothering Sgt. Mitchell was the thought of not being able to communicate. I had hoped that we would luck out regarding the interpreter situation, but apparently this was not to be the case.

The first operation was uneventful. The lieutenant said that this was considered a "safe" area. A South Vietnamese unit would walk through every now and then, but no VC units operated in the vicinity. According to the lieutenant, Charlie's country was to the north of Cao Lanh.

I caught Dai Uy Than surreptitiously eyeing me a few times. Of course, I was doing the same to him. He was my counterpart, a popular word in the advisory business. We were to be partners, or something, for the next four and a half months. Would I be anything more than a conduit for American material support for him? Based on what the junior officers at the Special Forces compound had been telling us, I suspected not. And if truth be told, Dai Uy Than probably didn't need a lot of "advice." According to the lieutenant, he had been fighting somebody or other for 20 years. The local Hao Hoas had just recently been won over to the government's side. Before that, they apparently strove for neutrality, but an armed neutrality. The 64th Dia Phon Quan was reportedly the descendant of some Hao Hoa warlord's private army.

Late in the day just to the south of Cao Lanh we intersected the road from Cao Lanh to the Tan Tich ferry. The lieutenant and I prepared to make our way back to the Special Forces compound. We had radioed that we were about to enter the town and requested that a jeep be sent for us if one was available. One was, and as we were about to drive off our interpreter stopped us. Through gestures and a word or two, he extended an invitation from the Dai Uy for a get together the next afternoon for the team. I looked over at the Dai Uy, smiled, shook my head yes, and said "Cam on," which is "Thank you" in Vietnamese.

Back at the Special Forces compound, I found my three NCOs at their new duty station, the bar. I grabbed a beer and sat down at the table. "Well, it wasn't too bad. Nothin' happened. The unit looks like its pretty well organized. They move with good spacin' and seemed to know what they're doin'. It was just a walk in the park."

No one said anything for a few moments. They just stared at their beers. I had obviously interrupted another gripe session. Finally, Sgt. Mitchell spoke: "How's the fuckin' interpreter?"

"Well, he wasn't great. But we managed to communicate."

"Shit. This sucks. I already wrote my congressman. I better damn well hear somethin' soon."

I was getting fed up with this crap. This day particularly burned me up. I was the one who had spent the time in the sun, strolling for 15 kilometers or so. These assholes had spent the day in a bar, working themselves up to a mutiny. "Look, you guys gotta come to grips with this. You're all goddamn professional soldiers. The Army's given you a home, a livin', for ten, fifteen years. I don't know what the hell you thought being a soldier was about, but even an ROTC guy like me knows it can be a fuckin' dangerous business. Now we're here, we've got a job to do, and we oughta start doin' it."

It was quite a speech for me, and they were somewhat taken back. But Sgt. Mitchell was only to be deterred temporarily. "Captain, I got no damn problem bein' with a U.S. unit. It's what I know, and what I was doin' before I got yanked for this. But I don't know this crap. I ain't been trained for this. I'm gonna be out in the middle of nowhere with a couple hundred little slant-eyes, and not be able to control nothin'."

I replied: "We're on radio contact. Somethin' happens to us, a Co Van My gets into trouble, we'll have U.S. assets comin' to get us. We'll be outta there quicker 'an shit." I didn't really believe it, but I was trying to give Sgt. Mitchell something. I continued, "My attitude is, I've been given this job, and I intend to do it. I already told you guys, I'm goin' on every operation. That means if you don't wanna think about puttin' two teams out, you'll just be goin' out once a week at the most. That ain't gonna be too tough is it? Maybe we'll be able to do somethin' more for this outfit, help'em with some trainin' or somethin'. Sgt Mitchell, ya know infantry stuff good. They'll be getting M-16s soon. Maybe we'll be able to help train 'em. Sgt. Blane, ya can hunt up their medics, see what they're carryin', see if you can show 'em a few things. The Army sent us here to do a job. The Army's been you alls' home for a long time. Now it's payback time."

No one said anything for awhile. I undoubtedly hadn't convinced anybody, but they could probably see that arguing with me was not productive. I was obviously gung ho looney. After a bit, I said: "The Dai Uy of the battalion wants us to come for grunts tomorrow. Vietnamese food and beer. I can eat most of that stuff. If you don't want any, just sorta play with it. We can bring some good ol' U.S. beer if you don't want Ba-Moui-Ba."

LTC Meathead

We arrived at the Hao Hoa pagoda early afternoon the next day. The Dai Uy had a residence off the left-rear of the building. The residence was a thatched hut. The interior appeared to have two rooms. The front was a porch of sorts. The thatched roof extended over the porch, and thatched sides about three feet high surrounded the porch on three sides. The floor was dirt, as was the floor of the interior of the residence. The porch was about six feet by fifteen feet.

The Dai Uy and several of his officers were seated around a table when we arrived. The officers were his three company commanders and his executive officer. The so-called interpreter of the day before was on hand to attempt to accomplish communication. Room was made for us, and we began eating and imbibing. At least I began eating. Of my three NCOs, only Sgt. Blane did more than toy with the food. There was plenty of rice and three or four fish or meat dishes. We all, both Vietnamese and Americans, sucked down the alcohol. The Americans stuck with beer. The Vietnamese were going mostly with local whisky.

One of the company commanders was a particularly boisterous guy. He was well-worn, appearing to be in his late forties or fifties. He had a mouth-full of really bad looking teeth, yellow and black and irregular in the extreme, which a perpetual grin kept permanently on display. He chained-smoked the sweet-smelling Vietnamese cigarettes. His ears intersected his head at a 90-degree angle. Appearance-wise, he was a brown-skinned Alfred E. Neuman. His company was located at the pagoda, and his residence was beside the Dai Uy's.

It was a convivial afternoon. Although the interpretation services were atrocious, we did manage to transfer a few thoughts back and forth. The main topic of interest was the team's residence. The Dai Uy was anxious for his advisors to get down with the unit. I was anxious for this also. Getting out of the Special Forces camp with its bar might halt Sgt. Mitchell's descent into the drunken disgruntled oblivion he seemed headed for. It was a long shot as we would still be close to temptation, but I was getting desperate enough about the deteriorating morale to be hopeful about anything. In addition, getting us living with the unit would increase the likelihood that we would focus on our mission—advising the 64th Dia Phon Quan. I was becoming extremely doubtful about doing much more than being radio connectors to American goodies, but at least we might try.

My NCO's weren't particularly anxious to leave the comforts of the Special Forces compound. They hadn't been resisting overtly, but the signs were all negative. I was determined, however, and assured the Dai Uy that we would move in as soon as Lt. Silver arrived with our equipment conex. He indicated a wide spot behind his hut where we could put up a team house. The area was swampy but other dwellings were there. They were on raised foundations of dried mud or on stilts. Until we had a house built, the Dai Uy said we could pitch the team tent in his front yard.

We departed late in the afternoon, pretty well snockered. As soon as we starting driving away, Sgt. Mitchell and Sgt. Roca started in. "Dai Uy, you sure you want to move down here? We got it pretty good where we are. In addition to air-conditioned rooms, a mess hall, and a bar, we got good security. I don't like the situation down here."

"Hey, there ain't nothin' wrong with this place. The Dai Uy lives here. We sure as hell ought to be able to. Besides, we want to get out from under the brass. We don't need them keepin' track of us, breathin' down our necks. Just reconcile yourselves to movin'. Sorry 'bout that, but there ain't no option on this."

There was a heavy silence for the rest of the drive. Mitchell and Roca hit the bar when we got back to the Special Forces camp, drowning their unhappiness and irritation with more beer.

No operations were scheduled for the next couple of days. We hung around the Special Forces camp waiting for Lt. Silver, drinking, and complaining. As we became more aware of the politics of the camp, even Sgt. Mitchell seemed to be coming around to the advisability of moving out. Major problems were a couple of coes and the meathead lieutenant colonel commander.

Two Vietnamese coes—girls—had the run of the camp. They were either in the Vietnamese military or were employees of U.S. Special Forces, I never could figure out which. They wore tight fitting tiger suits and strutted around as if every U.S. soldier in the place was at their beck and call, which was pretty much the case. One was a medic of sorts. She seemed to work out of the dispensary but was constantly hoping in a jeep with some Special Forces type and barrelling out of the camp. She was extremely attractive with a bubbly personality. The other was a tougher gal, not unattractive but hard, never smiling. She chain-smoked Tarleton cigarettes. Smoking among younger Vietnamese women was not particularly common, and those that did generally went for Kools or Salems. This broad, however, sucked now those double-filtered Tarletons with abandon. Both girls had quarters in the compound. Naturally, we asked about them shortly after our arrival but only got rolling eyes and smirks.

An incident during those first days revealed to us just how odd the place was, and what high but undefined position the girls held. It was the middle of the afternoon. We were sitting in a booth in the bar, having the usual gripe session. Except for the bartender, no one else was in the place. The tough gal comes in, sits at the bar, orders a beer, starts sucking down the Tarletons.

Our interest in hashing out what the team was supposed to do, where it was supposed to live, and so forth quickly waned. We were all devoting a good portion of our attention to this tiger-suited mystery. Eventually, Sgt. Roca threw down the gauntlet: "You oughtta check her out, Dai Uy. Gotta be hot stuff."

The others smirked. Truth be told, I didn't need much prodding. A few beers in my 25-year old belly quickly raised women to the top of my priorities. I said, "Yeah, well, no guts, no glory. I'll let you guys know what she likes." I moseyed over to the bar, taking a stool two down from hers.

"Hey, how you doin'?" I suavely ventured after a minute or two. She grunted something. I continued: "We're new here. I seen you 'round. You do translatin' and stuff?"

"Yes." She wasn't very talkative, and her expression didn't change. I would have shortly given up but my NCOs were watching. Pride required that I continue the attempt. So for ten minutes or so I made small talk, occasionally getting a mono-syllable response but not making any headway. I was about to admit defeat when LTC Meathead walked in. He strode purposefully to the empty stool between the tiger-suited coe and I. I said, "Howya doin', Sir?"

There was no response. The silence was deafening and deadly. All of a sudden I felt extremely small. Even an idiot could interpret LTC Meathead's message: scram. So I scrammed. Having to make an overt move to get out of the situation was embarrassing in the extreme. I slunk back to the booth, red-faced, grinning sheepishly, seething inside. My NCOs were so taken back by the colonel's conduct that they didn't even give me a hard time.

"That weren't right, Dai Uy. A senior officer shouldn't act like that." Sgt. Roca was talking. The other two nodded their heads in agreement.

I tried to sound nonchalant. "It's no big thing."

"Well, I never seen anything like that. This place is gettin' screwier by the day." It was Sgt. Roca again.

Sgt. Mitchell chimed in: "You'd better watch yo' ass, Dai Uy. The colonel's got it in for ya now."

I felt the need to salvage a little pride: "As I said, it's no big deal. But I'll tell ya one thing. I'm gonna nail that gal 'fore we get outta here. Ya heard me say it. That'll fix that SOB." Actually, I saw little possibility in "nailing" the tiger-suited coe. She was obviously in the hard-to-get category if nailable at all. I was not one to do a lot of courting. In fact, one of the things I found attractive about Southeast Asia was that you could get all the sex you wanted with a single thing: money. And not much of it was required. Personality, a smooth line, all that garbage that I had a dearth of was unnecessary if you didn't mind paying for it. I didn't. So I wasn't about to spend time trying to seduce some ice-queen just for the sake of a little revenge.

We spent the next hour or so assuaging my injured pride and speculating on the girl, what her real job was, and her relationship to LTC Meathead. The bar began to fill up with the after work crowd. We made some inquiries about the colonel and the girl, but didn't learn much. The incident did, however, break down a little the reluctance of my NCOs to move to the Hao Hoa Pagoda. Living in the midst of the Vietnamese couldn't be as bad as living in this looney ward.

But we couldn't move until Lt. Silver arrived with our conex of equipment. We were reluctantly given a jeep from the province's stock, and only because IV Corps in Can Tho had explicitly ordered that MAT teams needing jeeps be provided them. But all our other goodies were somewhere between Cam Ranh Bay and Cao Lanh, in Lt. Silver's tender care.

The days stretched into a week. Sgt. Mitchell continued hitting the bottle heavily and complaining. The drunker he got, the more mutinous was his language. I avoided him as much as possible. When I could corral my NCOs sober, I gave more pep talks on how it was now pay-back time as far as their Army careers went, but I felt it was like pleading with water to stop flowing. The longer we stayed in the compound, the harder I feared it would be for us to leave.

Another operation took place during the wait for Lt. Silver. This was the first for the team alone. I reiterated to my three NCOs that I intended to go on all operations. It was up to them how they wanted to work around my plans. Not surprisingly, they opted for the less demanding way: one of them would accompany me each time. The approach of sending two advisory teams on a regular basis was not something they gave much consideration to, and I wasn't going to press the matter.

The operation was an introduction to what the Mekong River Delta was really like. In fact, the operation started on the Mekong. Before dawn, I and Sgt. Roca—as the senior NCO, he had the honor of going first—rode with the battalion to the Tan Tich ferry. There, we loaded on some sort of landing craft, approximately 50 individuals to a boat. As the sky in the east gradually became light, we chugged downstream, in a southeasterly direction. The cool pre-dawn breeze, the smells of the river, the shadowy distant shore, the gentle throbbing of the engine, all worked to produce a contradictory combination of feelings. There was a peacefulness, a peacefulness belied by the fact that we were on the way to war. And there was an almost palatable sense of the exotic Orient. As the sun peaked over the horizon, the words of Kipling's *On The Road to Mandalay* came to mind: "...An' the dawn comes up like thunder outer China 'crost the Bay!" Five or six of these morning excursions on the Mekong occurred during my four plus months in Kien Phong Province. I never failed to fall into a semi-trance during the journey.

Another image the boat rides invoked was of World War II marines storming sandy beaches in the Central Pacific. The images of sandy beaches, of the exotic, of Kipling, however, were dispelled when the landing craft dropped its ramp onto a mud bank. Sandy beaches, indeed much in the way of beaches at all, were not to be found on our portion of the Mekong. The brown water stopped, and the thick reeds and undergrowth on the river bank started. If anything separated the two, it was mud, thick and deep.

Such a strip of mud greeted Sgt. Roca and me on this day. The strip was about ten feet wide. A narrow log crossed part of it, but the last few feet required a leap. The river bank beyond rose vertically for about three feet before leveling off. The leap put each individual on a little platform of earth about halfway up the bank. Some of the Vietnamese eschewed the log altogether and struggled through knee-deep mud. By the time Sgt. Roca and I traversed the log, made the leap, clung to the little platform, and were on top of the bank, we were as mud-covered as the Vietnamese who had taken the direct approach.

Sgt. Roca carried the radio. I tried to, but he insisted. We had the interpreter of several days before with us. About mid-way through the morning, he got the point across that the Dai Uy would assign someone to carry the radio for us by the next operation.

The area where we landed was considerably more rural than had been the area of our first operation. There were rice paddies and widely separated dwellings, and also patches of woods. The patches were not particularly thick. No machete work was required to get through them. But they didn't appear to have seen much recent human penetration. Women, children, and old men were at many of the dwelling sites. No young or middle-aged men were in evidence. Just about everyone wore the black trousers and blouses of the Vietnamese peasant. Most had a rag wrapped around their head or a large straw conical hat. Their attitude was indifference. As much as possible, they ignored the passing military columns, even when an NCO or an officer dispatched a soldier for a closer look at a dwelling.

Most of our stroll was on paths through shaded areas. A few times we crossed paddies on narrow dikes. Even many of the dikes, however, had trees providing considerable shade. The fields had obviously been configured many decades, maybe even centuries, previously.

For the first time, we—the two Co Van Mys—encountered one of the hazards of doing business in the Delta. That hazard was the foot bridge. In the rural areas, many of the small streams and canals were crossed by primitive bridges consisting of a few saplings resting on triangular supports of other saplings. Sometimes the bridges had flimsy handrails, and sometimes they didn't. The 130-pound Vietnamese who built the bridges negotiated them with no trouble. It was a different matter for us Co Van Mys. We didn't have the balance of those who had been trotting across these things all their lives. Also, we brought an additional 30 or more pounds to the task. A snapped sapling and a fall to the brown water and mud six or so feet below did not become a frequent experience, but it was not unknown in the weeks and months ahead.

At the end the stroll, about the middle of the afternoon, the boats picked us up and transported us to the dock at the Tan Tich ferry. There, I had another first-time experience. Lunch had consisted of only crackers and cheese, and I was famished. A Vietnamese vendor, an old woman, was selling a few food items from a basket. Some of the troops were buying, and I went over to see what she had. Among her inventory was what looked like hard-boiled eggs. I bought one, cracked it on a knuckle, and began to peel the shell. What I found inside, however, was not the cooked white of the outer portion of the egg. What I found inside made my knees weak and my stomach queasy, very queasy.

It was a nearly fully formed baby chicken. Its head, closed eyes, beak, legs, and wings were all readily discernable. I could also see the beginnings of the stubble that would have been the fuzz with which the chick entered the world. The cooking process had hard-boiled the creature in the shape of an egg, but that was the only egg thing about it.

I furtively glanced around to see if anyone else had purchased an egg. One young Vietnamese soldier had, and from a distance it also appeared to be a hard-boiled chick. He was nonchalantly eating away. Sgt. Roca had hung back at the end of the dock when we disembarked. He strolled up, saw what I was holding, and exclaimed, "What in the holy fuck is that!?"

"Just an egg." I was trying to hide by surprise, consternation, and distress. After all, I was the old Asia Hand. I was working on 26 months in-country. I was playing a role. I had tried to give the impression that I knew as much about Vietnam as any other ten westerners—glossing over the fact that my language ability was pretty much limited to communicating my basest needs to bar girls. The role of Old Asia Hand didn't allow for cultural surprises.

Sgt. Roca stared, open mouthed. "You ain't gonna eat that thing, are ya?"

Well, I wouldn't have if an audience weren't present. But there was no choice. "Sure. That's what I bought it for. Want one?"

He guffawed. "No way, Jose. Go to it Dai Uy." I suspected that he was beginning to suspect the truth. I was a man with no options. It was just me and the chick. I tried to avoid any tremors in my hand as it bore its burden to my mouth.

Most fortunately, the vision turned out to be much worse than the taste. It was actually a little like a hard-boiled egg, only crunchier. I finished it in three bites, avoiding looking each time my hand came to my mouth. With a big grin, Sgt. Roca watched. When I had swallowed the last bit, I said, "See? No problem." Then as causally as I could, I wandered away. When I saw that Sgt. Roca had turned his attention elsewhere, I drank half a canteen of water and gobbled the one or two crackers I had left. And prayed that the image burned in my mind wouldn't trigger an embarrassing eruption from my gut.

The fact that no one had been shot, blown up, or otherwise maimed on the first two operations alleviated just a tad the concerns of MAT-104's NCOs. Sgt. Mitchell was still hitting the bottle and being a belligerent drunk, however, and the others were no help. They egged him on, not directly but subtly, and probably not purposely. They had in effect reverted to the conduct of disgruntled PFCs and spec. 4s.

As promised, the Dai Uy assigned the team a radio humper. His name was pronounced "Mutt." He lived with a wife and several children in a fairly substantial thatched hut near the Dai Uy's. His English was nonexistent, but he was reliable and friendly. As time went by we also became familiar with most of the other members of the Dai Uy's headquarters entourage, which numbered about ten. One especially friendly and helpful character was Yum, who appeared to be the principal radio operator. He was small even by Vietnamese standards, maybe no more than five feet three inches and 110 pounds, but he was energetic and seemed to give as many orders as the Dai Uy did. He was solicitous of our welfare, frequently asking through hand signals on operations whether we had enough to eat and drink.

After almost two weeks, Lt. Silver finally arrived with our conex. It and he were in a truck convoy from Can Tho. The conex was placed in a line of conexes in the Special Forces Camp. I quickly inventoried the contents, as happy as a kid at Christmas. The day after our stuff arrived, I loaded the five-sided tent, three reluctant NCOs, and one reluctant lieutenant into the jeep and headed for the Hao Hoa Pagoda. I was determined to move out of the Special Forces camp as soon as possible. Maybe the new environment would improve morale. At least, we would have a little distance between us and the puzzle palace.

We set up the tent in the Dai Uy's front yard. The conex contained five cots, and they and our gear were the second load. We had the evening meal back at the Special Forces camp, soaked up suds at the bar, and returned for our first evening in our new home.

The tent was cramped, the floor was gradually being churned into a muddy mess, and Sgt. Mitchell was in a liquored-up rage.

"GODDAMMIT! THIS SHIT SUCKS! WE GOT NO BUSI-NESS DOIN' THIS!" He was literally screaming. We were making a fine impression on our first night with our charges. "WHAT THE HELL WE SUPPOSE TO BE DOIN' HERE, CAPTAIN?"

"Now, Sergeant Mitchell. Ya got to calm down. Ya can do whatever ya want to try to get out of this assignment, but until ya do, ya need to play by the rules. We're down here to stay. We've been over what we can do here. Sergeant Blane can give medic trainin'. You can give rifle trainin'. We can prepare these guys to fight their war." I was repeating the litany I had been running through since Di An. When Sergeant Mitchell was sober, he listened to it sullenly. When he was drunk, he was having none of it. The others weren't saying much. Sergeant Mitchell's ranting went on for a good half hour before he finally fell into an intoxicated slumber. I only relaxed when the loud snoring of the passed-out began emanating from his cot. A gradual increase in the sound of steady breathing indicated that the others were falling asleep also.

I lay awake for a long time, trying to decide what to do about Sergeant Mitchell and the drinking. Alcohol had been a major ingredient of my two-years-and-counting Vietnam experience. There had been the problems with the abuse of alcohol by others, starting with Sergeant Stratten back in the 716th MP Battalion in Saigon. There had been my own many episodes of getting shit-faced. And here in my final Vietnam adventure, I was being burdened one last time. I could lay down the law to Sergeant Mitchell, threatening dire action if he couldn't control his drinking. The difficulty was that it was a matter of degree. Forbidding drinking entirely was not really an option in 1968. Drinking in the military, especially in Vietnam as these pages have detailed, was pervasive. The fact that the Special Forces bar was open 14 hours a day said a lot about the drinking culture. And then there was the local bar just outside the Special Forces camp. It was open pretty close to 18 hours a day. The point was that absent going cold turkey, something I was not prepared to order, Sergeant Mitchell was likely to continue imbibing. The question was whether it was possible to keep his drinking within bounds. Based on my experiences with alcoholic NCOs, I was not hopeful.

Another alternative was to go to the senior NCO of the province team, an E-8, and ask that he have a talk with Mitchell. I had only met him briefly and didn't have a feel for his ability to deal with a problem such as this. Finally, I could go to the executive officer and try to get Sergeant Mitchell transferred or disciplined. The likelihood was that the inclination would be to sweep the problem under the rug, as the 716th had tried to do with Stratten. Mulling these unappetizing alternatives, I drifted off to an uneasy sleep.

Over the next few days, MAT-104 shifted, physically and mentally, to its new home. Shortly after we had arrived in the province, a U.S. Army engineer company also showed up. Its main mission was to improve the airfield, but it was also running a variety of errands around

Cao Lanh. Once they realized I was serious about living in a tent on the Dai Uy's front lawn, my NCOs developed a mild case of energy. They quickly made friends with the NCOs who laid on the tasks in the engineer company and got a commitment to build us a team house. I praised the three of them lavishly for their initiative, hoping by positive reinforcement to promote a change of attitude. The engineers also delivered a load of sand to us, the morning after our first night, in fact. So we spent portions of the second day at the pagoda filling sandbags to build a low wall around our flimsy shelter.

During this sandbagging effort, Lt. Silver managed to get on my wrong side. Each of the team members had been coming and going on various errands throughout the day. When two or more of us were at the pagoda at the same time, we had filled a few bags. Along about mid-afternoon, as the three NCOs and myself were there together and working away, I realized that everyone had put in a little manual labor but Lt. Silver. The NCOs realized it to and were beginning to make a few comments. Just then, Lt. Silver drove up from his latest excursion. Sergeant Roca sang out, "Hey, Chun Uy, just in time to fill a few bags." Silver disappeared into the tent without saying anything. After a few minutes, he emerged and headed to the jeep again.

Sergeant Roca called out impishly, "Where you off to now, Lieutenant?"

"Goin' up to province headquarters," he mumbled.

"Lt. Silver, how about givin' us a hand with these sandbags?" I was becoming unhappy with what seemed to be his avoidance of getting his hands dirty.

He paused, took a deep breath, and said: "Sir, I became an officer partly so I wouldn't have to do manual labor. I didn't go through ROTC for that. I don't think I should have to fill sandbags."

I knew a lot of officers thought like that, but actually to hear the sentiments expressed, and by a combat arms officer at that, was somewhat shocking. The four of us stared open-mouth. It was several moments before I found my voice. "Lieutenant, I'm a captain and these guys are non-commissioned officers. In theory, none of us is supposed to be doin' manual labor. But do ya see any EMs 'round? Whose gonna do it if not us? Up in the Central Highlands with the 173rd, I dug many a hole. This is war. It ain't no stateside parade ground. Now, how 'bout givin' us a hand?"

He reluctantly took off his shirt and pitched in.

Over the next week, the 64th Regional Forces Battalion went on several more operations, enough so that each member of the team received his baptism. Sergeant Mitchell threw a couple more drunken tantrums. I was concerned about the impression we were making on the Dai Uy and his men. Here we were parked in his front yard, engaged in evening shouting matches. What Vietnamese battalion commander wanted a rowdy insubordinate group of Co Van Mys living on his doorstep?

On the positive side, the engineers began constructing our team house. The members of the team not on an operation contributed. In fact, the engineers only lasted for a few days, long enough to get the frame built. Since the site was within view of the main road, the fact that a few engineers had been diverted to an unauthorized project soon came to the attention of some busy body. Fortunately, the engineers left behind enough material to finish the job. And working on the house gave the team members something to do besides drinking and whining.

As we put additional operations under our belts and talked to a few more old-timers, we began to get a feel for our surroundings. The area to the immediate southwest of Cao Lanh, where I had gone on the first operation, was the quietest. It was also where we were to visit the least. The 64th strolled among the well-built, sizeable dwellings and along the broad shaded paths only a couple more times over the next four months.

About five and a half miles north of Cao Lanh, an east-west canal bisected much of Kien Phong Province. The canal was often either a northern boundary or a southern boundary for an operation. Most of the area to the north, regardless of the side of the canal, was Charlie's country, at least in part. Undergrowth and trees were generally confined to the banks of canals and streams. The areas in between were large rice fields, some a click or so across. A village and an RF/PF fort, with an American advisory team, were on the banks of the canal almost directly north of Cao Lanh. No road connected Cao Lanh with the village.

The main road stretching in a west-northwest direction from Cao Lanh paralleled the Mekong. The road passed a large RF/PF training center, which also had an advisory team, about five miles from Cao Lanh. About a mile past the center, the road skirted a mid-sized village. Another village, one with a number of masonry structures, was to the north of the center. Just to the north of this village, and below the main east-west canal, was a sparsely populated region that the 64th always entered warily. The banks of the east-west canal in this vicinity had been extensively defoliated, a process that in truth didn't seem to reduce the concealment possibilities. Instead of a visually impenetrable green, the defoliated banks of the canal were a visually impenetrable brown.

In the area between Cao Lanh and the canal to the north were no villages, just a number of widely spaced farm dwellings. To the northeast and east, however, the nature of human habitation varied considerably. A meandering north-south river did a wide loop before finding its way to the Mekong. Just to the northeast along the river was a spread-out village that resembled the villages to the southwest of Cao Lanh. To the north of the village, the river banks were largely devoid of people. On the other side of the river to the east, what had been the main road was bordered by extended, elongated villages. Every few miles another river or canal interrupted the road. The interruption was literal because practically all of the bridges had been destroyed during the 1968 Tet offensive.

Charlie's stronghold seemed to be to the east and southeast. It was a diverse area of canals, streams, farm dwellings, a few small villages, and at least one sizeable one. The two biggest contacts we were to have during the next four months were to take place in this region.

We had arrived in Cao Lanh just after the end of the rainy season. For our first few operations, the fields and low spots contained considerable water. The level in the fields was as much as knee deep. Most of the fields were covered by what I supposed were rice stalks thigh and waist high. The fields looked like flooded wheat fields. Over the weeks as the dry season progressed, the water levels gradually went down until some of the fields actually became dry land. The canals and streams never dried up, however, and many of the fields remained soggy swamps.

Crossing the canals and streams could be an adventure. Wading or risking the rickety pole bridges were how we handled the smaller ones. Commandeered sampans provided transportation across the larger bodies. The term "sampans" encompassed, at least for U.S. soldiers, a wide variety of water craft. At one extreme were 30- to 40-feet motorized boats on which families often lived. These boats were constructed with planks and had awnings to ward off sun and rain. At the other extreme were dugout canoes—hollowed out logs. Practically every family living along a canal or stream had at least one of these. Power was provided by a pole. The operator would be balanced precariously on the stern, planting the pole on the bottom of the canal or stream and pushing. When the 64th needed to cross a body of water, the troops would round up several of these small sampans, with their owner-operators, from nearby dwellings, and the ferrying would begin.

Like the pole bridges, the small sampans posed a problem for the large Co Van Mys. The sampans had about a third the stability of a state-side canoe. Getting in one required a dexterity that most large clumsy Westerners lacked. The individual's weight had to be kept over the center of the boat, a nearly impossible task when a leap usually was required just to reach the boat. Once on board, the passengers often were packed tightly together and remained standing for a crossing. No shifting of weight was allowed during these journeys. Sometimes, if the line of march paralleled a canal or river and a column of troops was on each bank, the Dai Uy would have the command group proceed in a sampan or two on the water. As part of the command group, the Co Van Mys shared the dubious privilege of riding rather than walking. For these lengthier boat trips, sufficient room usually existed to squat or sit. Unlike for the Vietnamese, however, squatting for the Westerners was an unnatural act that turned to pain in a very short time.

One of the first operations after we started constructing the team house involved a float down a small canal. The operation was to the northwest of Cao Lanh. As with most operations, we were transported by truck to a jumping off place. From there, we were to make a swing to the north, west, and south, finishing on the main road from Cao Lanh to the Cambodian border. The final, south, leg of the trip was along a canal, and the Dai Uy commandeered several sampans.

Initially, the banks of the canal had no trees or undergrowth. The canal was just a straight murky brown slash across a wide expanse of paddies. After about a mile, however, the canal merged into an amorphous area of water and undergrowth. The walking columns on each bank angled away to the right and left as the sampans plunged straight ahead into the denseness. The course became obscure with two or three channels appearing to be possibilities. It was as if we had entered a flooded patch of forest. The river banks disappeared, replaced by large patches of bushes seemingly floating on the water. Whether they were actually floating, anchored in underwater mud, or growing on above-water soil was impossible to determine from our sampans a few yards away.

I noticed that the Dai Uy and his entourage were beginning to eye the undergrowth warily. If hostiles were about, we in our little dugouts were sitting ducks. One guy with an AK could wreck havoc. I figured if I survived the initial fusillade, I would be in the water heading down and toward the nearest clump of undergrowth. Then my main worry would be concussions from grenades.

By now, the Dai Uy was jabbering excitedly on his radio. I gripped my M-16 a bit tighter. Sgt. Mitchell was my accompaniment for the day. His eyes, though bleary from a hangover, nevertheless betrayed an apprehension. The sampan operators, natives to the immediate locale, also seemed uneasy. If anyone was getting ready to blow us away, it would be their neighbors. Getting whacked by the guy next door was probably not an appealing prospect.

But the rain of bullets didn't come. Instead, after about 100 meters we emerged into the open. The battalion columns were angling back in to the canal. The Dai Uy abandoned the sampans, and the command group joined the walkers for the remainder of the operation.

It was taking me awhile to acquire the knack of working with over-lays. Mounting the things on the map, folding the map for the plastic bag, and keeping track of coordinates while slogging through the muck initially seemed more than I could handle. One afternoon in mid-December, however, LTC Meathead brought me up to speed.

We were on a short operation just north of town. Though short, it was a multi-battalion effort, and the province chief was involved. Since he was involved, his counterpart, LTC Meathead, was on hand. The 64th's task was to proceed slowly north through a watery area, pushing any VCs into the arms of another unit waiting on a road. The Dai Uy loaded the command group into sampans—he and I were in separate boats—and we proceeded to thread our way through a swamp. Some of the rest of the battalion were in sampans. The remainder were on foot.

As we picked our way north, a muffled explosion sounded 100 meters or so off to the side. The Dai Uy immediately began jabbering on the radio. It didn't seem likely that any VC would be operating in the middle of the day this close to town, so I just rode serenely along, enjoying the bright sun reflecting off the flooded green fields. All of a sudden my radio blared: "Homestead Six, this is Cobra Six."

I answered: "This is Homestead Six."

"This is Cobra Six! You got a goddamn wounded man down there! You gonna get him out or what? Let's get on the goddamn ball! What are his coordinates!?" LTC Meathead was virtually screaming by the end of the transmission. I was caught flat-footed. Getting cursed so vehemently over the radio was a new experience for me. The fact that I couldn't immediately answer the good colonel's question was disconcerting. I attempted to communicate with the Dai Uy through our alleged interpreter, but it was taking awhile to get the process started.

"What the hell is goin' on down there Homestead!? I want those grid coordinates now!"

"We're workin' on it, Cobra Six, but we're havin' some interpreter problems." The real truth was that I was having map problems. I had folded the map in such a way as to hide the grid numbers. Thus I had no idea what my own coordinates were, much less the coordinates of the wounded man. I frantically began undoing my map paraphernalia in order to get at the coordinates. The fact that I was in a dangerously teetering sampan was not helping matters.

"I want those coordinates, and I want 'em now, Homestead!" The colonel was sounded more and more demented. He was also putting on quite a show. In this open terrain with the operating units in a tight little area, the medevac chopper did not need precise coordinates. Still, I was caught in a major gaffe for an infantry officer—I couldn't say where I was. I continued to flay away at my map mess. The Dai Uy was having his own problems. Apparently the province chief was on his butt as severely as LTC Meathead was on mine.

"Where the fuckin' hell's those coordinates, Homestead!? I said I wanted 'em now! That means goddamn now!"

Finally, I had the map spread out—though part of it was dipping in the water—and was getting my location pinpointed. We pulled up beside the Dai Uy's sampan, and through a few English words, a few

Vietnamese words, a few French words, and some acting, were able to establish where the wounded man was. I got on the horn. "Cobra Six, this is Homestead Six. The medevac is at," and I gave the coordinates.

"Bout fuckin' time, Homestead! You need to do a helluva lot better on that goddamn map!"

"We're have interpreter problems, Cobra Six. It's difficult to communicate with my counterpart without a decent interpreter."

LTC Meathead didn't reply. The medevac chopper appeared shortly, hovered within sight of us, took on the wounded man, and departed. The operation itself wound down not much later. LTC Meathead and the province chief were soon off the air, and I was left with my ears stinging. I had been publicly rebuked over the province radio net, and it wasn't a pleasant feeling. Truth be told, however, I deserved criticism. I had not been on top of the situation. I determined that it was not to happen again.

Little came of the incident. Apparently this was LTC Meathead's modus operandi. The XO did talk to me about interpreter problems, but that was about the extent of it. No decent interpreters were available. In addition, the new province advisor arrived shortly thereafter, and LTC Meathead retreated to his life as a Sneaky Pete. It would be too much to hope that he met his end on an excrement-covered punji stick.

A Third 'Nam Christmas

Work continued on our team house. I was even putting time on it myself. By mid-December it was finished, and we were moved in. It wasn't fancy, just a great big room on stilts. The bottom four to five feet of the wall was planking, the remainder to the ceiling was screen. The room had plenty of space for our five cots and lockers plus several tables and chairs. We built a bunker just outside the door. It consisted of sandbags about five and a half feet high. On top of the sand bags was a sheet of PCP, the airfield runway material. The PCP was approximately even with the landing going into the team house. We stacked several long narrow ammunition boxes filled with sand around the edge of the PCP and in essence made ourselves a small veranda. It was not an unpleasant place to wile away an off day.

Lt. Silver was assigned to duty in the province TOC. Team personnel were not supposed to be diverted, but I didn't object too strenuously. With me going on each operation, the others could go a week or more before having to do anything constructive. Getting Silver out of the rotation reduced a bit the amount of time the team NCOs were sitting around unoccupied or worse. Silver continued to live in the team house, but he was essentially on his own.

About the time we moved into the team house, an event occurred that both eliminated one of my major problems and in the years since has served to remind me that occasionally an individual can be redeemed. From his hangover one morning, Sgt. Mitchell announced: "I ain't drinkin' no more. I'm on the wagon."

And he meant it. He didn't have another drink during my stay. In real life, I've seen few people turn themselves around. It happens all the time on TV and in the movies, but in real life? Not in my experience. Sgt. Mitchell was an exception. He went stone cold sober.

But no good is unmitigated. To take up the slack, another problem drinker emerged on the team. He didn't become as disruptive as Sgt. Mitchell had been, but the booze certainly didn't help his job performance. He went on more than a few operations on only a few hours of drunken sleep and hungover as a skunk. He was me.

Nothing specific contributed to my increased drinking. In part, it was just due to free time and access. Even going on every operation of the 64th Battalion kept me busy only three or four days a week. So there was plenty of time to hang out at the Special Forces club and the bar at the entrance to the Special Forces compound.

Perhaps a contributing factor was the realization that the advisory team had few duties other than air liaison. We had certainly been warned that this was likely to be the case. But I had harbored hopes that we could contribute something more than communications with the My-My Whop-Whops—the Vietnamese term for choppers—and the fighter-bombers of the U.S. Air Force. In reality, however, what could we be beside liaison with air support? By definition, advisors don't command. Advisors may be able tactfully to offer advice to inexperienced commanders, but the Dai Uy and his company commanders had been combat commanders for many, many years. They had no need, or probably desire, for advice from the likes of me. And my attempts to have Sgt. Blane provide a little medical training or Sgt. Mitchell a little infantry or rifle training came to naught. The presence of advisors may have ensured that the Vietnamese didn't hold up in their compounds and actually went on operations, but by 1968 most advisors were dispensing little real advice. The Vietnamese didn't need it and didn't want it.

So for whatever reason—frustration, too much free time, lack of discipline, character flaws—my drinking increased, partly offsetting Sgt. Mitchell's redemption.

One of the few things I knew about war that the Dai Uy and his men didn't was My-My-Whop-Whops. As a unit, the 64th Regional Forces Battalion had not participated in a helicopter operation. A few individuals had some experience, but the unit as a whole did not.

But the first chopper ride with the 64th was also an experience for me. The reason was because the ride was on Vietnamese choppers. We loaded up on a road just to the north of Cao Lanh. Because at least two lifts were involved and thus more communications were needed, all four of us—myself and Sergeants Roca, Mitchell, and Blane—went. The choppers were pre-Hueys—the type of machines used by the U.S. Marines, and probably the Army also, in the early 60s. I was accustomed to the feeling of freedom in the Hueys—the open sides, the wind whipping through, the unencumbered view of the sky and ground. The ancient choppers of the Vietnamese, however, were like enclosed boxes. The fuselage had only tiny round windows. The single door was located well forward. Ten or twelve troopers entered and crowded to the rear. Only the two or three individuals in front had a view through the open door, and the view was limited. The cockpit with the pilot and copilot was about six feet above the floor of the fuselage. Thus a view to the front was nonexistent.

I was near the door and consequently had a view to the side, but I could have done without it. Once we were airborne, the choppers closed into tight formations of three each. And I mean tight. The chopper to our right looked close enough to touch. The whirling blades overhead had to be only a few feet from being intertwined. The machines were bouncing in the natural turbulence of the air and the artificial turbulence of their own making. I didn't see how they could avoid being slammed together. I sat with a racing heart and an empty feeling in the gut, waiting for a deafening screech of metal intersecting metal at high speed and the subsequent sickening plunge to the earth below. Grasping for any hope, I thought that if we went down in a paddy, the water and mud might allow some small chance of survival.

But we survived the trip and were set down near a canal. The battalion followed the canal south for several hours without incident until we hit the main road from Cao Lanh to the Cambodian border. We were just outside the sizeable village to the west of the RF/PF training camp on the Mekong. I expected trucks to pick us up there and return us home, but on this particular day the province had a surfeit of assets available. Over the radio, I learned that a U.S. chopper unit would shortly arrive to take the battalion back out for another little jaunt.

The Dai Uy heard of the change of mission about the same time I did. He and his entourage became extremely agitated. Orders were barked, and there was much scurrying hither and yon. Eventually it became time to approach the Co Van My with a problem. Through our barely borderline interpreter, the Dai Uy asked where and how he should get set for the pick up.

Well, if truth be told, I knew something about chopper operations, but I was far from being an expert. I had made decisions about setting a 30-man platoon up for an extraction, but the 64th had a strength of approximately three hundred troops. Plus, I was having difficulty learning how many choppers were inbound.

The first matter to be decided concerned exactly where the pick up was to be. The road was what suggested itself initially. It was straight, dry, and aligned with the prevailing breeze. But several old trees were growing along the stretch between the village and a wood line to the west. The trees would have to come down if the pick up were on the road. I got this point across to the Dai Uy. His men quickly located several axes and set upon the trees. An environmental pang hit me as I watched the chopping, however. For many decades, these trees had been providing shady spots on the road, had been part of this small segment of the Delta landscape. And here I was having them taken down for a one-shot, few-minute need.

There had to be a better way. I motioned to the Dai Uy to halt the clearing of these long-time guardians of the local scene. A field extended at a diagonal toward the north. It was marshy and not aligned with the wind but seemed like it might do. I finally got a fix on how many choppers were on their way: six. With much effort among myself, the Dai Uy, and the interpreter, I got across where the choppers would be coming in and how he should divide up his men. The process was still going on when a file of Hueys appeared in the sky to the east. I described to the leader where the PZ was and how he should approach. I concluded: "And there's one thing you should be aware of, Snake One. This is these guys' first time on Hueys. They are getting organized down here, but things might go a little slow. I hope ya got patience."

"Roger that, Homestead. We got all the patience in the world."

We popped smoke, the choppers came in, and the Dai Uy's men actually scrambled on like they knew what they were doing. We LZed several miles to the west and again walked to the road. This time the trucks were on hand to take us home. Thus the first day of air operations with the 64th Regional Forces Battalion went without incident.

The first beating of a prisoner took place on an operation to the northwest of Cao Lanh. We had been trucked to the vicinity of the sizeable town in that area and during the morning had made our way to the north. Eventually, we came to an east-west canal, on the far bank of which was a rural hamlet. We crossed the canal on sampans.

Women, children, and old men were the principal visible occupants of the hamlet. The Dai Uy's troops, however, flushed one teenage male who, by a stretch, could qualify as other than a child. He appeared no more than 13 or 14. But the Dai Uy had no sympathy for the youth's tender years. One of the Dai Uy's henchmen—a group that included several RTOs and a batman or two—was a mean looking guy who wore a uniform with a Vietnamese ranger patch, indicating that he had apparently served with this elite force. Shortly after the youth was found, the Dai Uy turned the ranger loose. The latter proceeded to pummel the kid, not seriously but enough to puff up his face a bit.

Questions were being shouted at the prisoner, but his sobbing answers were evidently unsatisfactory. Sgt. Blane and I watched the action from off to the side. The way South Vietnamese handled prisoners was common knowledge. Beatings, water treatments—holding a prisoner under water until he took in a good quantity—even killings were standard practice. How American advisors were supposed to handle these situations was not discussed much. The subject certainly hadn't been on our agenda at Di An. Such actions were of course contrary to some Geneva Convention or other, but we were advisors and not in positions of authority or responsibility. Probably in theory advisors should have reported such things up the advisory chain of command. But I never heard of such a report being made, and after more than two years in Vietnam, I was too jaded to raise any objections. Indeed, I probably wouldn't have complained during my first month in-country; apparently few others, if any, did.

The ranger wasn't having much luck extracting information, so the Dai Uy himself got involved. He took out his .45 and slapped the poor kid on the side of the head. Then he forced the kid to his knees, put the pistol next to the kid's ear, and fired a round into the ground. Then he fired several more. At first, the kid was hysterical. When he realized he wasn't dead, however, he calmed a bit, not much, just a bit. The Dai Uy apparently still wasn't getting the responses he wanted, but his interest was waning. After another few minutes of being slapped around, the kid was handed off to our favorite company commander, the one who looked like Alfred E. Neuman. Dai Uy Alfred immediately took the boy in his arms and patted his head. I didn't know if I was seeing real sympathy or just the second part of a bad guy-good guy routine. Whether real or faked, the performance was convincing. Dai Uy Alfred didn't untie the kid's hands, but he did take control of him and treat him with fatherly kindness. The kid was taken back to Cao Lanh with us. What became of him and others that were removed from the villages and rural areas in the weeks and months ahead, I never learned.

I did know what became of several who didn't get the opportunity to make the journey, however.

The first of these incidents occurred not too long after the kid-beating, and in the same general vicinity. We were moving across the wide open area of rice paddies to the south of the east-west canal where the kid's hamlet was located. A few dwellings were scattered here and there along the streams and canals that crisscrossed the paddies.

A male was flushed from a clump of bushes in a marshy field near one of the dwellings. He appeared to be in his thirties. The Dai Uy took an immediate dislike to him. The man's hands were tied behind his back, and he began receiving the standard thumping. He was responding to questions, but the responses weren't producing much satisfaction. The Dai Uy's voice was increasing in decibels and intensity.

The Dai Uy eventually called one of his henchmen forward and screamed some instructions. The guy carried a carbine. Apparently in accordance with the Dai Uy's instructions, he unslung the carbine from his shoulder and aimed in the direction of the prisoner, who was lying in the weeds and water. The henchman squeezed the trigger three or four times, and the carbine emitted its characteristic popping sound. Geysers of water rose in the air from the side of the prisoner.

Another set of questions was thrown his way. The answers, however, had apparently not become any more satisfactory. This time, the geysers of water were closer to the man. One of the rounds even found flesh, almost severing a finger. The guy lay in the weeds and grass moaning and whimpering a little but still not being sufficiently forthcoming to assuage the rising anger.

Finally, the Dai Uy had enough. He barked an order, and the command group resumed its sloshing march—all except the henchman with the carbine. After the rear of the group was about 15 meters from the prisoner and the rifleman, the Dai Uy yelled over his shoulder. I caught the Vietnamese word "ban," which means "shoot." The henchman again pressed the carbine into his shoulder and squeezed off several rounds. The geysers rising into the air were different from the results of the earlier bursts. These geysers were reddish, not bright red but a sort of pale, watery pink.

The carbine-wielder splashed to catch up with us. He was pumped and jabbered excitedly to his companions for some minutes. Initially, the Dai Uy was silent and purposeful in his strides. He was also avoiding my gaze. Finally, our eyes met. I said, "Numbah One VC."

A grin spread over his face, and he repeated, "Numbah One VC." We sloshed on toward the next blue line.

Sgt. Mitchell was my companion on the day of the first execution. He didn't have a lot to say at the time. When we got back that afternoon, he drawled to Sergeants Roca and Blane, "The Dai Uy found a new way to handle them VCs."

"Oh yeah? How's that?"

"Yeah, he found him a new way, didn't he Dai Uy?"

"He did that. No doubt about it."

"Well, what is it?"

Sgt. Mitchell said: "He shoots the muthafuckers. Bam. Bam. Must save on paperwork."

"Oh Yeah? He shot a guy?"

"Had the goofy-looking guy do it. Just blew his ass away."

Shooting prisoners didn't become an epidemic for the 64th Battalion, maybe because the unit didn't take a lot of them. Most people policed up on operations were questionables—youngsters, middle-aged men, and the like. Only one other outright execution occurred.

The operation was far to the northwest of Cao Lanh, sometime in mid-January. The battalion had been inserted by chopper onto one of the vast plains that stretched to the Cambodian border and beyond. We were following a blue line south when a couple of young men were flushed from a bit of watery undergrowth 100 meters or so out on the plain. The line of march of the Dai Uy and the command group was close to the bank of the blue line. The company on the left flank found the unfortunates.

The battalion stopped for a time awaiting instructions from higher headquarters. The command group was in a clearing and had an unrestrained view of the left flank company and the two prisoners. The Dai Uy had shown little interest in the individuals, although I suspect some of his radio conversations had concerned them. After a pause of a half hour or so, we received word to move on. And a decision was made about the fate of the prisoners.

One of the Dai Uy's henchmen was a jocular sort who was usually in the throes of some bit of merriment. On this occasion, however, he became all business when the Dai Uy issued him a harsh-sounding order and handed him a .45. The henchman sloshed off toward the left flank company and the two prisoners. When he got there, he talked for a moment with the company commander and then marched the two prisoners to the rear, behind some bushes that obstructed our view. A shot rang out, and after a pause, another. The jocular one was soon back amongst us, once again his fun-loving self.

On the outside, my reaction to the prisoner shootings was nonchalance. Inside, however, there were disturbing things. As I've noted, the South Vietnamese tender way with prisoners was widely known among American advisors. And making an issue of the matter was at least implicitly discouraged by the advisory hierarchy. It was a see-no-evil atmosphere. But a dark part of me wanted to actually embrace the evil. I had some vague desire to have more blood on my hands, to have more guilt for what was being perpetrated, by those on both sides, in this remote place. Perhaps some of the feeling came from knowledge about the French experience. My impression of that experience was that French and Foreign Legion units and individual French and Foreign Legion soldiers had gradually lost their humanity in Indochina and Algeria. As the years dragged on, torturing and killing prisoners became all too common.

Well, my years in Vietnam were dragging on. I was now over two and counting. And they were two straight. No intervening period of consequence had been spent back in a civilizing environment. The lieutenant who had stopped a prisoner from being beaten on Hill 882 over a year earlier was now a more cynical, more jaded captain who was perhaps reaching his saturation point of death and destruction.

Motivated in part by such grim thoughts, I began to feel early in my stay in Cao Lanh that it was time to go home. Actually, I had little choice. My ETS from the Army was in April 1969. No provision I knew of would allow me a further extension in the Army for a definite period. The options were to extend in the Army indefinitely or apply for a Regular Army commission. In either case, I would most likely have to return for a stateside assignment, probably the Infantry Career Course at Ft. Benning. But I didn't really give these options any serious consideration. I was in the Army for the war, not for peacetime garrison stuff. And there didn't appear to be any way for me to stay in the war.

So I had begun desultorily making some future plans. Shortly after arriving in Cao Lanh, I asked my mother to send me applications for law school at the University of Virginia and Duke University. By involving her, I figured I would give her hope that I might actually come home. The LSAT, the law school admissions test, was offered in Saigon in January, and I signed up. Still, the war had a hold on me. I toyed with the idea of putting in a ten-forty-nine for another five months in the Army and in Vietnam. The fact that I would have definite future plans—law school, assuming I was accepted—might be enough for someone to approve such short-term extensions. But in part because I did not hear about law school until I had left Vietnam, I never got around to the requests.

The future, however, was only a hazy blur on my horizon. I was conscious of the approaching end of my war, and I was half-heartedly making plans, but the present was what dominated. I lived for the operations, for tromping the paddies, swamps, and river and canal banks. Being only a glorified radio operator was a negative, but at least it had the potential of getting me to the sound of guns, the scream of shells and bombs, the addictive rush of adrenalin.

One thing I was not experiencing was much fear, the eminent feeling of my own demise that had been a large part of life as a platoon leader in the 173rd. Several factors accounted for the reduced level of personal fear. One was the cockiness that some survivors of combat acquire. After getting shot at a few times and not getting hurt, some idiots begin to feel invulnerable. The feeling does not comport with reality. Death when the bullets are whizzing is often only millimeters away. Nevertheless, surviving a few firefights can give one a Superman complex.

Another reason for the lack of fear was the overpowering dominance of the knowledge that I was coming down the stretch on my combat career. I had a desire to experience as much war as possible before I returned to civilization for what would probably be the rest of my life. Finally, when one is, as we advisors were, more an observer than a participant, one is more apt to adopt an attitude of bravado. Saying that a unit ought to be more aggressive is easy when there is no danger that the unit will act on the comment. The game is different when one is in command and actually making decisions that could result in excursions into harm's way.

Initially, however, my dearth of fear and desire for bang-bang were academic. Other than the prisoner shooting and a few booby trap explosions, operations in December were, from a combat standpoint, uneventful. Christmas brought a truce that combined with a certain inertia among the South Vietnamese to produce a week of inactivity. It was my third Christmas in Vietnam, my family's third Christmas without its son.

Naturally, I got drunker than nine skunks. About 11:00 p.m. on Christmas Eve, after lengthy stays at the Special Forces club and the bar at the compound's entrance, Sgt. Blane and I found ourselves carousing Cao Lanh's main drag. Actually, I was carousing; he was mostly trying to get me back to the pagoda. The streets were deserted. I suppose I was looking for women, but in my advanced degree of drunkenness, who knows? Noise from behind one door attracted our attention, and I commenced pounding. If a party was taking place inside, I wanted to be there. Eventually, the door opened a crack. A Vietnamese male eyed me warily. I asked, "Ba-Moui-Ba?"

He said, "Mot foot," meaning roughly "just a minute." He closed the door. In a few moments, he opened it wider and handed me something. The area behind him was dimly lit. Several other men were engaged in some activity. Through my drunkenness, I sniffed fresh bread. I glanced at my hand. What I was holding was a loaf of the long thin French-style bread that was a Vietnamese staple. Sgt. Blane and I were trying to crash a bread-making factory. The realization drained my desire for further partying. Sgt. Blane and I staggered back to the compound. The next morning, Christmas, I took a bite of the loaf. It was wormy. Merry Christmas.

Although from a combat perspective December was largely uneventful, other happenings made it an interesting month. High on the list was a growing acquaintance with the food of our Vietnamese comrades. The day-long operations encompassed the noon meal. The 64th Regional Forces Battalion would often stop and cook rice they brought with them and local delicacies found in the area. One local delicacy was field rat. Large rats inhabited many of the rice paddies. The soldiers of the 64th would catch the animals, which were the size of small cats, singe the fur off in a fire, place the bodies on spits, and roast away. The sinewy carcasses were devoid of fat. They reminded me of squirrels. Whether they tasted like squirrel I don't know: I've never had squirrel, and I didn't get around to accepting any of the offers to dine on haunch of rat.

I did accept an offer to partake of another bit of local fauna, much to my regret. Among the many types of aquatic life in the canals, streams, and ponds were snails. The soldiers would often gather these delicacies and boil them in a helmet or other container. I had tried snails once or twice during a trip to Europe in my undergraduate days. They hadn't been half bad, so on one operation in the middle of December, I accepted a plateful of boiled snails. And again, they passed the taste test.

They didn't meet with approval in a lower portion of my anatomy, however. I awoke early the next morning with racking stomach pains and severe diarrhea. This presented a problem because we did not have a toilet at our team house. We had pounded a large tube about five inches in diameter into the ground as a urinal, but for defecating, and showers, we went to the 44th Zone's compound or the Special Forces compound. I was not going to last the short jeep ride to either of these facilities, however. The alternative, other than crapping in my pants, was to make use of the Vietnamese's communal facility.

Within the 64th's compound at the pagoda was a large manmade pond. It was square, about 30 feet by 30 feet, and surrounded by a dike about six feet high. Two flimsy log bridges extended over the water to small platforms in the middle of the pond. The bridges had no hand-rails. Each of the platforms had a small wooden wall about two feet high around it. The platforms themselves were no more than a couple of slats tied to poles that were sunk into the pond.

This was the village shitter. A few of the more substantial huts in the compound had chamber pots, but most of the soldiers and their families did their business from the precarious platforms. What kept the pond from being nothing more than an open cesspool were what we Co Van Mys called shitfish. The pond contained a number of carp-like fish, the largest of which were maybe a foot long. These fish subsisted on shit, indeed craved it. A turd would no sooner hit the muddy brown water than be the subject of a wild thrashing melee of flashing silver bodies.

When the first wave of diarrhea struck me, I knew that the pond was my only alternative to crapping in my pants or on the team house floor. The pond was only 15 meters away, but a small swamp was between it and the team house. Getting to the far side of the pond where the bridges to the platforms were required about a 100-meter trip out to and along the main road and then in through another entrance to the compound.

Clinching my buttocks tightly together, pausing when the pains charged through my groin, sweating profusely, I made my slow way down the steps of the team house and toward the shitfish. My shuffling steps were no more than six inches in length. When I finally arrived at the pond, both of the platforms were occupied. Fortunately, there was no line. Squatting on one of the platforms was a grinning elderly mama-san, only her head visible above the small wall. Her mouth and few remaining teeth were stained red with betelnut. A young soldier was on the other platform. Both displayed a moment of astonishment when they saw that the next person in line was one of the big hulking Co Van Mys.

As I stood there, a feces dropped from mama-san's platform. The fish churned the water in pursuit of the delicacy. Having finished her business, mama-san rose and pulled up her black pants, all in one motion. Spry as a youngster, she scampered across the bridge, giggling as she passed me. It was now my turn, and none too soon. My legs were practically crossed trying to restrain the pending explosion. But first, I had to get to the platform, about 15 feet away.

I started across the flimsy logs. They groaned under the unaccustomed weight. I teetered first to one side and then the other, my arms flapping to maintain my balance. The possibility of falling in seemed very real. How would several dozen shitfish react to 160 pounds of Co Van My? Were they just interested in shit, or did they have a little piranha in them? But I made the platform without incident. At that point, I developed an appreciation for mama-san's ability to stand and pull up her pants in one motion. I now had to drop my pants and squat, and if they weren't in one motion, the surreptitious audience I was beginning to attract would get an eyeful. I did the best I could, but more than a few Vietnamese had a glimpse of a male round-eye's most precious possession.

The explosion occurred even before I was all the way down. Used to a single small bit of ordnance from directly above, the fish were at first puzzled by the carpet bombing. They recovered quickly, however, and scrambled about in search of the goodies. The Vietnamese adults who were watching were doing so out of the corners of their eyes, trying not to be obvious. A group of kids were not so bashful. About seven or eight had gathered on the bank and were watching the proceedings with, at first, restrained interest. The explosion and the resulting frenzy in the water sent them into gales of laughter.

Temporarily relieved, I simultaneously tried to rise and pull up my pants, with only partial success. Again, the watching Vietnamese got an eyeful. I started back to the team house. Before I could complete the journey, however, another attack struck. So I did an about-face and returned to the pond.

As it turned out, the pond was to be my second home for the next several days. The attacks were frequent and vicious. The novelty of a Co Van My using the local facility soon wore off for the Vietnamese. Thus my visits ceased to be a spectator event. The visits also ceased to be of interest to the shitfish. After the first visit, all I had in me was liquid. The fish apparently came to associate the heavy clopping on the bridge with something resembling rain. It certainly wasn't food. Between visits to the pond, I lay on my bunk, sleeping when the cramps were in remission. I even passed up an operation. Sergeants Roca and Mitchell did the honors.

Shitfish didn't just live in specially constructed sewer ponds. They were in all the waterways. The toilet facilities for many homes consisted of a bridge to a platform over a stream or canal. Falling defecation would be met by a melee of thrashing silvery bodies. The Vietnamese did not eat shitfish from a pond where the only food for the fish was, well, shit. The Vietnamese were not so discriminating about shitfish that had a varied diet, however. Shitfish from rivers and canals were standard fare.

Over several days, I gradually regained control over my bowels. Maybe some pills I was given by Sgt. "Doc" Blane helped, and maybe nature just took its course. I had dropped close to ten pounds and was weak as a kitten, but the trips to the pond were over.

A few weeks later, I actually ate a little shitfish. It was during the Christmas week slow-down. Sergeants Roca and Blane and myself were looking for something to do one afternoon, and we ended up at a so-called restaurant just to the north of Cao Lanh. The place had just opened. It was situated on a grassy clearing beside a canal. We had been drinking since noon at the Special Forces club and decided to try the new place for dinner.

The proprietor was effusively glad to see some clientele. No other customers were in evidence. We first had a few more beers at the bar. The proprietor then showed us to a picnic table outside, beside the canal. I don't know how we settled on the entree—maybe there was no choice. In any case, a whole two-foot fish was shortly laying on the table in front of us. Its head was attached, and its visible eye stared vacantly upwards. Its gleaming silvery body caused a nauseous little lump to rise in my throat. Sober, I wouldn't have touched the sickening thing with a ten-foot pole. But I was drunker than nine skunks.

We paused only momentarily, and then dug in. More beers lubricated our throats, although the fish was providing its own greasy lubricant. When the throat became a little too slick, a couple forkfuls of rice temporarily removed the feeling that an eel was sliding down my gullet. As we ate, we guffawed about telling Mitchell what a great meal we were having. Over the period of an hour and a half, we shoveled down the whole creature, except for the head. It was well after dark when we drove drunkenly back to the Hao Hoa Pagoda.

No operation was scheduled for the next day, so the morning was half through before the three of us began to stir. Sergeant Mitchell, now in his sober days, had been up for some time. He was sitting quietly smoking his pipe when Roca finally lurched out of the sack. "Hell, Mitch, you shoulda been with us last night. We had a great meal. This new little restaurant north of town. Had this big ol' fish that was really tasty. Ain't that right, Dai Uy?"

Just struggling to my feet, I was badly hung-over and not in a mood to be playful. Besides, Roca's tone had a bit of a malicious edge, and I could see Mitchell wasn't much amused. I said, "The goddamn thing was goddamn awful. I never had somethin' so goddamn bad. You lucky you weren't there, Sergeant Mitchell."

"Damn, Dai Uy, it weren't that bad." Sergeant Roca sounded hurt that I wasn't playing along. I regretted a little being so brusque, but the thought of that fish coupled with my pounding head and nauseous stomach overcame my innate human kindness.

Action In The Delta

War returned on January 6, 1969. The occasion was the first major operation after the year-end holidays. Early in the morning, the battalion conducted a helicopter assault northeast of Cao Lanh. As was the case with most helicopter operations, four Co Van Mys—myself and my three NCOs—were involved. The battalion moved south following a stream for most of the morning, finding the usual lack of anything interesting. Just a little after midday, we were told over the radio to gather for a pick-up and insertion into a new location. I thought maybe the province operations people were merely making full use of the U.S. Hueys, assets that the province probably had for most of the day.

The Hueys took us southeast of Cao Lanh, setting the battalion down in a large open area of relatively dry rice paddies. The terrain was not as unencumbered as that from which we had just come. The morning's operation had been in an area that except along the widely spaced streams had no appreciable vegetation. The new area in contrast was more like farm country in parts of the eastern United States. Fields were separated by various types of borders. Many of the borders were combinations of ditches and earthen dikes. Some of the dikes were as high as five or six feet. Most of the dikes were crowned with bushes or small trees. The smaller fields were in the neighborhood of 100 meters on a side.

Several lifts were required to transport the whole battalion. Sgt. Blane and I were on the first lift. As we waited for the subsequent lifts, I surveyed the situation and, over the radio with province operations and with the Dai Uy through our minimally adequate interpreter, tried to ascertain the mission. After some effort, I acquired a general understanding of what the battalion was to do. To the west, about a kilometer away, was a large stream bordered on each side by a band of trees about 50 meters wide. According to the map, several small hamlets also bordered the stream. One was directly to our west, within the trees. A Viet Cong unit was reported to be in the hamlet, and the battalion's mission was to throw it out.

Given my experience with the unreliableness of intelligence reports and the fact that after a month and a half in Kien Phong Province we had not run into anything but individuals that the Dai Uy wanted to shoot, I was skeptical. Most likely, this would be another false alarm.

It took over an hour for the entire battalion to get on the ground and ready to move out. The plan was to push to the stream and the hamlet in three columns, each consisting of one of the battalion's companies. On the left was a large rectangular field surrounded by a ditch and high dike capped with saplings. The far end of the field was about 200 meters from the treeline. One company was to advance through this field, cross the dike and ditch, move into a line formation, and proceed to the treeline. Sergeants Roca and Mitchell were to move with this company.

A second company was to advance on the outside of the right edge of the field. Once beyond a small hedge row bordering the LZ, nothing would be between this company and the treeline but an open field. By paralleling the dike bordering the field through which the first company was moving, the second company would have some cover and concealment. The Dai Uy and the headquarters group, with myself and Sgt. Blane, would accompany the second company.

On the right, the route for the third company was through a patch of trees and undergrowth and then a grove of banana plants that appeared to stretch to within 15 meters of the treeline. A large dike, visible even from our location, marked the end of the banana grove.

After a bit of getting organized, the battalion started off. The fields were mostly dry, with only a few wet spots. Much of the second company and all of the headquarters group stayed close to the dike running along the edge of the field. The edge was slightly higher than the middle of the field, so we were walking on dry ground. We covered the approximately 200 meters to the end of the field fairly quickly. There, we paused as the two companies on the left went into line formations. The company on the far left, accompanied by Sergeants Roca and Mitchell, had to go over the dike at the end of the field and then turn left or right to get on line. The company in the middle, with myself and Sgt. Blane, did not have to cross a dike and consequently was able to spread out more easily. The company on the right was in the trees and banana grove and stayed in a column formation. We could not see many of that company's soldiers.

Once the line formation for the two companies on the left had been attained, the Dai Uy gave the order to move forward. Many of the soldiers had been resting on one knee. Upon receiving the order, they rose, and the two companies began advancing en masse. The headquarters group was spread out abreast of the last 20 meters of the dike bordering the field to the left.

The line had advanced only about 15 meters when automatic weapons fire rent the air. Instantly everyone within my vision was flat on the ground, striving for concealment in the foot-high brownish grass. The distinct snap of in-coming bullets brought that familiar vulnerable-as-an-eggshell feeling to my skull. I clutched my helmet tighter to my noggin. Mutt, our RTO, was laying close by. Trying to keep my head as near to the ground as possible, I motioned for the handset.

"Bulldog, this is Homestead Six, over."

"This is Bulldog. What's happenin' there?" Evidently Bulldog was cognizant of something unusual from a sudden excitement on the part of his counterpart, who would be in touch with the Dai Uy.

"This is Homestead. The treeline has exploded with automatic weapons. We're takin' heavy fire. We're pinned out in the paddies."

"Roger. We'll be roundin' up some assets. Hold tight. Any casualties, over?"

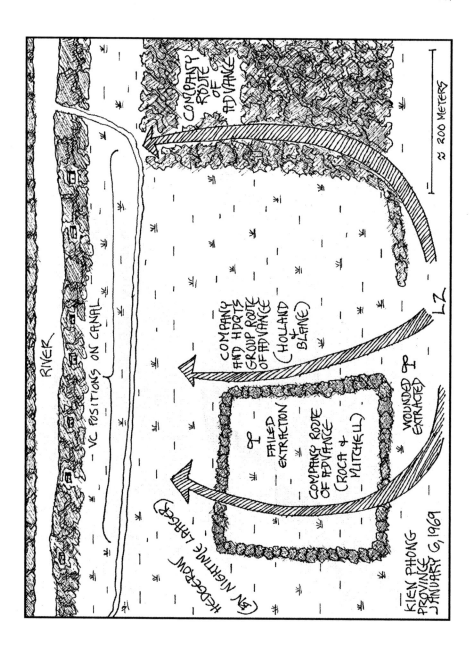

"This is Homestead. I don't know of any yet. But I don't know much beyond about ten meters, over."

"This is Bulldog. Understand. Be linin' up some targets for the air when it gets there. Bulldog out."

In the meantime, the Dai Uy, a few meters ahead of me, was jabbering to beat hell on his radio. I called Roca to see how he and Mitchell were doing. They were about 100 meters from me but out of sight—even if I had wanted to stand up—around the corner of the field. "Homestead Three, this is Homestead Six, over."

"This is Homestead Three." Sergeant Roca's voice was barely a whisper.

"This is Six. Howya doin' over there? Everybody okay?"

"This is Homestead Three. We're okay, but we need to get outta here." I didn't know exactly what Sgt. Roca meant. Maybe he was just talking about the company having to get off the open field.

"Hold tight, Homestead Three. You heard that air is on the way?"

"This is Homestead Three. Roger that. We're not in a good position here."

"This is Homestead Six. Just hold tight. Six out." There wasn't much else to tell them. We were largely at the mercy of things beyond our control. This wasn't like with an American unit where we would be decision-makers. Here, except for being able to provide some air support, hopefully, we were just along for the ride.

As these conversations were going on, firing was intensifying on the right, near the edge of the banana grove closest to the treeline. Some grenade explosions were mixed in. The snapping of bullets over our heads had slackened a bit, but the volume was still enough to keep us hugging the earth. I couldn't tell exactly where the firing was coming from, but I assumed it was from somewhere in the treeline. The map indicated that a small canal was perpendicular to our line of march and between us and the treeline, but I didn't give it much thought.

Although feeling fear, I didn't have the almost certainty of death or imminent harm that I had on occasions with the 173rd. My fear was a detached fear. I was also beginning to experience the adrenalin surge. The problem was that there was nothing to focus the surge on. Not being a decision-maker in this little scene, I didn't have a lot to do. The really interesting decision that might come up that afternoon would be whether to charge across the open field to the treeline. A part of me was relieved that I wouldn't have to make that decision.

"Homestead Six, this is Bulldog Five, over." It was the province XO, a major. There was throbbing in the background, which meant that he was in a chopper.

"This is Homestead Six."

"This is Bulldog Five. What's your situation down there, over?"

"This is Homestead Six. We're pinned down 'bout 200 meters from the treeline, but otherwise we seem to be okay, over."

"This is Bulldog Five. Roger. We've got some air comin' in. I'm gonna need you to mark your position, over."

"This is Homestead Six. Understand, but that may take a little time. We're spread out, and the interpretin' situation is not good." I threw that last in because the interpreting situation was indeed not good, and the XO was the guy who was ultimately responsible for doing something about it, assuming something could be done. We had brought the inadequacy of the interpreters to his attention several times, and now seemed like an opportune occasion for a reminder.

"This is Bulldog Five. Understand. You better get ready to mark. The first thing comin' is gunships. About what are the ends of your position, over?

"This is Homestead Six. We're spread out over about a, ah, maybe 300-meter front, about 200 meters from the treeline. That's where the fire is comin' from. The left, I mean right flank is closer, in a patch of trees. I'm gonna try to get smoke on our flanks and center now, over."

"This is Bulldog five. Roger, out."

The interpreter was nearby, his cheek pressed into the earth. I had begun to raise my head a little. I caught sight of Sgt. Blane about five meters to the side. He had his usual sardonic half-grin on his face, a look that seem to say, "this is the hand the world dealt me, and I'll live with it." I crawled to the interpreter and said, "Tell Dai Uy we need smoke, koei, at each end of battalion and in middle." I gestured in the various directions as I was talking.

He looked at me blankly. What little English he knew seemed to have been scared out of him. He was a relatively young looking guy, and it struck me that this might be his first time in combat. Not like being a Saigon cowboy, zooming around on your motorscooter, huh pal? I tried again, "Tell Dai Uy we need koiei! Planes come in! Drop bombs! Boom, boom! Combit?" The last word was Vietnamese for "understand," or so we had been told.

His eyes slowly began to focus, as if he were coming out of a deep coma. A look of mild comprehension appeared. He said, "Okay, okay! Koei! Okay!" He began crawling toward the Dai Uy. I followed. When we arrived, he and the Dai Uy jabbered a bit, and then the Dai Uy looked at me. I said, "Koei," raised three fingers, and then pointed to the left flank, to directly in front of us, and to the right flank. The Dai Uy immediately began barking instructions over the radio. Very soon, the smoke grenades were out. "Bulldog Five, this is Homestead Six. We have smoke out, over."

"This is Bulldog Five, I see it. You say the fire is from the treeline to the front of the smoke, over?"

"This is Homestead Six. Roger that, over." I glanced skyward and could just make out a chopper. Bulldog Five was at least 2,000 feet in the air. No heroics for him.

"This is Bulldog Five, the gunships are comin' in. There're about a minute out."

"This is Homestead Six. Roger." I said to the Dai Uy, "My-my whop-whop, skeech-skeech." The last phrase was supposed to be the sound of shooting. I then called Roca and Mitchell, "Homestead Three, didja monitor? We got gunships in-bound."

After a pause, Sgt. Mitchell's voice came on, "This is Homestead Three. We, uh, monitored." He sounded calmer than Roca had earlier, and I wondered momentarily about why they had switched possession of the radio.

The gunships interrupted my thoughts, however. Two of them, Hueys, swept perpendicularly across our front, following the treeline. They fired rockets and machine guns into the trees. We could see explosions. Two more Hueys followed shortly afterwards. The four of them made several more passes, always concentrating on the treeline. After about 15 minutes, they departed and the radio crackled, "Homestead Six, this is Bulldog Five. Now we got some big stuff coming in. You still takin' fire?"

Rounds were still intermittently snapping over our heads. A heavier volume of fire was occurring in the banana grove on the right flank. The gunship run appeared to have done little. "This is Homestead Six. We've still got incomin', over."

The first of several air strikes was about to start. We popped more smoke. The jets appeared. They were B-58s. They came in at a high angle, released their ordinance far from the ground, and pulled away, not getting too close to the action. They were followed after a bit by Phantoms, which took the nap-of-the-earth route, roaring over the treeline, sending napalm canisters tumbling end over end until they struck the trees or ground and burst in an evil mixture of fiery red flames and oily black smoke. Propeller-driven A-10s also put in an appearance. They chugged slowly along, seemingly sitting ducks for ground fire. But they were more precise in dropping their loads, and when finished they chugged away, apparently unharmed. In between the air strikes, helicopter gunships made their contributions.

None of this massive rain of steel from the air had any effect on the volume of fire coming our way on the ground. In the center and on the left, the battalion continued to take desultory automatic weapons fire. Fortunately, the VC did not seem to be actually trying to hit anybody. They appeared content that the two companies made no effort to advance. After awhile, officers and NCOs began moving about a little, crawling and crouching. Too great a display of energy would bring a

warning burst of bullets, a "Hey, you're making me nervous" state-
ment. But the VC weren't creating casualties in the field, and indeed
hadn't done so even in the first heavy fusillade.

This gentlemen's war didn't extend to the right flank, where the
banana grove and Charlie's positions seemed to be in close proximity.
On the right, the firing was heavy and punctuated by grenade explosions. And there were casualties. How many was difficult to tell. From
the interpreter, I understood that there might be more than a dozen
wounded and at least two dead. Several of the wounded were severe,
and an effort was to be made to evacuate them. One of the Dai Uy's
henchmen apparently volunteered to lead the attempt. He first ran
diagonally across the field to the banana grove, attracting a hail of bullets during the 200-meter journey. He could have taken a longer and
safer route by retracing our steps to the LZ and then proceeding up the
patch of woods to the banana grove but he chose the more direct route.
He survived unscathed, disappearing into the vegetation. After a few
minutes, he reappeared with two casualties and four helpers.

One of the casualties had a leg wound. He was hopping on his good
leg with his arm around the neck of the Dai Uy's man. The other
wounded man was on a stretcher that was being carried by the four
helpers. The group, crouching low, made their slow way back to our
location. They attracted a heavy volume of fire but none of it was finding flesh. I began to suspect that the battalion and the VC might have
some sort of silent understanding about casualty evacuations. Maybe in
exchange for not being pressed harder, Charlie was willing to allow
some removal of the wounded.

At first, I didn't understand why the wounded were being brought
to our location. Then it dawned that this was where the Dai Uy
thought the medevac should come. I called on the radio: "Bulldog
Five. This is Homestead Six, over."

"This is Bulldog Five, over."

"This is Homestead Six. I understand a medevac might be comin'
in. Do ya know anything about it, over?"

"This is Bulldog Five. It's not one of ours. It's Vietnamese."

"This is Homestead Six. Roger that, out."

So this was to be a Vietnamese operation. It should be interesting. I thought about trying to suggest to the Dai Uy that he move the wounded back to the LZ but couldn't work up the energy to tackle the translation problem.

Within a few minutes of the arrival of the wounded at our location, the noise of a chopper came from the left rear. I assumed that they would put down in the field to our right. This would give the Charlies in the treeline an unobstructed field of fire, but maybe their kind-heartedness would hold. The chopper pilot, however, had different ideas, or maybe just didn't have any idea at all. No one popped smoke for him or made any move to indicate a landing spot. The pilot put the machine, a 1950s-vintage item with wheels, down in the field to our left. Maybe he made a conscious decision to land in a place where some protection—the dike capped with trees at the end of the field—was between him and the VCs. Or maybe that was where the bird just happened to come into contact with terra firma. The erratic trajectory the pilot followed on the way in fostered the impression that he was not in complete control of this 20th Century piece of equipment.

The problem was, a tree-capped dike and a ditch stood between the wounded men and the chopper. The Vietnamese on the ground seemed frozen. The chopper on the other side of the barrier was dancing and bobbing. Unlike the field to our left, the field within the dike and ditch was flooded with approximately a foot of water. The pilot was reluctant to put down in this muck and risk getting stuck. I realized that some Western initiative might be helpful, so I raised to a crouch, grabbed a corner of the stretcher, and yelled "Come on! Chung ta di!" The latter phrase meant "We go." The stretcher bearers got the hint, and we started up the dike. The Dai Uy's man started a little further down with the hobbling wounded soldier.

But we were stymied by the ditch on the other side of the dike. In our vicinity, it was deep and about five feet wide. I discovered how deep when I went in the stagnant murky water up to my waist. The soldier on the front end of the stretcher with me lost his footing and fell in completely, disappearing from view for a moment. I grabbed both poles of the stretcher's front end and tried to clamber out of the ditch's far side, but it was futile. Getting across this obstacle was going to require a more thoughtful effort.

We were saved from the effort by the chopper's departure. The Charlies had zeroed in on the intruder, which was only partially protected by the dike at the end of the field. Even over the loud thumping of the chopper's motor, the sound of automatic weapons could be heard. Moreover, a few of the incoming rounds were tracers, and they appeared to be finding the top portion of the machine. The pilot wasn't about to be a sitting duck while these Keystone Cops on the ground tried to get their act together, so off he went.

Pissed, wet, and cursing, I struggled to push the stretcher back up the dike. When my compatriots finally understood that there wasn't any point in going into the field now that the chopper had departed, they lent a hand. Eventually, we rejoined the headquarters group. I tried not to glare at Sgt. Blane, who had not moved from his prone position through the whole episode. The two wounded soldiers appeared somewhat the worse for the experience. The one with the leg wound was obviously likely to survive, but the one on the stretcher did not look in good shape. I couldn't see exactly where the wound was, but the lower part of his shirtfront and the upper portion of his pants were soaked in blood. He was barely conscious. I suspected he might be going into shock. If Sgt. Blane carried medical supplies with him, he perhaps could have been of some assistance. All Blane had, however, was a canteen and a .45-caliber pistol. He wasn't prepared to function as a medic, and indeed we weren't supposed to be performing duties the Vietnamese were allegedly capable of performing. Still, I felt Blane could be of more assistance.

But there wasn't time to dwell on the matter. Bulldog Five was beginning to inquire about the possibility of getting into the treeline.

In other words, when were we planning to charge across the 200 meters of open field that separated us from the Charlies?

This was one time I was glad I was just an advisor. The ultimate fantasy of some infantry officers is to lead an infantry charge across an open field into the teeth of an enemy. The fantasy is rooted in romanticized history: the vast charges of the wars of the 18th and 19th Centuries. Few are the bona fide infantry officers who don't harbor a secret longing to be part of a successful effort such as the Union's breaking of the Confederate line at Missionary Ridge in the Battle of Chattanooga in 1863. The problem is that frontal charges were a chancy thing even in earlier centuries—the slaughter of Pickett's men at Gettysburg was a more typical outcome—and were pretty close to suicide in the 20th. The machine gun turned infantry charges into massacres. A principal lesson in military tactics from World War I, a lesson that took four years to register, was that charging machine guns was not wise.

Full-fledged infantry charges were rare in Vietnam, although not totally absent. Often times, particularly in III and IV Corps, VC defenders were grossly outgunned and outnumbered. If the attackers, whether Americans or ARVNs, could muster the courage to stand up and advance, laying down a heavy base of fire as they did so, they had a chance of success. A determined effort at advancing could quickly deflate the spirit of the young adolescents manning the VC bunkers, and they would likely break and run. But making that determined effort was a monumental endeavor. It required overcoming an inertia of immense proportions. And if Mr. Charles didn't break and run but stayed with his automatic weapons, there would be hell to pay. One gritty individual who remained with his gun, firing waist-high two-second bursts, could decimate an attacking unit that persisted in attempting to advance.

South Vietnamese units in Kien Phong Province had conducted a successful charge sometime during the previous year. After softening up the VCs with air strikes and artillery and gearing up their own courage, a force of several battalions rose from the paddies and made it across several hundred meters of ground. So Bulldog Five had a precedent for thinking a charge might be productive. Bulldog Five was not LTC Meathead, however. The hand-off of the province advisory responsibilities had occurred between Special Forces and MACV, although the new advisor was not yet on board. Thus Bulldog Five, the province XO, was for the moment the man responsible, and he was not the type to push a charge.

Moreover, what the Co Van Mys wanted to do was largely academic. The Vietnamese made the decisions. Indeed, the absence of responsibility often gave rise to a false bravado on the part of the Co Van Mys. We could rant and rave about the need for our boys to charge whereas a charge would be unlikely if we were actually in command.

When Bulldog Five tentatively brought the matter up, I gave my best assessment: "This is Homestead Six. I don't think these boys'll be doin' any chargin' today. The incomin' fire is still pretty heavy. And the air strikes aren't havin' much effect, over."

"This is Bulldog Five, roger that, out." And so the matter was dropped. What would I have done if it had been a U.S. unit and I was in command? I don't know.

The battle had been joined around two o'clock in the afternoon. With the air strikes, the probing on the right, the failed evacuation, the minutes stretched into hours. Time flies when you're having fun. Toward dusk, the decision was made to pull back to the vicinity of the LZ. Crawling at first, then crouching, the two companies on the left and the headquarters group retraced their steps. Sergeants Mitchell and Roca joined up with Sgt. Blane and myself. All three of my NCOs were unhappy cowboys. Sgt. Roca was especially angry. Stuck out in the middle of the rice paddies with night coming on, reliant for protection on a ragtag collection of little brown people, no evening meal, no sleeping gear, these were not things conducive to the morale of my troops.

I had a few concerns myself. They mostly involved our defensive posture. The headquarters group and a good portion of the two companies seemed to be congregated in one large mass just outside the corner of the dike-surrounded field at the other end of which we had been pinned down. We were shortly joined by much of the third company. It had extracted itself from the firefight in the banana grove and pulled back, bringing two dead and about ten wounded. We still had the two wounded from the failed evacuation attempt. I could not see any evidence of security, so with our interpreter, I approached the Dai Uy. After the usual battle of the translations, the Dai Uy assured me that he had security posts at the end of the field nearest the hamlet and in the woods and banana grove. At least that's what I thought him to assure me of. Given the level of the translation, he might have been telling me where the VC had set up their security posts.

Shortly after dark, the province home base—Bulldog Five in his chopper had long since called it a day—radioed that a U.S. medevac was coming to get the wounded. We would need to talk them in. Fortunately, the Dai Uy was able to produce a flashlight. (Daytime operations had gotten me out of the habit of carrying a flashlight; this experience corrected the omission.) I tried to get the point across to the Dai Uy through the interpreter that once the chopper was within reach of the ground, the wounded had to be put on quickly. And the dead weren't supposed to go out by medevac. This flight was only for the living. The Dai Uy looked dubious at this bit of news, and I suspected he would try to sneak his dead on anyway.

"Homestead Six, this is Dustoff One-Two. Do you read me, over?"

"Dustoff One-Two, this is Homestead Six. I read you Lima Charlie, over."

"Roger, Homestead Six, we should be near you in about two minutes. Let me know when you can hear us. What's the security situation down there, over?"

"This is Homestead Six. There should only be friendlies in the immediate vicinity. The VC are about a click to the west, but there isn't any sign that any are nearby, over."

"This is Dustoff One-Two, roger. How many packs do you have, over?"

"This is Homestead Six. We have 12 whiskey-india-alphas and two straphangers that I think they'll try to get on, over."

"This is Dustoff One-Two. Helluva load. We could do without the straphangers."

"This is Homestead Six. Understand. We'll, ah, do what we can, over."

"Roger, Dustoff out."

In about two minutes, I heard the distinctive whump-whump of a Huey approaching from the southeast. "Dustoff One-Two, this is Homestead Six. I hear ya. You're on an azimuth of about 140 degrees from my location, over."

"This is Dustoff One-Two. Understand that we're southeast of you. Do you have a light, over?"

"Roger, I'm blinkin' now, over." I was standing at the edge of the field that had been the LZ in the afternoon. The dustoff found my light without much trouble, made a couple of circles to the east at about 750 feet, and then began an east-west descent. I handed the flashlight to Mutt to free myself for the effort of getting the wounded on board. I was concerned about the battalion's lack of familiarity with choppers and about what seemed to be a tendency for no one to take charge of loading operations.

The chopper came on a descending path across the field. At about 100 meters out and 100 feet up, it switched on its big front ground lights, bathing the area in brightness. It continued its descent, coming to contact with the earth just in front of Mutt. The chopper did not put down solidly but engaged in a sort of hovering tap-dance with the ground. Sure enough, no one made a move to load the wounded. I shouted, "Come on! Di di mau! Di di mau!" and reached down for one of the wounded. As I was picking him up, my back was to the chopper and I was facing west, the direction of the VC. Two bright red tracer rounds streaked through the night, passing a few feet over the Huey. Spurred by this added bit of incentive, I shoved my burden on and reached for another. The soldiers responsible for the wounded and the two dead finally realized the need for speed, and sprang into action. The chopper was loaded in short order. I ran to the front of the Huey's bubble and gave the pilot a thumbs-up. He pulled up a few feet, turned the machine east, raised the tail, and began crossing the field, gaining speed. The chopper finally rose into the night.

"Dustoff One-Two, this is Homestead Six. Great job. We 'preciate it. But I'm 'fraid ya got the straphangers on board, over."

"Homestead, this is Dustoff. That's alright. We'll drop 'em off at the right place. You take care. Dustoff out."

I returned to my NCOs. They sure as hell had been a big help. Frustrated, unhappy, they were basically sulking. "Well, I guess this is our home for the night," I said. About all I got in reply was a grunt. None of them appeared to be in the mood for conversation. The headquarters group was bedding down for the night on the inner side of the dike surrounding the field that had been on our left all afternoon. The Dai Uy seemed to have set up a perimeter on the dike. There wasn't any place to get horizontal except on the top of the dike, and that location didn't seem particularly safe. So we each struggled for a comfortable position on the 45-degree slope. Fortunately, I had insect repellant, so the mosquitoes were kept at bay. Nevertheless, sleep was fitful at best.

We were up by dawn the next morning. As with the evening before, no meal, not even coffee, was in the offering. The question was whether Charlie was still in the vicinity. If so, we would be in for a long day. The company that had been on the right the previous day retraced its steps through the trees and the banana grove. It tentatively probed beyond where it had been stopped, a dike at the end of the grove, and discovered that Charlie had departed. The rest of the battalion started toward the treeline, 200 meters from the end of the dike-surrounded field where we had been pinned down the day before and at the other end of which we had spent the night.

Halfway to the treeline, I discovered one reason the air strikes and helicopter gunships seemed to have had no effect. Charlie hadn't been in the trees after all. He had been along the small canal that paralleled the treeline and was about 50 meters from it. A low dike, no more than three feet high, was on the far side of the canal. Approximately every 30 meters along the dike was a bunker with at least two feet of overhead cover and beaucoup camouflage. There were maybe eight bunkers in all, and each could hold at least four people. Three or four of the bunkers were configured for machine guns, with an earth platform inside the bunker on which the gun was placed. The gun ports had unobstructed fields of fire in the direction from whence we had come. Both the dike and the bunkers were practically indiscernible from a hundred meters out in the field.

Thus most of the ordnance from the air had missed the VC positions by at least 50 meters. The trees and the hamlet were trashed while Charlie relaxed.

On the right, the opposing forces had been within 20 meters of each other. At the end of the banana grove was a high dike, about ten feet tall. Just on the far side was the canal. The dike on the other side of the canal at that point was higher than the portion out in the field, but not as high as the dike on our side in the banana grove. The battalion's company on the right had made several attempts to mount the large dike, cross the canal, and get over the small dike. It had been unsuccessful. Most of its casualties had been taken as soldiers reached the top of the large dike.

We spent an hour or so checking out the bunkers and going through the hamlet. All of the inhabitants had departed before or during the fighting, and no one had yet returned. Some of the houses were substantial structures of lumber. Others were thatched huts. Many of the trees and structures had sustained damage, but surprisingly no building seemed totally destroyed.

After the exploration, the battalion followed the stream to the south. The stream joined a larger one that was a tributary of the Mekong. Landing craft were to pick us up on the larger stream and take us to the Tan Tich ferry. The battalion waited in one large mass. No security was out as far as I could tell. We were packed so tight that one twelve-year old with an AK-47 could have sprayed the area and produced a casualty per bullet. After a short time, however, the boats arrived and we proceeded to Tan Tich and then by truck to Cao Lanh.

The NCOs were still disgruntled, but basic needs were the first order of business upon our return to Cao Lanh. It was mid-afternoon by the time we arrived. The rest of the day and the evening were spent mostly at the Special Forces camp showering, drinking, and eating. I ran across the province XO and told him of the bunkers along the canal and how we had been dumping ordinance on the wrong spot. He seemed mildly interested.

It was the next morning, after a sound night's sleep, that the real explosion hit. My three NCOs had obviously been talking among themselves, although I suspect Sgt. Roca had been doing most of the talking. He started off: "Dai Uy, we can't be in a situation like that again. We need more support out there. That was just damn ridiculous."

"What kind of support do ya suggest?" What the hell. Did he think we were going to have a U.S. infantry company on standby to rescue our little butts? The absurdity of it struck me as, well, absurd.

"I'm in the U.S. Army, Captain. I'm not supposed to be stranded out in some rice paddy with a bunch of goddamn incompetents. We're lucky we ain't dead. I'm gonna see the XO about this. We just can't be going back out there under these conditions. We ain't doin' nuthin' there anyway."

"Well, I ain't gonna argue that point. And ya can certainly see the XO anytime ya want. But I'm not with ya on this. I've said it before.

You're soldiers. Uncle Sam has given ya a good life. He's given ya a home, a profession, and three meals a day. Now it's payback time. He's askin' ya to do a difficult, unclear job. Look, I know this is hard. We don't know what we're really suppose to be doin' here. We give these guys a little air support, and that seems to be 'bout it. Maybe we're doin' somethin' more. Maybe we're supposed to be doin' somethin' more. I don't know. But I intend to go on doin' it. And hey, I been in this country 27 months now, and I ain't even a professional soldier. If I can do it, you professionals oughta be able to hack it. I never yet asked for any slack, and I ain't 'bout to start now."

The speech wasn't great, and Sgt. Roca kept grousing for a little longer, but it seemed to take the wind out of his sails. The other two, Mitchell and Blane, kept silent, resulting in Roca being alone in his revolt. Whether he ever actually went to the XO, I don't know. If I had been completely fair, I probably should have been more sympathetic. Although he was a professional soldier, Sgt. Roca was a man with a family and approaching middle age. Judging him by the standards of a gung-ho youth was maybe being a little too harsh. Moreover, this advisory business was different from regular soldiering. Being an advisor was not for everyone, and I thought the Army was making a mistake in believing or at least acting otherwise.

And if truth be told, if an American unit had run into the kind of contact we had made, the support would have been close to unlimited. The air strikes would have been continuous. There would have been beaucoup artillery—we only had a few erratic rounds from two 105s located back in Cao Lanh. And reinforcements would have been inserted to set up a cordon around the area to keep the Charlies from waltzing away as they had done.

But the world ain't perfect.

Although my speech was nothing to brag about, one word survived, caught on, and became part of the team's vocabulary. That word was "slack." It became part of phrases expressing an attitude of reluctant acceptance of our predicament, as in "Don't gimme no slack" and "I don't need no slack," phrases that were the equivalent of an expression I had often heard during my time with the 173rd: "Take two salt tablets and drive on."

Several mornings after the fight, the interpreter appeared and made known that the Dai Uy wanted us to attend a funeral service. It took place at a Buddhist temple on the north side of Cao Lanh. The main room was bare except for two rough wooden coffins in the middle of the concrete floor. The coffins were surrounded by flowers and smoldering jasmine sticks. Members of the battalion were standing in a circle around the coffins and flowers and about 15 feet away. Two large flower wreaths were on stands. The Dai Uy motioned for me to pick one up. He picked up the other, moved forward, and placed it next to one of the coffins. I followed his lead with the other wreath and coffin. There were no speeches or prayers, just a minute of silent contemplation in the heat and the slightly sickening smell of flowers, burning jasmine, and decaying flesh. Then we turned and left.

Feudin' and Lovin'

Our relationship with our charges—the Dai Uy and the 64th Regional Forces Battalion—took a dip after the January 6 fight. Ostensibly, the reasons weren't attributable to the fight, but the depressing unclear outcome certainly didn't improve anyone's mood. The immediate cause concerned a complex situation involving the team's radio and machine gun.

The Dai Uy coveted our M-60 machine gun. When we arrived, the battalion's automatic weapons were BARs and .30 caliber machine guns, both World War II-vintage weapons. The battalion began getting M-60s within a short time after our arrival, but few infantry commanders ever feel they have enough firepower. The Dai Uy saw our M-60 sitting unused and could discern no reason why it shouldn't be helping his troops out in the field. His hints to this effect began early on and rapidly increased in overtness. We had been warned at MAT training school about lending our equipment, particularly our weapons, to our unit. For one thing, we were supposed to be advising our charges on how to get by with what they had. For another, the distinction between "lending" and "giving" was, in the view of many Americans, not always apparent to the South Vietnamese.

So I resisted letting the M-60 out of our control. The Dai Uy persisted, however, and I finally relented. But I imposed a condition: the weapon had to be returned after each operation. This would, I hoped, prevent the question of the gun's ownership from being muddied. In addition, we would have the gun at night, the most likely time of need. In case Charlie came charging into downtown Cao Lanh, I wanted to be able to put a steady stream of tracers into his ranks. The agreement about the gun was reached shortly before Christmas and was adhered to for the few operations between then and January 6. Within a few days of the battle, however, the company that had been borrowing the gun was moved to quarters and a defensive area to the west of Cao Lanh. This new location apparently made picking up and returning the gun inconvenient.

The first afternoon the gun wasn't returned, I hunted up the interpreter and sent him to the Dai Uy to find out what was wrong. It was a not-so-subtle way of saying, "Get the damn gun back here pronto." We didn't get the gun back that night, so the next day—there was no operation—I again sent the interpreter, this time to ask specifically that the gun be returned. It eventually was, late in the afternoon. We went through the same game after the next operation. Consequently, I decided that the time had come for a lesson. Nobody was gonna make a fool of this Co Van My.

Thus, when the two grinning Vietnamese came for the weapon before dawn on the day of the next operation, they didn't get it. The interpreter showed up a few minutes later to find out the problem, and I told him to relay the message that because we couldn't count on getting the gun back when we wanted it, I wasn't going to allow the battalion to use it.

Retaliation was swift. Mutt didn't show up to take the radio. The trucks were about to leave. Sgt. Mitchell, whose turn it was to accompany me, started to pick up the radio's backpack harness. I said, "No, let me have it. If we're gonna play this game, let's play it all the way."

"Now Dai Uy, you don't wanna make too big a thing outta this. You carryin' the radio is just gonna make the Dai Uy mad."

"I don't give a crap whether he's mad or not. I'm pissed my own self. Besides, I like carryin' the radio."

So I humped the radio for the next several operations. The Dai Uy and I ignored each other more than normal, but otherwise we generally pretended as if nothing unusual was occurring.

Wasps and a broken bridge eventually put an end to the childishness. The operation was along the Mekong, to the southeast of the Tan

Tich ferry. Landing craft had deposited us on a muddy bank, and we were making our way along well-worn but heavy-foliaged trails. We were a long way from Cao Lanh and there was no intermediate field headquarters, so I had put the long antenna on the radio. As I walked along, the extended antenna hit the vegetation that stretched overhead. At one spot, the antenna encountered more than vegetation. It brushed a wasp nest. I learned of the encounter through a sudden intense pain on the back left of my neck. Almost simultaneously, a similar pain struck on the right side. With my free hand, the one not holding the M-16, I swatted my neck. I mashed an attacker against flesh, grabbed him in my fingers, and brought the still-moving body in front of me. My brain interpreted the visual evidence in my hand fairly quickly: "Wasp!" I yelled. As the word came out, I became aware of many more of them, buzzing angrily in close proximity to my face.

I took off up the trail. About 20 meters separated me from the rear of the headquarters group—about 20 meters and a small log bridge over a muddy ditch. The bottom of the ditch was about six feet below the bridge. Maybe in a gentle crossing, the bridge would have held the weight of a Co Van My. Mine was no gentle crossing, however. I hit the bridge in full sprint. My second step broke its two logs with nary a pause, and I and the logs went into the mud. Fortunately, the wasps did not follow me downward. I was mired up to my knees and immobile.

Sgt. Mitchell had been behind me. He had not gotten into the wasps' killing zone. He left the trail and made his way through the brush. He appeared on one side of the ditch just as the Dai Uy and most of the headquarters group were gathering on the other side. They all looked down at the cursing, thrashing creature who had two huge welts rising on his neck. The merriment was general.

On the morning of the next operation, several days later, Mutt appeared at our door for the radio. After we had returned that evening, I sent the interpreter to tell the Dai Uy that the M-60 could be carried on operations. I told the interpreter to emphasize, however, that the weapon had to be back at the team house after each operation. The M-60 was picked up before the next outing. I never saw it again.

Two months later, the question of the gun's whereabouts surfaced. I was preparing to depart, and Lt. Silver, who had been returned to duty with the team and was to be my replacement, at least temporarily, was inventorying the team's equipment in preparation for signing for it. When we reached the listing for the M-60, I said: "Oh, uh, that company on the other side of Cao Lanh has it. The Dai Uy will get it back whenever ya want it." Silver looked at me suspiciously. I assumed my most angelic face. Reluctantly, he signed. I and my wallet breathed a small sigh of relief.

Life for the members of MAT-104 had fallen into a routine. Generally, an operation took place every second or third day. Unless it was a helicopter assault, only two members of the team went—myself and one of the NCOs. Lt. Silver was still detailed to the province TOC. He lived and slept in the team house, but his work days were spent elsewhere. We hired a maid, a middle-aged wizened mama-san, who made our cots and a pretense of keeping the place clean. Mostly what she did, however, was try to keep out of the reach of Sergeants Roca and Blane.

Initially, we ate most of our meals at either the Special Forces camp or the 44th's compound, but as time went on we did a greater amount of our own cooking. The sergeants tapped the NCO back-channel supply network for goodies. A favorite dish was lima bean soup. We would simmer canned lima beans for half a day, sometimes with the added ingredient of canned bacon. With a few hot peppers to spice it up and local French bread to sop it up, the concoction was quite good. On operations, my standard lunch fare became rice supplied by the Vietnamese, to which I added canned tuna. Sometimes I would take along a piece of the chewy French bread and have a tuna sandwich instead of tuna and rice.

Often, an operation would end near the local version of a lemonade stand. If we did a swing just to the northeast of town, we would normally not ride back to the pagoda in trucks but would walk through town. Just to the north of town were several stands that made a delicious and refreshing sweet limeade. Of course, the ice and water were questionable, and I always expected a return bout of dysentery, but fortunately the bug did not reappear.

Occasionally, I ate at a local restaurant just across the bridge from our compound. With unpainted rough wooden planking for a floor and small cheap linoleum tables, it was not a fancy place, but the food was good. It served a spicy hot soup that cleared the sinuses. Slices of tiny peppers were in bowls on the tables as condiments. I usually added a spoonful of the peppers to the soup, making it even more searing. One evening, I unthinkingly picked up a few slices of pepper with my fingers and put them in the soup. Then I happened to rub my eyes. The pain was immediate, and blindness soon followed. My eyes were watering so heavily that I literally could not see anything. I sat there feeling like a complete idiot and more than a little vulnerable. This was downtown Cao Lanh, but Charlie was just outside town and most likely in town too. Several other patrons, all Vietnamese, were in the restaurant. There was no front door, the side of the restaurant facing the street being completely open. I always sat facing the street so I could keep an eye on things and be ready to move if a grenade came flying from some passerby. In my current condition, however, someone could have walked up and slit my throat.

I knew the soup was in front of me. I located it and the spoon with my hands and tried to eat. The intent was to make like nothing was wrong. I had to abandon the effort, however, when I couldn't navigate the spoon to my mouth without jabbing my check and dragging the utensil across my face. This also added to my discomfort by depositing burning pepper residue on my cheek. Finally, after what seemed like the proverbial eternity, vision began to return. I resumed eating. When my eyes had cleared enough for me to see beyond my immediate vicinity, I furtively glanced around the room. The other patrons and the restaurant owner were staring at the loony American, probably wondering what his next trick would be. So much for being an Old Asia Hand.

Most evenings when an operation was not scheduled for the next day, and a good many evenings when an operation was, were spent in drink. The Special Forces camp and the local bar at its entrance were the two drinking places. The latter was the more intriguing and attractive locale. It was the preferred watering hole for the Special Forces contingent commanding the airboat Mike Force just across the street. Even for Special Forces personnel, the 15 or so members of this contingent were a colorful group. They paraded around in an assorted mixture of tee shirts, shorts, tiger suits, jungle fatigues, Rolex watches, Montegnard bracelets, and beach sandals. They appeared to have as much time on their hands as we did, and at least one or two could be found in the bar at just about any hour of the day or night. It seemed to me that the airboats rarely went out. One explanation was that the wet season was their primary period of operation, and this was the dry season. Given the lies that these characters could tell, however, the truth about the nature and frequency of their employment was elusive.

Many of them seemed Old Asia Hands, with at least as much time in Vietnam as me. In addition, their conversations were filled with cryptic references to clandestine excursions into the Middle East and Africa. From time to time, several of them would disappear for a few weeks. When asked casually where they had been, they would respond somewhat theatrically with mumblings that were just clear enough to drop a few names of exotic places in the Delta: the Plain of Reeds, the U Minh Forest, the Seven Mountains.

Once, I asked one of them who hadn't been around for several weeks about a couple of the others. He nonchalantly said they had been killed in the Seven Mountains, and proceeded to tell a harrowing tale of the firefight. I expressed sorrow and regret at the loss of his buddies. Given these guys' propensity to bullshit, however, I wouldn't have been surprised to learn that the missing pair had returned to the Land of the Big PX. In fact, I suspected that many absences were the result of extended visits not to swamps, jungles, or mountains but to Saigon or Bangkok. By 1969, Special Forces had as many big-talking, role-playing cowboys as it had true hard-core anti-communist freedom fighters. Like the rest of the Army, Special Forces was not what it had been five years earlier.

The Mike Force itself was composed mostly of Cambodians. They appeared to be a mean lot, but again I was never aware that they actually did much. Some of the Cambodian NCOs had enough money to habit the bar, which I thought was unusual. A regular was the unit's first sergeant, a short heavy set character who looked as if he had been slitting throats since Japanese times. He snaked one of the bar honeys—there were only a couple of them—that I had set my eyes on. She was attractive in a pert sort of way, and had a curtained area, with a bed, in the basement of the bar. I realized I had lost in the battle for her affections when I parted the curtains one evening and found the first sergeant grinding away at her. I wasn't about to contest his claim.

Besides, I had found another honey, and I had even gotten to first base with the dour Tarleton-smoking tiger-suited gal that LTC Meathead was so protective about. That latter event occurred one evening during the Christmas period. The gathering at the bar was larger than usual, large enough to be classified as an outright party. The drinking was heavy, and I was drunker than nine skunks. Tiger-suit appeared, morose as usual. She had a beer at the bar, and then wandered out to the patio in back. I was sitting with Sgt. Mitchell, who was maintaining his commitment to the wagon, and Sergeants Roca and Blane, who most definitely were not on the wagon. When Tiger-suit went out back, Roca, with a touch of maliciousness, said, "Now's yer chance, Dai Uy. Ya said you were gonna nail her 'fore we got outta here."

"Yeah, I guess it's time to make my move. Let's see what this coe's got," I slurred. The booze was talking. I ordered another Ba Moui Ba and lurched out back. The night was made for romance—the blackness was lightly broken by the brilliance from ten thousand stars. A soft breeze took the edge off the tropical heat. I approached Tiger-suit, who was sucking down another Tarleton. "Howya doin'," I suavely ventured. We talked for awhile as I moved closer. Finally, I nuzzled her neck. She didn't resist. We kissed. I prepared for some real stuff. She said, "I must go" and was gone.

I regained my composure and staggered back inside. "Well, how'd it go?" Sgt. Roca asked.

"The coe's mine. I'm gonna get her."

"In other words, ya didn't get her just now."

"Hey, she ain't no bar whore. Ya gotta put in a little time. I'm on the case. I got beaucoup time left in this place."

But I wasn't on the case. As I was talking, a coe in an ao dai caught my eye. I had seen her around but hadn't paid too much attention. She was attractive but in a hard sort of way. She seemed to have some sort of secretarial job with the Vietnamese province administration. She must have had a thing for drunks because she took me home that night, to a small one-room apartment in downtown Cao Lanh she shared with another girl.

Early the next afternoon, nursing a nauseous hangover, I went to the bar in the Special Forces camp for a little hair-of-the-dog. Tiger-suit was at the bar, sucking on a Tarleton and nursing a beer. I went up and said, "Hi." She glared, slid off her barstool, and stomped out. So news of my two-timing had gotten around quickly. Whatever real or imagined tragedy had soured this gal on life, I certainly didn't help the situation.

A month or so later, I made an attempt to make amends, in a drunken lustful sort of way. The Special Forces camp was visited by a rock-and-roll band. Kien Phong Province being so off the beaten track, however, it was no USO-sponsored stateside group. It was four or five soldiers with musical backgrounds who had somehow gotten together and persuaded the Army to let them travel around entertaining. Several of the group had spent some real infantry time before becoming Army rock-and-rollers.

The group began an evening concert in the courtyard of the Special Forces camp. They actually seemed to be quite good, but most anything sounds good to a tin-eared drunk. Approximately 45 minutes into the festivities, just as the lead singer had taken a deep breath, closed his eyes, and thrown his head back in preparation for another song, LTC Meathead stormed into the picture. He put his hand on the chest of the unsuspecting singer, shoved him forcefully to the rear, grabbed the microphone, and announced: "The music's over. A Charlie battalion is at the Tan Tich ferry, marching on Cao Lanh. Everyone go to your posts."

Talk about a wet blanket. The singer recovered his balance and stumbled forward wide-eyed, looking for whoever had almost sent him sprawling into the drums. But LTC Meathead was already moving brusquely toward the camp's operation center. After a moment of incomprehension, the audience gathered itself and began to disperse, moving more quickly as visions of marching VC legions took hold. The four members of MAT-104 raced for their jeep. With the sober Sgt. Mitchell at the wheel, we barreled out of the camp, roared across town, and screeched into our compound at the Hao Hoa Pagoda. We gathered weapons and the radio and took up positions on top of our bunker.

Nothing happened. There wasn't even much chatter on the radio net. After about 30 minutes, I put in a call: "Bulldog, this is Homestead Six."

"This is Bulldog, over."

"This is Homestead Six. Any sign of those Victor Charlies advancin' from the ferry, over?"

"This is Bulldog. That was apparently a false alarm, over."

"This is Homestead Six. You've got to be kiddin'. How can a report of a marchin' battalion be a false alarm?"

"Your guess is as good as mine, Homestead. This is Bulldog out."

Crap. If I didn't have so much respect for brother officers, particularly higher ranking ones, I might have concluded that LTC Meathead had just gotten tired of that infernal rock-and-roll racket. Hoping that the concert would resume, I decided to return to the Special Forces compound. None of the others wanted to come, so I went alone. The band members were drinking in the bar. Not many of the audience had reconvened, and no plans were evident to pick up the concert where it had left off. I had another beer. Something triggered an urge to foist my attentions on Tiger-Suit.

She had a room at the back side of the messhall. The location was out-of-the way and thus could be approached without the approacher attracting attention. I knocked on her door. "Go way." The phrase sounded well-practiced. I was probably not the first amorous drunk to come calling. I knocked again. "Go way or I'll call someone." The direct approach was obviously not going to work. Through the alcoholic fog, the thought sprung up that maybe an overhead envelopment was called for.

A nearby pile of lumber gave me access to the roof, which consisted of sheets of corrugated tin. I was standing on the slope of the roof planning the next step when my feet flew out from under me. I hit the tin with a loud thud and slid off onto the pile of lumber, which disintegrated under the impact. When everything came to rest, I was on the ground entangled in two-by-fours. I had on jungle fatigue shirt and trousers, but my feet were only protected by beach sandals. Pain from the direction of my feet was general. I disengaged myself from the two-by-fours and, just as doors began to open, hobbled around the corner of the building. Noises of a gathering crowd hurried me to the jeep, which fortunately was parked some distance away near the front of the compound. The next morning my NCOs wondered about the scratched and mutilated condition of my feet. I explained that I had fallen in the parking lot. Their faces registered skepticism.

This was my last effort at Tiger-suit. As for the coe for whom I had forsaken Tiger-suit, I paid her a few more visits, always when I was in an advanced state of inebriation. How inebriated? One night after a particularly lengthy session at the bar outside the Special Forces compound, I followed my loins in the direction of the coe's apartment. I made it as far as a pile of sand at a nearby construction site. Sometime long after midnight, I was awaken by her shaking me. An ARVN guard had found my prostrate, snoring form, guessed my destination, and fetched the coe. He could just as well have slit my throat.

In general, the coes in Cao Lanh proper were an exceptionally attractive lot. Maybe it was the shitfish diet. Whatever the cause, the beauty of some of the school girls was breath-taking. The light brown skin against the whiteness of the flowing ao dais, the large dark luminous eyes, the delicate fragile features—in some of the coes, the combination was enough to make you ache.

Approaching the locals in beauty was the female Vietnamese who was a Special Forces medic and lived in the camp. She had a room close to Tiger-suit, and in fact wore tiger suits herself. She was apparently from a very well-to-do family in the Saigon area. She was taken out of circulation by the captain who commanded the engineer unit that arrived shortly after MAT-104 did. The guy, a graduate of an Ivy League school and seemingly the stereotype of a scion of the Eastern Establishment, was certainly a fast worker. Within six weeks, the two were married—a bona fide Catholic Church marriage that would result in a move to the states for the coe. Much of the courtship was conducted at the bar outside the Special Forces camp. In the years since, I've often wondered how Mom and Dad back in Boston greeted their Asian daughter-in-law, and how the marriage fared.

The coes I dealt with during my years in Vietnam were not ones I was ever tempted to take home to Mom, and my female acquaintances during the Cao Lanh months were no exception. I gravitated toward the lower strata of society. I was not the only member of MAT-104 who sometimes thought with his loins. Sergeant Blane also had occasional difficulties. One particular incident provoked a rare overt assertion of authority on my part. As I returned to the teamhouse one evening, Sgt. Roca was standing at the foot of the stairs, by the entrance to the bunker. Because of the darkness, I couldn't see his face well, but it struck me that he was acting oddly. I asked, "What's happenin', Sgt. Roca?"

"Oh, nothin', Sir, nothin' much." My suspicions increased. He usually addressed me as "Dai Uy," not "Sir." Then I heard a giggle from the depths of the bunker. I was instantly pissed to beat hell. One of the few rules that I had laid down early on was, no women at the compound—none, absolutely. This was not only to avoid offending the sensitivities of our charges, many of whom resided with their families in our immediate vicinity, but also for our own protection. If we pissed the locals off by bringing girls into the compound, some disgruntled benshee—Vietnamese private—might one night toss a grenade our way. So I was vehement about the rule.

"You get that girl outta here pronto! Is Sergeant Blane in there? You and him get her th' hell outta here, now!"

"Yes sir."

I went to the top of the stairs, stopped, turned, and looked down. Sgt. Roca had his head in the bunker, and there was inaudible mumbling. "Get her outta here now, Sgt. Roca!" I yelled.

Three forms shortly emerged from the bunker and went quickly to the jeep. They drove off. I went inside the teamhouse. The room was dark, but I could tell Sgt. Mitchell was under his mosquito net on his cot. "I can't believe those two are that damn stupid! Didn't ya say something to 'em?"

"Roca outranks me, Dai Uy." I was not happy with the response, but I didn't pursue the matter. I lay down on my cot. After a bit, Roca and Blane returned. They silently undressed and turned in. The silence hung heavy. I eventually said, "I don't want that to happen again. That was stupid as shit. Not ever again."

There was an operation the next day, a walk to the northwest of Cao Lanh, and Sgt. Blane was my accompaniment. We plodded along in awkward silence for most of the morning. I finally said, "Ya realize what ya did last night was dumber than dog shit, don't you? I ain't kidding. I don't want that happnin' again. That's not usin' yer head. It could cause us big trouble with the Dai Uy and his men."

Sgt. Blane grunted in acknowledgement. Maybe I should have been harsher, perhaps gone to the XO for a bit of nonjudicial punishment. I was too nice a guy, however. Nevertheless, the point seemed to have been made because there were no reoccurrences, although I suspect that from time to time Sgt. Blane drilled the old mama-san maid.

The team's junior NCO was a quiet wizened little guy who looked older than his years—he was in his mid-thirties—but who had an above average interest in the opposite sex. And that is saying something because the average interest in sex among U.S. troops was pretty damn high. Sgt. Blane seemed particularly attracted to the unusual, such as our mama-san maid. One group that turned him on consisted of females in the Vietnamese army. These babes were for the most part not your sweet delicate little coes. Maybe Vietnamese WACs had a minimum weight requirement because they stretched their uniforms to the utmost. Whenever we passed a Vietnamese WAC, Sgt. Blane would start making lustful comments about "big-butted benshees," "benshee" being the Vietnamese word for private. The phrase still has a certain resonance for me.

Although normally inconspicuous, Sgt. Blane was capable of suddenly becoming the center of attention. On one early operation, he and I were accompanying the battalion on a circular route just to the northeast of Cao Lanh. The last portion of the route before reentering the town required the crossing of a large canal. Local sampans were slowly ferrying the battalion over the water when Sgt. Blane took it into his noggin to speed things up. Part of his motivation for the decision might have been that several of the sampan operators were mamasans, and one was even a sweet young coe. Whatever the motivation, Sgt. Blane was suddenly as naked as a jay-bird, his member, which was in fact well above average size, dangling aggressively. "Here Dai Uy, take mah clothes over. I'm gonna swim."

An accomplished swimmer he wasn't. He plunged into the canal and dog-paddled to the other bank. It was a few minutes before I arrived with his clothes. He waited with his hands on his hips, as unashamedly as if he were in the shower back at the Special Forces camp, his whiteness in stark contrast to the greens of the vegetation and the browns of the earth and the Vietnamese. The soldiers of the battalion giggled and commented among themselves, undoubtedly discussing how well-endowed the Co Van My was. The women avoided openly glancing in his direction. The Dai Uy looked glum. I felt inadequate. Sgt. Blane nonchalantly dressed, and we proceeded into town.

Commingled with the fun and games, with the drinking and the women, was the war. One evening soon after the January 6 fight, we were lounging around the team house. It was one of the rare evenings when one or more of us weren't out boozing. Suddenly, pounding footsteps came charging up the stairs. It was the interpreter. The Dai Uy urgently wanted our help. The Tan Tich ferry had been attacked, and the 64th Dia Phon Quan had been ordered to send a reaction force. Several trucks were on their way for the troops, but the Dai Uy himself wanted to be transported in our jeep. I got on the radio. "Bulldog, this is Homestead Six."

"This is Bulldog, over."

"This is Homestead Six. We just got word that there's action at Tan Tich. Know anything about it, over?"

"This is Bulldog. Yeah, there's been a rocket attack on the construction barge, over." A large construction barge with a superstructure three decks high had recently tied up near the ferry pier. The barge was from the ubiquitous U.S. construction company RMK-BRJ and was the living quarters and operational base for a crew renovating the pier. Most of the crew were Filipinos.

"This is Homestead. Uh, our unit's apparently been ordered there. Any information on that, over?" I was reluctant to discuss the subject in the clear on the radio. No telling who was listening.

"This is Bulldog. No, nothing."

"Well, if they go, we'll probably go too, Homestead out."

I turned to the team. "Well, any volunteers? This could damn well be an ambush. There's three miles of dark road between here and there."

After a pause, Sgt. Mitchell said, "I don't think this is a good idea, but I'll go."

"There's one other thing. The Dai Uy'll have to ride in the front seat. Since I'm gonna drive, that puts you in the back. Unassing that thing from the rear seat if we get hit ain't gonna be easy."

Sgt. Mitchell just shrugged. We went down to the jeep. A deuce and a half and a three-quarter ton were just pulling in. The Dai Uy was jabbering excitedly into his radio and to his entourage. Sgt. Mitchell pushed the front passenger's seat forward and climbed in. Six of the Dai Uy's entourage tried to follow him. Both Sgt. Mitchell and I said, "Hey, whoa." I held up three fingers, indicating only three more bodies could crowd in. The back seat would still be cramped, but they were little guys. An argument erupted over who would ride in the jeep and who had to go by truck. Finally, the agitated Dai Uy grabbed one of his men by the collar and pushed him toward the trucks, aimed a kick at several others, and thus got the matter sorted out.

I pulled the jeep out on the road, in front of the trucks. Sgt. Mitchell was in the back with the radio, his M-16, and three companions, all with carbines and one with one of the Dai Uy's two radios. Two of Sgt. Mitchell' companions were squeezed on the seat with him, and the third was sitting on the driver's side wheel-well. The Dai Uy and his other RTO were scrunched together on the front seat, with the Dai Uy's other radio. I had my M-16 across my lap. In the event we encountered an ambush, I was ready either to drive like hell through it or to unass the jeep.

In my excitement, however, I almost didn't make it past the first bridge, 100 or so meters down the road. The bridge was a narrow single-lane structure. Steel girders held the roadbed and extended up the sides and overhead. The roadbed consisted of thick cross-wise ties on which were laid two parallel rows of planks for the tires of vehicles to roll on. The approaching road at each end of the bridge was several feet lower than the roadbed. The differences in elevation were traversed by sharp inclines as the road at each end met the bridge. Ten miles an hour was a safe speed at which to make the crossing.

By the time I had covered the distance from the compound to the bridge, I was doing about 40. I had a quick glimpse of the guard in the bunker beside the bridge ducking behind his sandbags. The jeep became briefly airborne as it topped the incline of the approach. We landed with a spine-jarring thud, and the rear of the vehicle immediately did a sharp fishtail to the left, the back tires coming off the length-wise planks of the roadbed. We proceeded down the bridge in a diagonal skid. At the incline on the far end, we again became airborne. When we finally landed on the road, however, we were going slowly enough for me to regain control. I glanced briefly to the right and the rear. All that was visible in the darkness were the whites of six pairs of eyes. Given the sizes of the whites, the eyes had to be in the "wildly staring" position. No one spoke.

The bridge crossing worked to counter the adrenalin surge, and I throttled back a little. Still, I was not about to become a statistic because of slowness in getting out of the kill zone of an ambush. Consequently, we sped through the night, expecting at any moment to encounter the flashes of gunfire. Every new object that made its abrupt appearance in the headlights—trees, bushes, dwellings—was thoroughly scrutinized for evidence of danger. But the expected fusillade never came, and our small convey arrived intact at the Mekong.

A small Popular Forces unit had secured the area. The construction barge had taken two B-40 rockets into its second deck, but the damage was superficial and there were no casualties. The Charlies had evidently been no more than a small team and had quickly departed. After an hour or so of uncertainty about what was to happen next, and no further sign of the Charlies, the Dai Uy was instructed to spend the night at the ferry with the reaction force. We hadn't thought to bring over-night gear, but the Dai Uy coerced the locals into providing some reed mats. The headquarters group with Sgt. Mitchell and myself curled up on the veranda of a small one-story school building.

The next morning, the reaction force did a more thorough search of the area. A trampled-down patch of grass was found about 75 meters from the barge. This spot was apparently where the rockets were fired. A trail extended into the distance along the bank of the river. Near the ferry, the trail was bordered by residences. The buildings thinned out as the distance from the ferry increased. The reaction force searched the trail for approximately a kilometer or so without finding any fur-ther evidence of the attackers.

Every few nights for the next two weeks, the 64th Dia Phong Quan had to provide a force at the ferry. The force included the headquarters group and two Co Van Mys. During my last two nights at the school, the Dai Uy for some reason decided that my status warranted more than a reed mat or my air mattress. So he had a four-poster bed set up in the school yard. He showed it to me with great pride and an obvious expectation that I would be immensely pleased. His joy was such that I felt I couldn't refuse the hospitality. So I spent the final two nights at Tan Tich on a big thick mattress on a large bed in a school yard, sur-rounded by little brown people sleeping in the dirt. Much to their relief, my NCOs didn't rate the royal treatment. Moreover, they took great pleasure in my discomfort.

The Advisory Business

The 64th Dia Phong Quan conducted a number of operations to the immediate northeast and east of Cao Lanh. A common route was to go northeast until the sizeable river in that area was encountered, and then to follow it as it did a wide bend first to the east, then to the south, and finally to the west. Charlie frequented this area, and the battalion could usually count on finding evidence of his presence.

Booby traps were the most common evidence. Charlie's booby traps in Kien Phong Province were not fancy. A grenade laid horizontally on its handle with the safety pin removed was an effective casualty producer. Just a slight disturbance would cause the grenade to roll, which would result in the handle being released and, in two to five seconds, an explosion. Set in the high grass on the edge of a trail, these grenades awaited a careless foot or even the vibration of a nearby step. When the Dai Uy's boys found a booby-trapped grenade, they generally did not attempt to neutralize it. Instead, they marked its location with a piece of paper and gave it a wide berth. The grenade could just as well get an unwary VC as it could one of the good guys.

Sometimes, the Dai Uy's boys found a grenade the wrong way. Casualties were not uncommon, and a number of them were incurred in the area to the northeast of Cao Lanh. No deaths from booby traps occurred during my months with the battalion, but some of the wounds were serious. For example, an older platoon leader in one of the companies took the main force of an explosion in his legs and groin. By the time the headquarters group arrived at the location, the lieutenant's pants had been removed. Cuts from shrapnel covered his legs, but these wounds were not what attracted attention. A spoonful-size drop of very dark blood had formed just behind the tip of his penis, and the tip was at an odd angle to the shaft. Obviously, the tip had been partially severed. The lieutenant was in a state of delirium with his head lolling from side to side and his eyes unfocused and rolled upwards.

The service the Co Van Mys provided in such instances was medical evacuation. Province operations could generally put its hands on air assets, usually from a medevac unit based in Can Tho. We on the ground would then talk the pilot in, giving him the location and general situation. U.S. medevac did not mean U.S. medical care, however. The U.S. Huey would deposit the casualty at a Vietnamese hospital. The lieutenant with the partially severed penis received the benefit of our services. He was medevaced, but I never learned how he and his penis fared in the tender hands of the Vietnamese medical system.

Because of the inadequacy of our interpreters and the battalion's unfamiliarity with U.S. procedures, medevacs did not always go smoothly. Unless the Co Van Mys were on the actual scene, the Dai Uy's boys could be at a loss as to what to do. And because the battalion was often widely dispersed as it moved over the landscape, sometimes even with elements on the opposite banks of a wide river, we sometimes could not be on the scene.

One day on an operation in the booby-trapped infested area to the northeast, one of our favorites suffered from the problems that could arise. The company commander who had a home next to the Dai Uy at the Hao Hoa Pagoda and who resembled Alfred E. Neuman became riddled with shrapnel. Initially, the headquarters group was close by. Alfred was bloody but conscious. I had the impression that his wounds were mostly superficial, but he was not bearing up well. He looked at me imploringly and said in his limited English, "Help me, Dai Uy, help me."

Unfortunately, this was one of the occasions when province operations had trouble locating uncommitted air assets. I reluctantly told the Dai Uy that nothing was available. So the decision was made to put Alfred in a sampan and take him by river to the road leading to Cao

Lanh. The boat set off with Alfred lying on his back, still looking at me with soulful eyes. Shortly after the sampan had rounded a bend in the river and was out of sight, province called and said that a passing Chinook on a supply run could make the pick-up, but the mission would have to be accomplished within the next few minutes. I frantically tried to get across to the Dai Uy what was needed. Alfred had to be taken from the sampan to an open area beyond the vegetation on the river bank. Smoke needed to be popped. And Alfred needed to be put on the chopper. As we broke into a trot along the bank, the Dai Uy began barking instructions into his radios.

My radio crackled: "Homestead, this is Windy Three."

"This is Homestead, over."

"This is Windy Three. We're inbound about three minutes out. What's the situation, over."

"This is Homestead. We have one whiskey-india-alpha. There don't seem to be any hostiles in the area."

"This is Windy Three. Are you with the whiskey-india-alpha?"

Uh oh, this sounded like it might be trouble. The guy was asking embarrassing questions.

"This is Homestead. We're on our way to his location now, over."

"This is Windy Three. Are you sure the area is secure? What's in the treelines?"

"This is Homestead. We haven't seen any hostiles all day. I can't vouch for all the treelines, but I don't think anything's there."

"This is Windy Three. Okay, doesn't sound good. I'm not gonna be on the ground long. I need to see smoke now."

I told the Dai Uy to have his people throw a "koei." We were rushing along the bank. I heard the Chinook off to our right. As the sound got lower, the column turned from the river and headed quickly along a path leading to the open fields. Over the radio came, "Homestead, this is Windy Three. I'm on the ground but no one's doing anything."

"Roger, Windy. I'm comin' to your location now. Just hold on a second."

"Sorry, Homestead. I've got to leave. Windy Three out." At that moment we broke into the open. The Chinook was just beginning to lift off. A group of soldiers was crouching about 25 meters away, surrounding a stretcher on which Alfred lay. I didn't know who to be more pissed at: the Chinook pilot for cutting and running so quickly or the Dai Uy's men for not taking a little initiative. They had simply crouched there as the chopper waited, not being able to react without specific instructions.

We reached the group, and Alfred fixed me with his pathetic gaze. "Help me, Dai Uy, help me."

"Bulldog, this is Homestead Six. We missed Windy Three. Ya got anything else available, over?"

"This is Bulldog. You're in luck. There's an inbound dust-off, about ten minutes out."

"This is Homestead. Thanks. We'll be waitin', out." I gave Alfred a smile and a thumbs-up. He smiled weakly in return. He was shortly in the air and on his way. After a week, he was back at the pagoda. His mood was good, but it seemed to us that he milked his injuries for all they were worth. He didn't get back to operations until shortly before my departure.

Although it took casualties from VC booby traps, particularly in the area to the immediate northeast of Cao Lanh, the battalion was lucky in one respect. Mines were rarely encountered. During my months, the battalion came across no bouncing betties, claymores, or pressure mines that detonate underfoot. Such mines were far more lethal than the rudimentary booby traps found in central Kien Phong Province.

On a few operations in the area to the northeast of Cao Lanh, we ran into real live Victor Charlies. The most significant contact occurred one day when the whole battalion crossed to the far side of the river. Usually, the Dai Uy's orders were to stick to the more populous western side or at most to put a small unit across. On this particular day, however, his instructions were to stride boldly into the unknown.

The vegetation on the far side was a mixture of fields, patches of woods, banana groves, and swamps. After closely following the river bank for several kilometers, the battalion swung out to avoid an area of swamp. When it turned back toward the river, it found the elusive Mr. Charles.

A burst of automatic weapons fire was how Charles announced his presence. We were moving across a large open field, with the left flank brushing a treeline. To the left front was a meandering stream. On its far side was a patchy area of palm trees and banana plants. Straight ahead, about 250 to 300 meters away, was an L-shaped row of trees and bushes, a sort of hedgerow. The battalion was moving into the open face of the L. The long side of the L went to the right, ending to our right front. The short side met the stream to our left front. Approximately 100 meters beyond the long side of the L was the treeline along the river. In back of the short side of the L was what appeared to be a banana grove.

En masse, the battalion hit the dirt. The initial burst was the extent of the incoming fire, however. After a short period, officers and NCOs began standing and walking around, but there was no move to resume the advance. The left flank was now beyond the trees and was anchored on the meandering stream. Except for a small bare area, the field was covered by grass, or maybe rice stalks, two to three feet high. The bare area was where the left flank met the stream and seemed to be a place where the thrashing of rice was done.

The Dai Uy and the headquarters group moved to the bare spot. Both the Dai Uy and I had informed province operations that we had contact. Some air assets had been located, and I prepared to put in air strikes. A forward air controller, or FAC, in a small Cessna was to coordinate the effort. Two B-58s were soon on station. The FAC marked the target with white phosphorous rockets, and the B-58s performed their high altitude approach and release. The bombs seemed to be hitting in the vicinity of the L-shaped row of trees and bushes. The FAC reported seeing several figures in black pajamas running from the area.

The B-58s expended their loads and departed, and province said that nothing else would be available for awhile. The Dai Uy then spent close to an hour ineffectively trying to adjust rounds from the two 105-howitzers at province headquarters. Most of the rounds landed well to the rear of where the VC appeared to be.

I spent the time wondering how I would approach the L-shaped row of trees and bushes if I were running the show. Following the stream bed would seem to provide considerable cover and concealment. Also, a route through the swamp along the river bank might be worth trying. But however the attempt was made, the guys on point would be tempting fate.

Finally, it was time to fish or cut bait. The Dai Uy had the center and right advance so that the battalion line was generally parallel to where we assumed the VC positions were. Once the unit was ready, a strange thing happened. The Dai Uy gave an order, and the entire battalion dropped into the grass, disappearing from view. I didn't know whether the plan was for the battalion to crawl forward, or what. After several seconds, the VC reacted with a sustained barrage of automatic weapons. With the distinctive popping sound of incoming fire, the rounds whipped just overhead. Based on the volume of fire, it would seem that we were facing at least a platoon-size unit.

Whatever the plan had been, the barrage changed it. A general retreat began. It was hard to tell whether the move was ordered or spontaneous, but suddenly everyone was heading to the rear. The experience was a new one for me, and without really being aware of it, I broke into a run. I only realized I was running when I felt several hard whacks on my shins. I looked down to discover that Mutt, our RTO, was surreptitiously working me over with his walking stick, a long rod about three-quarters of an inch in diameter. The rest of the battalion was retreating, but it was a controlled retreat with each individual walking and units maintaining integrity and formation. The Co Van My, on the other hand, had been about to engage in head-long flight.

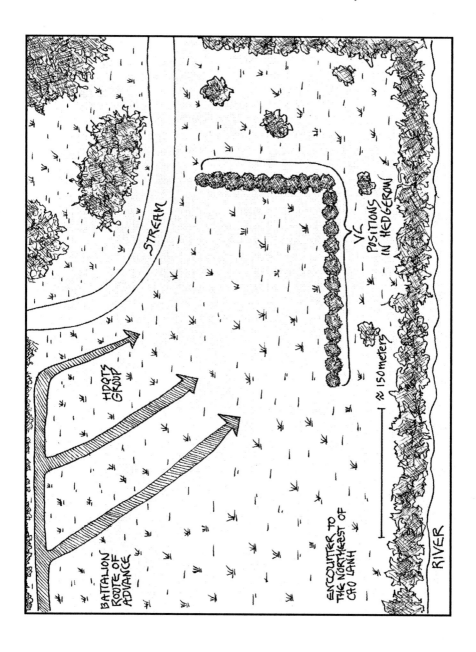

The experience was sobering. I realized how quickly a unit breaking contact with the enemy could disintegrate into an undisciplined and uncontrolled mob. And I began to look at Mutt and indeed the entire battalion in a different light. Lowly Regional Forces PFC Mutt had prevented the exalted U.S. adviser from appearing to fall victim to panic. The battalion had shown itself to be a more professional unit than I had thought. It might not be an aggressive offensive force, but it was a bona fide military outfit that understood some of the often overlooked finer points of the military art.

On this particular day, Charlie ruled the field. The battalion had sustained no casualties, but it was ordered to return to Cao Lanh. No other units were available for the battle, and the battalion had nighttime defensive missions that were deemed more important than keeping a fix on Mr. Charles. We returned the next day but the hostiles had gone. Along the L-shaped row of trees and bushes, we found approximately ten freshly constructed fighting bunkers. A bomb crater was within 50 meters of one of the bunkers. The occupants would have had a helluva headache. Perhaps they were the ones that the FAC had seen fleeing. Unlike the case with the January 6 fight, in this instance where I thought the VC were was where they in fact were. With enough air strikes, we eventually would have done some damage. But maybe that's a commentary on the whole war.

Sometimes the forward air controllers did more than coordinate and adjust air strikes. Sometimes they weaseled their way into the action. One such incident of greater involvement occurred in that same area to the northeast of Cao Lanh. The operation was a simple blocking operation. The battalion was sent to the point where we usually intersected the river and began following it as it swept to the east and south. This time, however, instead of proceeding along the river, we stopped. Another unit was conducting a sweep a few kilometers to the north, and the battalion was to watch for any Charlies that might be flushed by the activity.

The Dai Uy set his men up on the southwest bank. The opposite bank at this point was clear of bushes and trees, and we had a view across open fields for at least two kilometers. I settled back for a nap.

I was awakened by excited chatter. The Vietnamese had congregated on the bank and were pointing and gesturing toward the open area beyond the opposite bank. Almost a click away, five or six black-clad figures were splashing through the paddies. They were running parallel to our position, in a northerly direction. I informed province operations that we were seeing actual hostiles.

After several minutes, the fleeing group gained the cover of the jungle to the north. But then another small group appeared. Earlier, the Dai Uy had commandeered several sampans to stand by in case the battalion had to get to the far bank. He began transporting a portion of the battalion across the water. Meanwhile, a FAC in a piper cub appeared on the scene. This was a once-in-a-tour opportunity: Charlies in the open.

The FAC circled, floating lower and lower. The Charlies had a long way to go, and the FAC was taking his time scouting the situation. Perhaps he was hoping for the arrival of a flight of Phantoms, B-58s, or prop-driven A-10s. No other planes appeared, however, and with the Charlies getting closer and closer to cover, the FAC made his move. He got to the rear of the group, went into a shallow dive, and from a height of only about 200 feet fired one of his target-marking rockets. A geyser of paddy water rose into the air close to the frantically fleeing figures, and one of them collapsed. The FAC swooped over the group and turned for another run, but by the time he was in position the Charlies were almost within the safety of the trees and undergrowth. He fired one more rocket just as the group disappeared, the smoke from the explosion suddenly materializing at the woods' edge.

By this time, the headquarters group and two of the battalion's companies were across the river. The Dai Uy gave the order to move out, and we began sloshing forward. In short order, we arrived at the freshly dead body. He was face down in the water. Shrapnel had torn open his right side, and his blood and some internal organs were seeping into the adjacent muck.

The excitement was over. No more Charlies appeared. After a bit the operation was called completed, and we returned to Cao Lanh.

In late January, we were to spend a number of days in the same locale. A new Popular Forces outpost was being constructed, and the 64th Regional Forces Battalion was assigned to provide daytime security. As the Dai Uy's boys manned a broad perimeter, the PF troops put up, on a little piece of high ground, a triangular fort with mud walls. At night, the battalion returned to Cao Lanh, and the PFs provided for their own protection.

My experience with FACs in their piper cubs was not limited to talking to them on the radio or to watching their occasional cowboy antics. Shortly after I arrived in Kien Phong Province, I was invited by one of the two Air Force FACs permanently stationed there to go for a little orientation ride. On the appointed day, we took off from the airfield in his two-seater piper cub. We went north, over the southern portion of the Plain of Reeds. Here and there, isolated individuals were working in the large fields. The whole area was a free-fire zone. No friendlies were supposed to be there, and in theory everybody was a justifiable target.

In addition to the people, we also saw dwellings that appeared to be occupied. Evidently, not all the Vietnamese had gotten the word that this was a free-fire zone. The FAC ignored most of the individuals and dwellings until one dwelling caught his interest. He circled it several times, then asked province operations for permission to fire it up. Permission was granted, and he said: "Hold on. We're gonna have a little fun."

He put the plane into a steep gut-wrenching dive. Down we plummeted. Finally, my driver fired a rocket. It penetrated the thatched roof, and the explosion inside quickly ignited the dried grass and reeds. We pulled up in another gut-wrenching maneuver. We circled the area for a bit but saw no human activity. I was struck by the arbitrariness of the action. The pilot had seemingly ignored other apparently inhabited dwellings and a number of individuals. What led him to focus on this particular thatched hut was not evident to me. Vietnamese who sought a life in this uncertain area most definitely led a precarious existence.

Within two months, the pilot who provided me with the excursion was dead. Those many hours cruising the skies, randomly firing up huts, water buffalo, and individuals, might have given him a feeling of invincibility. That would seem the most likely explanation for how he died. He was flying the little piper cub up the river where we had watched a FAC—perhaps it was him—wax the Charlie in the open paddy. Reportedly, he was only a few feet above the water and below the level of the treetops. A VC unit was relaxing on the river bank when suddenly one of its principal nemeses comes around a bend—fat, sassy, and ripe for the plucking. A burst from an automatic weapon would have been all it took. After months and years of quivering under the assaults from the skies, the Charlies must have taken a great deal of pleasure in bringing down an enemy at such close quarters.

The plane with bullet holes was located by the South Vietnamese in short order, but the pilot was gone. LTC Meathead seemed to think he was dealing with a bunch of Old West banditos. He offered a reward for the return of the pilot, disseminating the offer by a massive leaflet drop. But if the pilot survived the crash, it was not for long. His body was found about five days later less than two kilometers to the north. He seemed to have died as a result of injuries from the crash. It was impossible to tell whether he had been killed immediately and for some reason the VC had moved his body, or whether he had survived for a time and died during an attempt to remove him from the area.

It was about the time of this incident that certain feelings of sympathy, or perhaps envy, I had for the VC were at their strongest. For Old Asia Hands, the feelings were not uncommon, although not often expressed. It was difficult not to at least admire an enemy who operated under such adverse conditions and suffered such hardships. In terms of firepower, mobility, and military hardware, Charlie was definitely the underdog, and routing for the underdog is human nature, not to mention a tradition embedded in the American experience. Also, at the ground level the larger issues the war was being fought about were not all that apparent. Freedom and democracy? The South Vietnamese did not seem to enjoy an over-abundance of freedom, and their political system certainly wasn't a shining example of democracy. Anti-Communism? In the reality of the jungles and swamps, the heat and bugs, the maiming and death, the abstraction of Communism was difficult to grasp. No, at the ground level, "our" Vietnamese and "their" Vietnamese were in many ways indistinguishable.

So a true professional soldier was likely to feel a certain affinity for an enemy who did so much with so little. And in his fantasies, that professional might just wonder what it would be like on the other side. Such fantasies were another reason a more realistic part of me was saying, "Time to return to the Land of the Big PX, Cowboy. Twenty-eight months in the 'Nam is long enough."

In very early February, I took a trip to Saigon to take the LSAT, the Law School Admissions Test. It was also one more opportunity, approaching my last opportunity, to sample the pleasures of the Pearl of the Orient. The LSAT was given in a U.S. Embassy building in the quiet, tree-shaded northeast area of the city—Dao Kao, my old stomping grounds. Most of the others taking the test were junior enlisted personnel or junior officers. And most of them seemed to be rear-echelon types. Someone should have clued the grunts that taking the LSAT could get them out of the field for a few days.

Taking the test was an other-worldly experience that was to foreshadow the emotions during my first years—actually, the emotions have never completely disappeared—back in the World. A couple of days before I had been slogging through the paddies. Blood, gore, and death were very recent acquaintances. And here I was in an air-conditioned room puzzling over words, ideas, and abstract concepts. At the very moment, somewhere not so far away, a unit was undoubtedly in contact. The shells and bombs were raining down. The automatic weapons were slicing the bamboo just overhead. Fear was palpable. Life was tenuous. And I wondered whether to apply my No. 2 pencil to box A or B.

After the test, I spent a couple of days checking out my old haunts—the Tu Do and Dao Kao bars, the city's lone pizza place, the Chinese restaurant near the Capitol Hotel in Cholon. I also saw a coe who had been a cashier at one of the BOQ eateries when I had been an MP. I had run across her when I came through Saigon on the way to Di An a few months previously, and felt the need to look her up. She was virginal and the relationship was platonic, so I don't know what I had in mind. Maybe I was just trying to have some contact with a part of Vietnamese culture a little removed from the sleaze and the war. Whatever the case, I took the girl to dinner, a movie, and then her home, and finished the evening with a bar honey.

I returned to Kien Phong with less than two months before my combination DEROS/ETS. The level of activity kept me from dwelling on the pending end to my war. Also, I had one more R&R coming to me, and I was looking forward to five days in Bangkok with Trachit Pangbon in early March.

On one of the first operations after returning to Cao Lanh, I lost a cherished possession, an item that I had brought with me to Vietnam way back in August of 1966. It was nothing expensive or unique, just a simple sheath knife. But it had become part of my identity. And perhaps the worse thing about the loss was how it occurred—the knife was stolen, STOLEN, by one of the Dai Uy's troops.

We were on an operation to the east of Cao Lanh, just to the north of the site of the January 6 fight. Choppers had put us next to the river flowing to the hamlet the battalion had tried to enter that day. We moved for about an hour and then paused for a break. I took off my web gear—the pistol belt and suspenders—and walked over to confer with the Dai Uy and the interpreter for a moment. The knife was in its sheath, which was on the pistol belt. I was only about ten meters away and for no more than three minutes. When I returned, the sheath was empty.

I was livid. My companion of more than two years, a tool that had seen me through Tuy Hoa and Dak To, not to mention uncounted bars and disreputable places, was gone, ripped off by people whose way of life I was helping to preserve. The ungrateful little bastards! I threw what was close to a temper tantrum. Sgt. Roca, my fellow Co Van My for the day and the team member who most enjoyed creating or exacerbating situations, was concerned enough to try to calm me down. He was probably afraid that I would cause such a ruckus a Vietnamese would blow me away and he would be left alone with a couple hundred irate Ruff-Puffs.

The Dai Uy was obviously embarrassed and made an effort to find the knife. My conduct was so outrageous, however, that his sympathies soon seemed to shift. If the Co Van My was such an asshole, he deserved to lose his frigging knife. After a time, he ordered the operation to continue. For the rest of the morning, I loudly expressed my unhappiness.

To complete the day, the battalion was sniped at. As we approached the hamlet where the January 6 fight had occurred, the Dai Uy swung the battalion out into the fields and paddies. We were avoiding the hamlet, and the reason soon became apparent. Several shots came winging our way from the treeline. Charlie was definitely in residence, but the Dai Uy evidently had orders not to become engaged. This gave me something more to rant and rave about. "Hey Dai Uy, tysou?" "Tysou" was the word for "why." In essence, I was questioning his manhood.

His executive officer called my bluff. A slim mid-thirties usually quiet lieutenant, the XO had probably had enough of the obnoxious Co Van My. He grinned at me, starting walking toward the treeline, and said, "We go. Get VC." I quickly caught up with him, and we moved abreast toward the enemy. We had gone about 25 meters when the reality of what I was doing took hold. I turned tail. He had won the game of chicken. I consoled myself with the rationale that I would have been the preferred target when the Charlies opened up. Still, I had been put in my place. We resumed the march, and although I continued to mutter about the lost knife, my complaining was at a much subdued level. But I did not let my charges forget my loss: I kept my empty sheath on my web gear for the rest of my tenure.

A few days after the knife incident, a sniper came close to drowning half the battalion. The action occurred at the end of a multi-battalion operation on the Mekong, southeast of the Tan Tich ferry. The landing craft transported us to a muddy landing spot early in the morning. We moved northwest paralleling the river for most of the day, not finding anything of interest. The spot where we were to be picked up by the landing craft in late afternoon for the trip back to Tan Tich was far from ideal. It was at the mouth of a marshy channel between the mainland and an offshore island. The channel was about 75 meters wide at the mouth, and the water was only two to three feet deep. The mud on the river bottom, however, added another foot of depth.

The boats could not negotiate the shallow water and muddy bottom, so we had to wade about 100 meters past the mouth of the channel out into the river. The Dai Uy had commandeered a father and son guide-team in the morning. They were to wade to the boats with us and were to be given a ride back down the river.

In short order, the loading operation destroyed unit discipline and cohesion. The mud was of the clinging, sucking type. The short Vietnamese were struggling in water up to their chests in some cases, trying to hold weapons and radios overhead. Some individuals became stuck and had to divert all their energies and attention to extracting themselves. I became stuck myself, unable to pull my boots from the mud. Indeed, my right foot was threatening to come completely out of the boot.

Three landing craft were waiting at the start of the deeper water. Initially, three columns were snaking their way to the boats. As more and more troopers had to engage in their own personal struggles with the water and mud, however, the columns disintegrated. By the time the rear of the battalion had entered the water, the front and middle had become a churning mass of individuals, each attempting with growing desperation to gain the solid deck of the nearest landing craft.

Just at this moment, a burst of automatic weapons fire came from a few meters back in the jungle near the spot where the battalion had entered the water. Panic ensued. Individuals renewed their scramble for the perceived safety of the boats. A few even abandoned items of equipment, although no one seemed to have lost a weapon. There were a number of bursts of return fire, including one from me. I was still mired in muck up to my boot tops, with the water waist high. I was about 25 meters from the nearest bank, which at that point was covered with swamp grass six to ten feet high. All of the Vietnamese near me, including Mutt, had scrambled off. Sgt. Mitchell was my companion this day. He had taken a somewhat different route and was almost at a boat. I was quite alone and getting lonelier.

Partly in frustration at not being able to move, partly in real concern and fear at what the grass just a short distance from me was hiding, I leveled my M-16 and fired a burst. The rounds, their path etched by several tracers, whipped into the vegetation. If there had been any disciplined Charlies, my unaimed firing would have been pretty much ineffective. Nevertheless, the power evidenced by the kicking M-16 had a calming impact on my psyche. I returned to the effort to extract myself. Attempting to pull my legs upward wasn't working, so I tried a short rocking motion. It worked, and soon I was headed for the nearest boat.

Fortunately, the single burst of fire was all that Charlie sent our way. It was probably an individual or very small unit that was shadowing the column and saw an opportunity for a laugh. No members of the battalion were hurt in the panic but there was one mystery. The father-son local guide team that the Dai Uy had commandeered disappeared in the confusion. They had been near the front of the battalion and had almost reached one of the landing craft. A trooper thought he saw them dive under water when the shots were fired. I never learned whether they drowned or made it to a bank.

Over the next weeks, the battalion took several more trips down the Mekong. One was in response to an attack on a district headquarters. Districts were subdivisions of provinces. This particular district headquarters was a town just off the Mekong, on a tributary. Many districts in Vietnam had American advisors but this one did not. The headquarters building was a nondescript thick dull-grey masonry structure, one-story high, surrounded by a gargantuan amount of barbed wire. The wire was in a number of circles, the closest about 20 meters from the building and the outer about 50 meters. There were rolls of concertina, fences of various arrangements, and low-lying aprons designed to catch the feet of anyone running.

A sapper team had apparently tried to get through this barrier. It wasn't successful. Two of its members were still draped over the wire. That they had managed to get almost half-way through the maze was quite an accomplishment. Of course, they weren't able to appreciate this testimony to their training, preparation, and perseverance. The only damages sustained by the headquarters building were several sizeable craters in the masonry walls. The craters were caused by B-40 rockets. The thickness of the walls kept the damage to the superficial level.

The battalion conducted a sweep into the hinterland, mostly to show the flag. The Charlies were long gone. The headquarters group paused for lunch outside a well-constructed plank dwelling in a patch of thinned-out woods along a stream. A porch ran the length of the building. It was a fairly impressive structure to find in such an out-of-the-way place. By the time we returned to the town in the afternoon, the bodies had been removed from the wire.

On another operation to the southeast, I learned a little something about deep stream crossings. Most of the streams we encountered were either shallow enough to wade or traversed by bridge or boat. This particular stream turned out to be over my head, and there was no bridge or boat. The battalion strung a rope across the water, and individual troopers dragged themselves across holding their weapons and radios over their heads. The process was slow. Being larger than the Vietnamese, I somehow got the idea the water would be no more than chest deep. Sometimes haste has a negative impact on reasoning.

About halfway across, holding my M-16 and map overhead, I took a step and went completely under. I pushed up with my foot, broke the surface, gulped a mouthful of air, and sunk again. The bank was only about ten meters away, but I had no idea how deep the water might get. If it didn't get much deeper, I perhaps could bounce the distance. If it became deeper, however, I was in trouble. The rope was about ten meters to the right and no help. Turning around and retracing my steps would be as difficult as continuing.

So I proceeded forward. Each time I broke the surface, water cascaded off my helmet. Through the blur on my glasses, I could see a gathering group of Vietnamese on the bank watching my slow progress with interest. My arms began to ache from the effort of holding the rifle and map aloft. At best, each bounce was taking me forward only a foot. Fortunately, the stream did not get any deeper. Finally, just short of the bank, the river bed began a steep ascent. To the grins of the crowd, I struggled from the water. "Numbah one," I said, trying to maintain my savoir faire. Sgt. Mitchell was still on the opposite bank. He called across: "I'll think I'll take the rope, Dai Uy."

In mid-February, I had the honor of making a contribution to Mr. McNamara's computerized score-keeping system for measuring progress in the war. McNamara was no longer the head man at the Pentagon, but many of his systems and procedures were still in place. One target of those systems and procedures was the Vietnam conflict. McNamara's legacy, the systems analysis boys, were intent on proving with numbers that the war was being won.

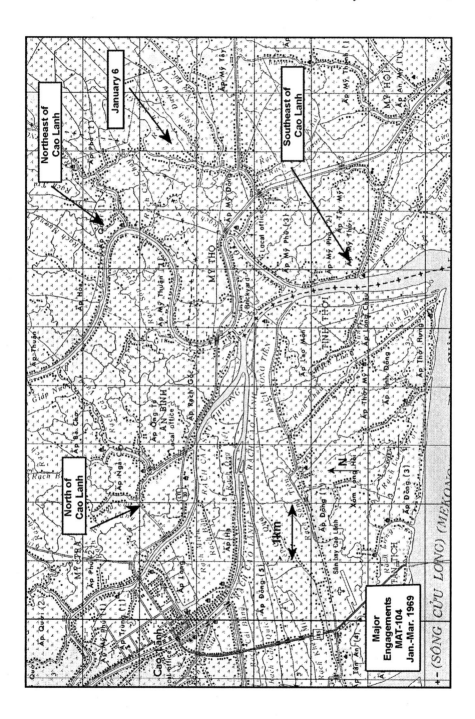

My contribution was to a village and hamlet rating system. I was given a map of the Cao Lanh area of Kien Phong Province on which colors indicated the extent to which the various locales were controlled by the VC. White indicated a government-controlled village or hamlet, while red indicated a VC-controlled one. In between the two extremes were three or four shades of red indicating different degrees of control and sympathy. I was to make any changes that I thought appropriate.

The problem was that there was no way to show reality. If government soldiers were in or passing through a village or hamlet, the community was controlled by and sympathetic to the government. If Charlies were in or passing through the village or hamlet, it was controlled by and sympathetic to the VC. If no soldiers of either side were present, who knew?

Nevertheless, I played the game, making a few upgrades and downgrades. And I suppose my input was combined with others to produce a composite of the province that was pondered, scrutinized, and analyzed at MACV headquarters in Saigon and in the bowels of the Pentagon, enabling some desk jockey to conclude we were or were not making progress, most likely the former, a conclusion dutifully communicated to the White House, the Congress, and the American people. But the whole process could be described no more aptly than by the basic cliché of the computer business: garbage in, garbage out.

Finishing With A Bang

It was supposed to be an off day, but we were awakened shortly after sunrise by the interpreter's excited voice: "Dai Uy, Dai Uy, VC outside town! We go!" I contacted province operations and was told that the battalion was indeed being sent just to the north of town to meet a VC unit that had taken up residence.

The hamlet where the Charlies were located was no more than a kilometer from the northern edge of Cao Lanh and was the Vietnamese equivalent of a suburb of that town, a plush suburb at that. Most of the dwellings were large, substantial multi-room plank structures. The dwellings were located along a wooded river bank, and the approaches required the crossing of open fields. Apparently the VC had moved in overnight, thrown the inhabitants out, and constructed hasty defensive positions. The 64th Dia Phong Quan was to approach the hamlet from the Cao Lanh side. Another Regional Forces battalion and a Ranger battalion were to probe from the north and east.

We strolled the short distance to the site of the coming battle. From the main road running east from Cao Lanh, a side road led north to the western edge of the hamlet. This approach road was about 400 meters in length and about four feet above the surrounding fields. A few trees and bushes grew on the steeply sloping sides of the approach road. The Dai Uy led the battalion along the road until about the halfway point and then had two companies pivot out into the field to the right. Thus they were on line facing the hamlet. The third company pushed cautiously another 50 meters up the road, which terminated at a stone foot bridge over the river. For its last 75 or so meters before the river, the road ran between several dwellings and scattered trees and bushes. Ini-

221

tially, the company on the road stopped short of the dwellings and vegetation.

At this point, things halted for a bit. Evidently, we were waiting for air support, further instructions, or divine intervention. The headquarters group was standing on the road in plain view of the alleged Charlies in the trees only 200 meters away. On top of a four-foot high roadbed, the tallest guy in the crowd, obviously a Co Van My, I began to feel very conspicuous. I said to Sgt. Mitchell: "I don't know 'bout you, but I'm gettin' down in the field behind this road. We're just targets up here."

"Think you're on to something, Dai Uy."

So the two Co Van Mys, as nonchalantly as possible, took cover. The Vietnamese in the headquarters group grinned down at us condescendingly. Then the VC expended their first shots of the day, just a few short bursts. The headquarters group quickly joined us. The shots also caused the Dai Uy to pull back his two companies in the field. They lacked any cover, and concealment was impossible because the field had been cut to just stubble.

Also, air support was on the way. Province operations called: "Homestead Six, this is Bulldog, over."

"This is Homestead Six, over."

"This is Bulldog. We have some air on the way. Are you prepared to put it in, over?"

Something was not ringing right. The two 105s at province headquarters, only two clicks away, had not been firing any support. The amount of incoming fire we had received thus far was not indicative of a large force. I was hesitant to put 500 pounders and napalm on these well-built old structures if the only thing there was a few snipers. "Bulldog, this is Homestead Six. I got some qualms 'bout this. How come no artillery has been fired? If this village is gonna be destroyed, it seems to me the Vietnamese ought to participate. The whole blame shouldn't fall on the U.S. Air Force. You got any idea why there's no artillery?"

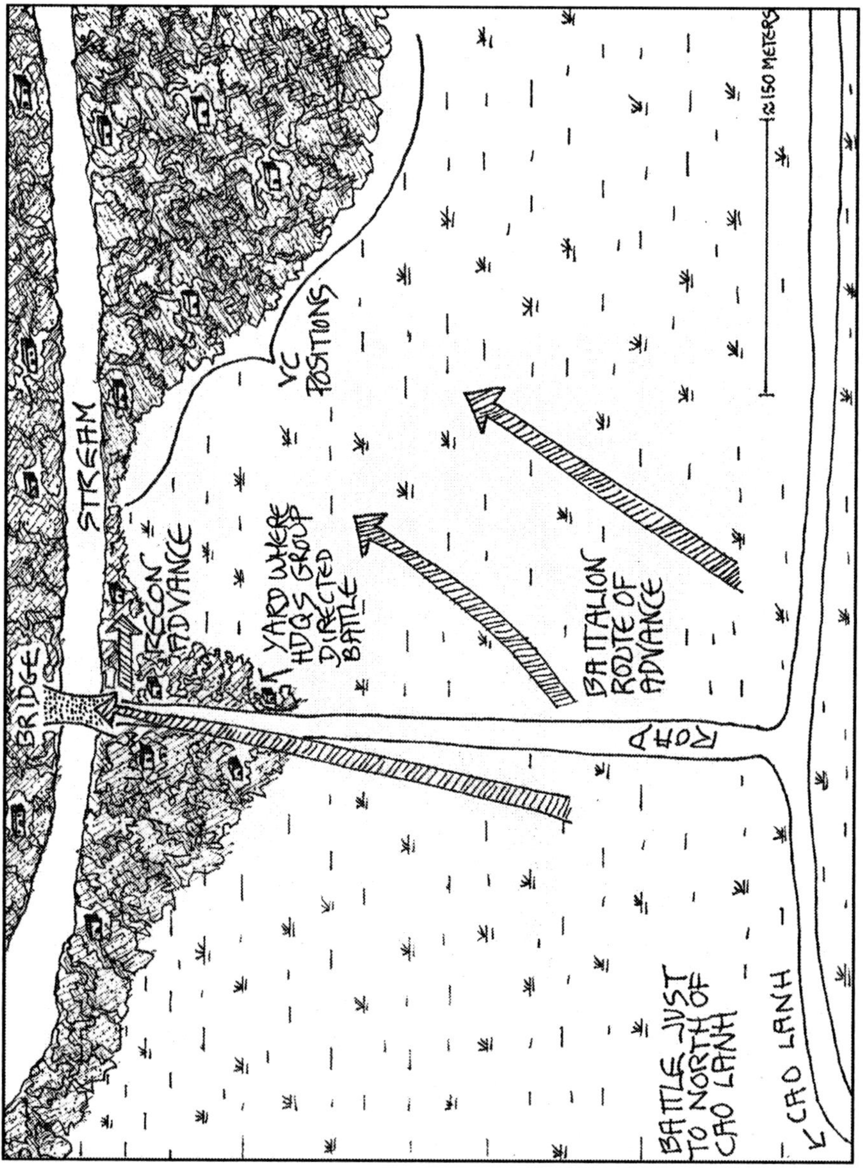
BRIDGE
STREAM
RECON ADVANCE
YARD WHERE HDQS GROUP DIRECTED BATTLE
VC POSITIONS
BATTALION ROUTE OF ADVANCE
ROAD
≈150 METERS
BATTLE JUST TO NORTH OF CAO LANH
CAO LANH

There was a long pause. Then, "I don't know, Homestead. I'll check it out. Bulldog out."

One thing triggering my concern was the negative propaganda effect of the enormous amount of destruction that had been wrought in urban areas during the Tet offensive a year earlier. The famous remark of the adviser in the town of Ben Tre—also in the Delta—came to mind: "We had to destroy the town in order to save it." By unleashing the full power of the U.S. Air Force on this quiet suburb, we might be doing just what Charlie wanted us to do. I couldn't figure out any other reason he would instigate a fight against a much larger force. He had to know that he couldn't hold the position for much longer than a day, if that.

Word of my reluctance evidently filtered back through the Vietnamese chain of command. The Dai Uy began an extended radio conversation in which I seemed to be the subject. He occasionally looked at me and gestured in my direction. He seemed more perturbed with who he was talking to than with me, however, so maybe he saw my point. Finally, Bulldog called: "Homestead Six, this is Bulldog, over."

"This is Homestead Six, over."

"This is Bulldog. The province deputy chief is complainin' you won't put in air strikes, over." The deputy chief was a youngish Vietnamese lieutenant colonel who favored mirror sunglasses, camouflage scarves, and considerable strutting.

"Now hold on, Bulldog. Ya know what I said. I just asked how come our allies aren't firin' their artillery. If this place has to be destroyed, they ought to participate. Seein' only those big jets with their white stars and U.S. Air Force on the side is gonna make the locals view us as the only bad guys. What the hell's wrong with that thinkin', and why no artillery?"

"Wait one, Homestead." Apparently a major discussion was underway at province operations on what was to be done about this audacious VC move almost into Cao Lanh itself, and the attitude of this lowly Co Van My with the 64th Dia Phong Quan was only adding to the consternation. A partial solution eventually evolved from the fact that air assets were limited. A flight of two U.S. Air Force propeller-driven A-10s appeared on the scene, and at province's instructions I coordinated the dropping of their loads, but this was all the air available. Some artillery was finally fired into the trees. From our vantage point, the damage done by either the A-10s or the artillery was difficult to detect.

As the air and artillery were supposedly loosening up the enemy position, the powers-that-be at province were busily concocting the next step. The idea of advancing across the open field was abandoned in favor of a move up the road. And the honor of conducting this maneuver was taken by my new buddy, the province deputy chief. He would show those Co Van Mys how things were done. Actually, it wouldn't be him himself but an outfit under his personal control, the Province Recon Team.

This bunch of clowns was no more a fighting force than the mess hall crew at the Special Forces camp. The Recon Team had about 25 bodies. They wore an outlandish collection of uniforms, most of which were topped off with extremely large bush hats. They also sported a variety of scarves and cravats, some camouflage, some brightly colored. The unit did little, in any, actual reconning. Its main function was apparently to guard the province chief and deputy chief.

One of the battalion's companies moved cautiously up the road, getting all the way to the bridge. The bridge was in the shape of an arch, and the point element of the company crawled to just below the crest of the arch. The sides of the bridge were concrete walls about two feet high. The company set up a machine gun pointed over the wall on the bridge's right side and aimed in the direction of the Charlies. The headquarters group went as far as the first dwelling. Trees and several sizeable depressions in the yard surrounding the house provided cover. Between the end of the yard in the house's rear and the treeline where the VC were located was an open space of about 150 meters.

Shortly after the battalion was in position, the Recon Team came barrelling up the road in a deuce and a half. The truck went almost to the bridge, and the team piled out. The province deputy chief shouted orders, emphasizing them with exaggerated posturing and gestures. The lead elements started moving forward through the trees along the river bank, jogging in a crouch. They were soon lost sight of.

Only a minute or so elapsed before all hell broke loose. Automatic weapons fired, grenades exploded, individuals screamed. The Dai Uy received excited instructions on the radio and in response crawled forward in the yard to the last depression before the field began. Sgt. Mitchell and I followed. One of the company's machine guns began firing bursts across the field into the trees. Popping sounds just overhead indicated that the Charlies were returning fire.

The good thing for the Recon Team was that it didn't get trapped and pinned down. The bad thing was that it had at least five members shot up. The deuce and a half soon came back down the road. Bloody bodies were visible lying on the seats. An ashen-looking province deputy chief was sitting beside the driver. In a cloud of dust, the truck disappeared toward Cao Lanh.

We spent the next several hours doing not much more than fiddling around. Bursts of automatic weapons were traded, but no effort was made by the battalion to advance. In late afternoon, the bulk of the battalion was ordered to return to nighttime defensive responsibilities. So Charlie was left in command of the hamlet. Sgt. Mitchell and I went to the team house and then to the Special Forces camp for a meal and a shower. In the shower, I ran into my new boss, the MACV province advisor. I hadn't had much contact with him since his arrival six weeks or so previously and so hadn't formed much of an opinion about him. He proceeded to begin the development of that opinion by asking accusingly why I hadn't gone by province operations after the battalion returned to Cao Lanh. There might have been important matters for me to learn, such as what was to happen next, and I might have been able to impart some insight on what was happening. He was right, but I had fallen into a stay-away-from-the-puzzle-palace mode of operation. The less contact I had with headquarters people, the better.

The lieutenant colonel was a big guy, but he didn't inspire fear. Consequently, I gave him a little lip, a smart-ass answer about what was the need. Nevertheless, after the shower I stopped by province operations—in jungle fatigues and shower clogs—and did learn some things of interest. The Charlies had escaped to the north, leaving the hamlet somewhat the worse for wear but in friendly hands. And a company of ARVN armored personnel carriers was on the way to teach them VCs a lesson.

The level of activity in Kien Phong had apparently reached a threshold of concern for the IV Corps planners in Can Tho. When Mr. Charles threatened a province capital, a response was called for, although a response might be just what Mr. Charles wanted. Maybe he was trying to divert attention from some other area. But the option of not responding in some fashion to a VC show of force was an alternative that most of those responsible for military operations viewed as unacceptable.

So in response to the VC moves in Kien Phong, IV Corps dispatched a company of mechanized infantry—infantry in armored personnel carriers, or tracks. The APCs were M-113s, the same kind used by U.S. mechanized units. The ARVN unit arrived two days after the fight just outside of Cao Lanh and was given a joint mission with the 64th Dia Phong Quan.

My knowledge of mechanized infantry operations was pretty close to nil. Not having been to infantry officers basic at Ft. Benning, I, of course, had no formal training on the topic. Moreover, unlike on-foot infantry operations, mounted infantry operations were not something that playing war or cowboys and Indians as a kid was even a limited preparation for. Fortunately, the 64th's involvement with the tracks was to be only as passengers. In fact, the mechanized unit had its own Co Van Mys—a captain and a staff sergeant E-6. So my ignorance was not likely to be dangerous. Indeed, this was an opportunity for me to learn a little something.

The tracks and the battalion were given a mission of making a broad sweep to the northwest of Cao Lanh. Trucks transported the battalion to the jumping off place on the main road to the Cambodian border. There, the Ruff-Puffs clamored onto and into the tracks, and we took off towards the north. For soldiers accustomed to the slow pace of traveling by foot, the speed of the tracks was exhilarating. The by-the-book way for infantry to travel with tracks was inside. The usual preference, however, was sitting on top. That is where the crews of this mechanized outfit rode, and that is where most of the Ruff-Puffs found a place. The honchos of the company—the Dai Uy commanding, the other officers, some of the NCOs—even had short-legged lawn chairs strapped on the tops of the armored behemoths. The Co Van My Dai Uy had his own chair in back of his ARVN counterpart. The Co Van My Dai Uy was an armored officer and had thus received his training at Ft. Knox, Kentucky. I doubt if he received any instructions there on lawn chairs.

We raced at least 15 kilometers to the north. The vast fields were relatively dry, and the few dikes and canals were easily traversed. Eventually, we encountered a number of suspicious mounds along a dike. The mounds were seven to nine feet high and up to ten feet in diameter at the base. They weren't fighting positions, but they were large enough to contain hiding places for humans. The Dai Uy's boys tried digging into several of them. Random arrangements of logs the thickness of an arm made digging an extremely difficult endeavor, however. After 30 minutes or so of not much progress, the battalion loaded onto the tracks, which backed off about 100 meters. Several of the tracks had 106-mm recoilless rifles mounted on them instead of machine guns. The rifles began firing high explosive rounds into the mounds. One round was not enough to destroy a mound, but it made quite an impact.

After the first few salvos, a figure appeared from nowhere and began walking along the line of mounds. Machine guns on the tracks commenced a fusillade. Tracers streaked into the line of mounds. Miraculously, the figure kept walking, finally disappearing behind a mound. A command was given and the tracks charged forward. Several of the mounds had been sufficiently opened up to reveal hiding VC, now dead or dying. About 15 bodies were counted, and a like number of weapons—mostly AK-47s—retrieved. We had evidently surprised a small VC unit in what it must have considered a safe area. A little armor certainly simplified war-making in Kien Phong Province.

The task force turned to the west. As we proceeded along, I made the mistake of discussing with the armor captain advising the tracks my unhappiness with the advisory business. I made the further mistake of personalizing the discussion by putting the onus on my Dai Uy—he didn't solicit my advice, he didn't listen to what I had to say, and so forth. In reality, the advisory business and I were just incompatible. The only thing the Dai Uy could have done to satisfy the gnawing inside me would have been to give me command of the battalion, and that wasn't going to happen. But the armor captain seemed to think it was just a matter of the relationship. If I made my desires known subtly and tactfully, the Dai Uy would come around. The armor captain even offered to have his Dai Uy intermediate. The armor captain probably went on to a career running encounter groups.

When I realized I was yapping with a guy that took my griping seriously, I eased off. I didn't need to be unburdening myself to some character who thought problems were actually solvable. Meanwhile, the task force had come to a sizeable river. The depth wasn't deeper than the tracks' height, but the river was at about the limit of what the vehicles could cross without adding swimming equipment. The crossing took a considerable amount of time. Once on the other side, the task force turned south, aiming for the main road.

In a farming complex of several huts, we found an old man and a boy. For some reason, they aroused the interest of my Dai Uy. One of his henchmen proceeded to give the old man the water treatment. The henchmen held the poor guy's head underwater for close to a minute, yanked him up, shouted a few questions, and shoved him back under. This went on for 15 minutes but apparently didn't yield whatever the

Dai Uy was looking for. Maybe my Dai Uy was just trying to impress the Dai Uy of the armored force.

Finally, we started the final leg of the return to the road. The old man and the boy were brought along. Their hands were tied behind their backs, and they were made to crouch in a small V-shaped area in the front of a track. The V was made by an armored plate, approximately five feet long by three feet high, that was attached with hinges at the bottom to the sloping front of the vehicle. Even if their hands had been free, the two prisoners would have had difficulty maintaining their balance in the uncomfortable V. With their hands tied, the two took a beating. They kept falling forward, smashing their faces on the metal. Their feet were cramped down awkwardly into the bottom of the V. They survived the bouncing trip over the rough field, but they were definitely the worse for wear.

That night, I took a shower at the Special Forces camp and got a measure of one-upmanship over one of LTC Meathead's flunkies, a master sergeant E-8 who was in operations. I was telling another occupant of the shower that the operation had resulted in 15 VC bodies. The sergeant piped up sarcastically, "Another 15 of them unarmed civilians, huh Captain?"

"As a matter of fact, Sergeant, there were also 15 weapons, mostly AKs but also an SKS. Yeah, those civilians sported a little hardware." I almost forgot that I was just a Co Van My.

One day toward the latter part of February, Sgt. Roca announced that he wasn't going on anymore operations. He was short, with a DEROS just two weeks away. I had no problem with cutting him some slack—"no slack" was most definitely not his personal motto—but his public announcement in the presence of Sergeants Mitchell and Blane in the team house was too much of a direct affront. I said: "Hey Sergeant Roca, I'll try to keep you outta the field if possible, but how 'bout not tellin' me what to do, okay? I'm the guy in charge, remember? If we need four people for a chopper assault, you're on call."

The more I thought about it, however, the more I concluded that keeping Roca out of the field was the best thing. With the approach of his DEROS, his testiness level had been sharply rising. And the relationship between him and Sgt. Mitchell was deteriorating. They even became engaged in a little pushing match at one point. My manpower problem was partly solved by the return to team control of Lt. Silver. The province advisory team had received several new junior officers and consequently now had sufficient personnel to man its radios. So Lt. Silver was returned to field duty.

Shortly after his return, we did indeed undertake a chopper operation requiring four Co Van Mys. The operation was uneventful, but there was a moment of note for me. As we were waiting on a road just north of town to load up, the province advisor spied my extremely well-worn field boots and chewed my butt, mildly, for setting a bad example for the Vietnamese. Almost four months of tromping the Delta mud and water had rotted a huge hole in the left front of my left boot. Several toes were exposed to the elements. I wore the boots with a certain pride. They were a clear expression of a "no slack" attitude, but they obviously offended the province advisor. I had little more than five weeks left in my 30 months in the 'Nam, and I resolved to stay out of the colonel's way and keep wearing my badge of honor.

Sgt. Roca departed at the beginning of March. He was relatively subdued the last few days, and didn't even throw a goodbye drunk. His departure eased tensions considerably. Since Sgt. Mitchell's adoption in December of a no-booze policy, Sgt. Roca had been the principal source of disruption in the team, not major disruption but still disruption. His complaining and whining kept Mitchell and myself—Sgt. Blane was impossible to provoke—on edge. To be honest, however, Sgt. Roca had adequately done the job the Army pushed him into, a job he did not want and that he was not suited for.

At about this time, I had an opportunity to discuss the matter of who indeed was suitable for a Mobile Advisory Team. An inspector team from MACV was traveling the country, ascertaining how the

MAT program was doing. I spent about 45 minutes trying to convince the captain in charge that the procedure of levying line units was not going to result in getting the cream of the crop for the "Vietnamization" program. Units were far more likely to unload malcontents and disrupters. Another source-group raided by levied units—individuals in transit—might provide some suitable advisors, but overall the process was sorely lacking. The captain, however, did not want to talk about the inadequacies of the process. Instead, he wanted specific instances of unsuitable personnel in order to raise hell with the units that provided the individuals. I soon realized that he was not going to focus on my point, and I certainly was not about to focus on his, so our conversation ended.

Nevertheless, others at a much higher level apparently were realizing the inadequacies of the MAT manning procedures. For the last years of the war, personnel for MAT teams were assigned directly from the states. In other words, you arrived for your year in Vietnam trained for and already assigned to a MAT. Whether this resulted in an appreciable improvement in the quality of personnel, however, was something I know little about. The new procedure certainly didn't lead to a successful Vietnamization of the war, unless it was North Vietnamization.

In early March, shortly before my final R&R, the battalion returned to the area where the joint operation with the tracks had taken place. This time, the operation was on foot, a long slow stroll across the drying fields. A little to the east of where the slaughter of the Charlies in the mounds had occurred, the battalion found several more mounds. They weren't as formidably constructed as the first mounds. Indeed, they seemed to be no more than graves. The soldiers dug into them and found eight or nines bodies in an advanced state of decay. The flesh was mushy, putrid, and falling away from the bones. The sight and smell were a not a good send-off for Bangkok.

Naturally, the last R&R was a bit of a disappointment. I arrived in Bangkok on a dull grey humid day. After the interminable orientation,

I was deposited at a new hotel in the heart of the main bar area. It was so new that I seemed to be the only customer. No one else was in the lobby, and the only people around were the various preyers upon those in possession of dollars. I checked in and sent a message by taxi to Trachit Pangbon. After about 45 minutes, she appeared. In her own mercenary way, she apparently was not unhappy to see me, although she seemed somewhat distracted. She invited me to stay in the house over the klong, so to the great disappointment of the hotel's staff, their one guest checked out. I learned later that as I was engrossed in the paperwork, the equivalent of the concierge put a hammerlock on Trachit Pangbon and extorted a wad of cash from her.

The five days were a drag. Trachit Pangbon was having both physical and emotional problems, neither of which I was able to learn much about. The upshot was that on my last visit to the sex capital of the world, I was stuck with a no-fun companion. I was glad when the five days were over. I made some promises to return after I had left the Army, but I knew I wouldn't, and she probably knew it also.

On the way back to Cao Lanh, I lingered a few days in Saigon. Some chores needed doing. The Dai Uy had asked that I buy him a television at the PX. The interpreter swore that the Dai Uy would repay me. Reluctantly, I made the purchase, promising myself that I wouldn't part with the thing without money in my hot little hand.

I also wanted to see my chaste Saigon honey. I went to the U.S. facility where she was a cashier and made a date to meet her at my favorite Chinese restaurant in Cholon. She didn't show, and I actually felt relieved. Maybe she had a valid reason, but I took the opportunity to call the relationship—such as it was—at an end. She didn't know where I was staying, so there was no danger of seeing her again. Finally, I had to pick up a little tailoring at the tailor shop near the Five Oceans. When I was with the 716th MP Battalion, the shop had been where I bought patches and had my sewing done. On my subsequent travels through Saigon, I usually stopped in. The main attraction was a teenage girl of incredible beauty and flirtatious manner. On the trip to

Saigon a month earlier to take the Law School Admission Test, I had left my going home uniform to be altered.

When I entered the shop, it was deja vu all over again. An individual from my childhood in Williamsburg, Virginia, was standing there in the camouflage uniform of a ranger Co Van My. Like myself, Pinky was a captain. We had been in boy scouts together and had lived not far apart. With him was a platoon sergeant E-7. Pinky was Pinky for, of course, his red head. I had always called him that, but I wasn't sure the childhood nick-name was appropriate in front of his sergeant. Consequently, I awkwardly stammered out his given name, David, the same as mine.

Pinky was an FNG, having been in-country only a month. Before that, he had been in Germany for almost two years. His sergeant, however, was close to being an Old Asia Hand. He was on his second or third tour, and in fact had been with the 173rd at Dak To. He had been in the company of the 4th Battalion that had rescued the Charlie Company task force on November 12, 1967, the day Alpha Company was bogged down at the entrance to a bunker complex. The three of us talked for a while and then parted. I told Pinky I would try to look him up when I came back through Saigon in a couple of weeks.

For that's all I had left in my two and a half years in Vietnam—a couple of weeks. They were not to be a quiet couple of weeks, however.

I flew by C-130 to Can Tho and from there caught a chopper heading for Cao Lanh. It put me, my gear, and the Dai Uy's TV down on a landing pad near the Special Forces compound. I struggled the few hundred meters to the Hao Hoa Pagoda. The Dai Uy was sitting in the small open front of his house when I came by. At the sight of the TV, his eyes lit up like a kid's at Christmas. I grinned and waved and continued on to the team house. I had no intention of parting with the TV before I had the money. Two and a half years of the good people of Southeast Asia chasing after my dollars had made me a cynical bastard.

Shortly after I entered the team house and greeted the remaining members—Lt. Silver and Sergeants Mitchell and Blane—the interpreter appeared. The Dai Uy was anxious to get his hands on his TV. "Tell Dai Uy I need money first," was my blunt response. After the interpreter departed, I said: "That SOB ain't gettin' his hands on this thing before I get my money. And if there ain't no money comin', my last day I'm puttin' this sucker on the berm and zappin' it with an M-16. This boy's got taken by his last Vietnamese."

But the interpreter was soon back with the Dai Uy himself. Money changed hands, and we unpacked the TV and tried it out on the small line that provided us with a dim light bulb. There wasn't enough electricity to operate the picture tube, nor was there enough at the Dai Uy's. Our maid lived nearby in a more developed part of Cao Lanh. We carted the thing over to her house and tried it. A picture only filled about half the screen, but the Dai Uy was ecstatic. Bright and early the next day, he was busy supervising the running of a bigger line to his house from a pole along the road. The man was happy as a clam.

The battalion had been out four times during the week that I was gone but each operation had been uneventful. Two days after my return, we headed southeast. Lt. Silver was my accompanying Co Van My.

A sizeable town lay not far from Cao Lanh in that direction. It could not be reached by road, however. Late in the morning, we boarded landing craft at the Tan Tich ferry and followed a meandering course on canals and tributary rivers of the Mekong in order to reach the place. The start was late because the operation was a last minute thing apparently in response to intelligence reports. Once at the town, we unloaded and began a trek on foot on the east bank of a broad river—probably 200 meters wide—that flowed south to the Mekong. About three kilometers to the east was the site of the January 6 fight.

After we had gone little more than a kilometer, an explosion of automatic weapons fire rolled from the direction of the battalion's lead elements. The distinct snapping and popping of incoming rounds sent everyone to the ground. After the first fusillade, the firing tapered off to intermittent bursts every 30 seconds or so. At least half the bursts seemed to be outgoing. The Dai Uy barked on the radio for awhile and then started working his way up the column at a crouch. I followed. The vegetation on the bank was fairly heavy and seemed to extend for at least 100 meters to the east before the open fields began.

The lead elements had reached the bank of a canal that flowed into the river from the east. The canal was about 20 meters wide. For the Delta, the elevation of the land in the area was relatively high, and the river and the canal had ten-foot banks. The Victor Charlies had been on the far bank of the canal. They seemed to have moved up the canal to the east but were still close enough to put fire into the battalion's lead elements and to cover the canal itself. The Dai Uy's mission was apparently to get part of the battalion across the canal and then move on both sides of the canal to the east where the main VC body was suspected to be.

A U.S. patrol boat of some sort was in the river about 100 meters offshore, sporadically firing an automated 40-mm grenade launcher and a machine gun toward the south side of the canal. We had no communications with the boat, and province operations did not know how to get in touch with it. The Dai Uy and I were concerned that because of the lack of communications, the boat might fire us up. So I moved back up the trail to where a sampan had been commandeered. It took me out to the boat. The water was a fast-flowing muddy brown flecked with free-floating aquatic plants. The members of the boat's crew were a scruffy bunch from the U.S. Navy, a description some would consider an oxymoron. The crews of river patrol boats had a reputation as being on the wild side. Charging up and down remote rivers and canals in their powerful heavily-armed craft, they certainly had an interesting war. We exchanged information on radio frequencies and on the battalion's plans, and I returned to the bank.

The battalion spent the rest of the afternoon trying to get an element across the canal. The VCs had an unfettered view and field of fire down the canal, so getting to the other side was no easy task. The Dai

Uy had two companies work their way to the east on the north side of the canal, and eventually they pushed the VC screening outposts back far enough to permit a crossing. By the time the battalion was situated to the Dai Uy's satisfaction on both banks, darkness was rapidly descending. The headquarters group settled down for the night on the bare-earth yard of a thatched hut on the north bank. Rice was prepared and consumed, and we curled up for uneasy, uncomfortable sleep.

Early the next morning, the push to the east was resumed. About 400 meters up the canal, the battalion ran into stiff resistance on both banks. A trail paralleled each bank, providing a path through the vegetation. On the north bank, dwellings, some of them well-built of finished planks, interrupted the vegetation every 50 meters or so. The dwellings had obviously been recently occupied, but the occupants probably had departed in anticipation of the coming fight. The south bank had fewer buildings.

The stiffening resistance brought the advance to a halt. Intermittent automatic weapons fire was taking place on the south bank about 150 meters forward of where the headquarters group was stopped on the north bank. After a time, the Dai Uy moved forward on the north bank past the lead elements. He apparently wanted to perform a personal reconnaissance. The lead battalion elements on the south bank were still about 75 meters ahead of us, but we were now the furthest forward element on the north bank. Smoke and dust from the activity obscured the area, adding to the feelings of unease and foreboding. The point man crossed a high-banked muddy ditch perpendicular to the canal. After climbing the far bank, he took several steps and was suddenly enveloped in a cloud of smoke. The explosion was muffled but his scream wasn't. Two others quickly crawled to him and manhandled him back across the ditch. His right pants leg was ripped and bloody, but the damage to the exposed limb seemed superficial—no jutting bones, no spurting severed arteries, no great gouges in the flesh, just a number of relatively small shrapnel wounds.

Thus ended the effort of the headquarters group to lead the battalion charge. For the rest of the morning, there was much heated discussion on the radio, periodic exchanges of gun fire on the south bank, but little movement. The battalion sustained several more casualties, none serious. Lt. Silver and I spent the time lounging on the porch of one of the deserted houses.

Early in the afternoon, the headquarters group retraced its steps for a few hundred meters, crossed to the south bank of the canal, and went forward. The band of vegetation on the south bank gradually shrunk to about 30 meters wide. The fields beyond, however, were not well-kept. They contained a fair amount of undergrowth, and lines of trees and bushes criss-crossed the area in random directions. The Dai Uy put the two companies in a line formation and attempted a general advance. The line stretched from the canal south for about 200 meters. The advance was barely underway before it attracted a crescendo from the direction of the Charlies. The VC positions were easily discernible on a dike about 100 meters ahead. The dike intersected the canal at approximately a 45-degree angle, or from our direction a 135-degree angle. That is, the closest VC position to us was where the dike met the canal; from there, the dike angled away to the southeast.

The VC barrage brought the advance to a halt. At about the same time, province operations informed me that the air assets they had been trying to get for most of the day were finally on the way. So we settled down to wait for the heavy stuff. After a short time a FAC called and said a flight of F-4 Phantoms was on-station. For some reason, he wanted to put the air strikes in over the top of our position and not parallel to it. This was not the school solution: the error factor in air strikes was much greater along a plane's axis of flight than perpendicular to that axis. The ordnance was likely to fall anywhere within an ellipse-shaped area, and you wanted that ellipse parallel to your front, not including you within its tail.

But the school solution was not to be applied here. Since the battalion's line was as close as 100 meters to the VC positions, I asked the

FAC to hold off a few minutes while we moved back a bit. When the movement was completed, we were still no more than 150 meters away, but the FAC was getting anxious. If the air strikes weren't used shortly, the planes would likely be diverted to other targets. So I said, "Okay, Hound Dog, put the stuff in, but tell them guys not to hiccup."

The Phantoms came screaming in, right down on the deck, passing directly overhead. They seemed close enough to touch. The release points for the 500-pounders and napalm were to our rear, so unattached diagonally falling ordnance zipped over the battalion's line. The headquarters group was on that line, protected only by a small clump of bamboo. Each of us flattened our bodies into the ground, seeking what cover we could from the slender bamboo reeds and other bits of vegetation. After the first run, the FAC called: "Homestead, this is Hound Dog. How ya doin'? Everything okay?"

"Yeah, this is Homestead. We're gettin' some shrapnel overhead, but it's not bad. Keep it comin'. Out."

The two Phantoms completed their runs, and then we got two more. The bombs seemed to be impacting in the vicinity of the dike, but none of the visible bunkers had taken a direct hit. If these VCs had the usual discipline, they would not be panicked by a near miss. Only a crater where a bunker had been would be helpful.

After the planes had made their final runs and departed, the battalion resumed its advance. And the Charlies resumed their automatic weapons fire. It took only the first evidence of the Charlies' continued presence for the Dai Uy to abandon the effort. The headquarters group recrossed the canal. It was late in the afternoon, and the Dai Uy became embroiled in a lengthy radio conversation with province about what the course of action was to be. Meanwhile, who should appear but Sergeants Mitchell and Blane. A supply boat had been sent to the battalion, and they had come along with C-rations and other goodies. They weren't there long, but it felt good to know that someone still remembered us. "Hey Dai Uy, when you comin' back?"

"Well, I don't know. Looks like we'll be here at least another night. Thanks for the stuff."

Just as they were about to leave, Lt. Silver comes up with a small dog. "Sergeant Mitchell, take this back to Cao Lanh for me." Mitchell and Blane looked at the animal dubiously. So did I. Until now on this operation, Silver had been pretty much an inoffensive presence.

"Uh, Lieutenant. Where d'ya get the dog?"

"At one of those houses up the trail. He was just running around."

"Ya know, he might belong to somebody. Also, uh, you sure this is a good example for the Vietnamese? Ya know, we're trying to break them of their lootin' habits."

Silver looked at me as if these thoughts had just occurred to him for the first time, which I guess they had. "You mean, I shouldn't keep the dog? He'd make a good team mascot."

I muffled a guffaw. Mitchell and Blane didn't impress me as taking well to a team mascot, particularly in Sgt. Blane's case one that couldn't be screwed. "Well, I don't think we need to get one by plunderin' these houses. Think how the owners will feel when they return and their dog is gone." The way they would feel would be the same way they would feel about a lost chicken—a meal uneaten. But I didn't remind Silver of this different cultural outlook. Crestfallen, he trudged off to part with his prize. Relieved, Mitchell and Blane left with the departing supply boat.

Evening was approaching, and the Dai Uy pulled the headquarters group back to the laager site of the night before. I didn't have much problem with this action, but then I realized that he was pulling the whole battalion back. The VCs would be free to depart, which I strongly suspected was what the Dai Uy and his superiors wanted. I tried to make my case to the interpreter and the Dai Uy: "VC di-di mau. Numbah ten. Put benshees up trail." I gestured up the canal toward the VC positions. The Dai Uy just grinned sheepishly. The effort was in vain, but I kept muttering loudly to Lt. Silver about the matter as we ate and settled in for the evening.

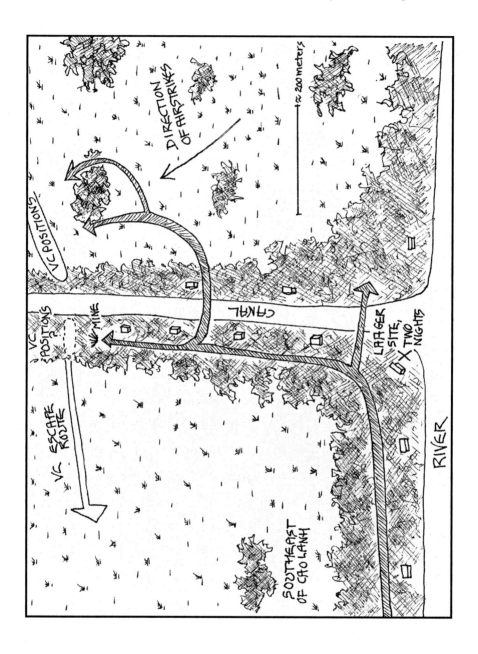

Sure enough, in the morning the VCs were gone. A fresh path in the open fields indicated that they had departed to the north. A machine gun in the treeline could have wrecked havoc on their departure. We examined the abandoned positions. They were formidable with excellent fields of fire, and a frontal assault would most likely have been disastrous. But the VC could have been prevented from leaving. Eventually, air and artillery would have taken their toll. The South Vietnamese in Kien Phong Province, however, appeared reluctant to go for a knock-out blow.

Finally, in mid-afternoon we were back in Cao Lanh. After a shower and a meal, I headed for the Special Forces bar. The only other occupant was a lieutenant. He had been my main radio contact at province operations for the three days. Although he had been in-country for only a few weeks, he had been to ranger and airborne schools as well as Infantry Officers Basic, and fancied that he had the answers. His theory was that we should have called in smoke and assaulted the VC positions under its cover. I listened mostly in silence, thinking 29 months down, less than nine days to go. Maybe seven and a wakeup.

Later, the FAC came in and made me feel a little better. He was relatively new himself, the replacement of the guy who had been shot down while hot-dogging up the river. He was in awe of the fact that we had been within range of the shrapnel from the bombs yet had kept the stuff coming in. Half-heartedly, I tried to convince him that this was standard practice having more to do with being too tired or lazy to pull back sufficiently far to create the buffer zone required by the manual. Still, it was nice to be the object of a little admiration, undeserved though it was.

No Slack

Seven and a wakeup. Two and a half years, 30 months, three Christmases, the Saigon cops, Tuy Hoa, Dak To, Hill 882, Bong Song, the Delta, and the Old Asia Hand was down to a week. Time enough for a couple of chores and one last operation.

One of the chores was to get Lt. Silver his team mascot. The agricultural adviser on the civilian side of the province advisory team was giving away chickens. As a suburbanite in my youth, I had a yen for the farming life, the yen of one who has no practical experience in a matter. I took a dozen of the half-grown birds and constructed a rough pen in the space between the floor of the team house and the ground. I figured those good ol' southern boys Sergeants Mitchell and Blane would know how to care for the animals, and Lt. Silver could provide tender loving care. None of the three showed much enthusiasm for the project.

A second chore was to try to reverse a decision by the province XO to transfer Sgt. Blane to another MAT team. The transfer was to be made because the other team was short personnel. But MAT 104 was down to four people, and I was about to leave. I hauled a reluctant Sgt. Blane to the province XO's office. Blane didn't really care if he went or not. He was the original roll-with-the-flow guy. I made my case. MAT 104 itself was short personnel and about to be getting shorter. The XO countered that two replacements were in the pipeline. Moreover, since the team was in Cao Lanh, it could be augmented by members of the province team. I smelled the desire of the "attack under smoke" lieutenant to get into the field. I also argued that Sgt. Blane had established a rapport with the members of the 64th Dia Phong Quan, a rapport that should not be thrown away. This argument, of course, was a crock. If Blane had any rapport, it was with the team's maid. My arguments were to no avail, and the transfer of Sgt. Blane stuck, although he wasn't to leave for a couple of weeks. By then, I would be long gone.

The final operation was a chopper assault to the north of the main east-west canal bisecting the province. The pick-up was at the usual location just outside of Cao Lanh. The operation was a multi-unit affair, and the province advisor was conspicuously present. In violation of his explicit order, I had not discarded the jungle boots with the hole that exposed the side of my foot. So I strove to stay out of his sight.

After a short delay during which I surreptitiously scurried about the pick-up zone keeping distance between me and the colonel, the Hueys arrived. We were soon in the air, winging north. The choppers put us beside a stream that flowed south to the canal. The operation started as the usual stroll in the sun, except that we were well-shaded in the growth along the banks of the stream, which was deep, sluggish, and hemmed in by high muddy banks. A little after noon, however, several shots rang out from the direction of the head of the column, 100 meters or so to the front. The headquarters group soon arrived at the site of the commotion. Two large mounds, each about six feet high, sat in a small clearing. Several thatched huts were also in the clearing. About a dozen soldiers were attacking one of the mounds with entrenching tools and pointed sticks. Others were talking excitedly and gesturing at the mound.

The mound that was the center of attention had no entrance that I could see. The second mound, the larger one, did have a crawl-way opening. I felt the need to investigate, or perhaps just to tempt fate on my final day in the field, so I borrowed a flashlight from one of the Dai Uy's henchmen and crawled in a few feet. The tunnel took a sharp right. It was extremely narrow and cramped, and I could not squeeze my body around the bend. Stymied and becoming engulfed by a crushing claustrophobia, I backed out.

In the meantime, the diggers had made some headway on the other mound. They were digging at its base. After about a foot of very hard dried clay they reached a layer of sticks. The sticks were the size of a thumb and about an inch or so apart. As the dirt was cleared away, parts of several bodies became visible. The rhythmic rise and fall of torsos showed that the individuals were alive, although how that was possible was difficult to understand. The space into which they were squeezed was little more than six inches high. From the layer of sticks to the dirt below was barely enough vertical room for a head turned sideways. How much lateral room existed was impossible to tell, as was the location of the entrance to the cramped space.

As more dirt was scraped away, there was much jabbering and laughter from the onlookers. I thought the Dai Uy might dig the poor bastards out entirely, but such was not to be their fate. Instead, the barrel of a carbine was brought to within several inches of the exposed cloth and flesh. A dozen rounds were squeezed off, the barrel being moved a little after every couple of shots to ensure that all the occupants were attended to. Blood and gore oozed into the dirt. The rhythmic rise and fall of the torsos was replaced with a stillness except for one, which began a spasmodic heaving. As we resumed the march, the struggle with death was still underway.

The choppers came for us an hour later. Just prior to their arrival, I decided to fire my M-16 one last time. To the right of our line of march a vast plain extended for at least a mile before being interrupted by a treeline. I put the weapon on semi-automatic and started to squeeze off a round in the direction of the emptiness. Only it wasn't a squeeze. Just like the newest recruit in basic training, I jerked the trigger, sending the bullet angling into the sky. Sgt. Mitchell snickered: "Damn, Dai Uy. If ya wasn't so short, I'd have to give ya some marksmanship trainin'."

As I was still coping with the ignominy of my last shot, the choppers descended for the pick-up. We were soon back in Cao Lanh.

I was scheduled to leave for Saigon in two days. I picked up the necessary paperwork and packed on the intervening day, and didn't even get sloshed. Time was passing too quickly to speed it up with a last binge. I spent the final evening sitting on top of the team's bunker, watching the sun set in the west. Lt. Silver and Sgt. Blane turned in early—they had an operation in the morning. Sgt. Mitchell and I sat in the darkness until close to midnight, not saying much, he smoking his pipe and me sipping beer.

Lt. Silver shook me before dawn the next morning. I could hear the trucks out on the road, ready to carry the battalion to the day's jumping off place. He said, "Captain Holland, I've enjoyed serving with you, Sir. I've, uh, learned a lot."

"Well, uh, thanks. You take care of yourself, ya hear?" I sleepily replied.

"Yes Sir. And Sir, one other thing."

"Yeah?"

"Could you put me in for a Bronze Star? It'll really look good when I get out of the Army. You know, on my record."

I assumed we would all automatically get an appropriate trinket and so hadn't checked to ensure that the paperwork guys were on the case. As the man in charge, I should have been more on top of the situation. Still, this idea that a war medal was a step toward success in later life had been voiced by a number of others during my time in the 'Nam and indeed seemed widespread. Too bad the powers that be back in the World could give a hoot. I responded, "Uh, yeah, they're handlin' that at province. I'm sure you'll get the standard stuff."

"Thanks, Sir. You know I'm just asking for my record. It might help get me a job sometime. Have a good trip, Sir."

He left and I went back to sleep.

Sgt. Mitchell and I arose after daylight broke. The daily Caribou was scheduled to leave from the airfield sometime after nine. I had a cup of coffee and then performed one last chore. I tied the laces of my field boots together—the pair with the hole that had aggravated the province advisor—balanced the boots on the end of a bamboo pole, and raised them to the end of the roof beam, which extended over the landing at the top of the stairs. I said to Sgt. Mitchell: "This'll give you guys somethin' to remember me by. When the goin' gets tough, just look at that hole and think, 'no slack.'"

We drove to the airfield. The Caribou had already arrived from Can Tho and was preparing for its return journey. I turned to say farewell to Sgt. Mitchell. From starting out as the bane of my existence, he had become the most dependable member of the team. He was one of the few people I had known, or was to know, who actually turned their lives around, at least for awhile. He had a little speech prepared: "I'm sorry to see ya go, Dai Uy. You done good here. But I'm glad you're gettin' out. You're too nice to be a career officer. A career man's gotten be mean sometimes, and you just don't get mean. Good luck to ya. I'm glad to have served together."

"Well, uh, thanks Sergeant Mitchell. I think. Ya don't think I'm mean enough, huh?"

"No Sir. But hey, that ain't necessarily that bad. You just ain't no lifer."

"Well, look. You take care. I 'preciate what you done here. Keep yourself safe for another couple months."

"That's right. Fifty-four and a wake-up. Adios Dai Uy."

"Adios." I threw him a salute, turned, and walk to the plane. We were shortly airborne and in Can Tho not long after. A flight to Tan Son Nhut wasn't leaving for a couple of hours. I whiled away the time in the Special Forces bar near the terminal, and late in the afternoon was descending into Saigon.

I went to the old hotel on Nguyen Hue Street, the one with rooms around a second floor open-air courtyard. I had no desire for a last fling, either with beer or women. My mood was melancholy. My desire was to slow the inevitable movement of the clock. I had a pizza at the restaurant at the top of Tu Do Street—still the only pizza place in the city. I then read until sleep intruded.

The next day I returned to Tan Son Nhut to turn in my M-16 and equipment and to out-process. The tasks took only a few hours. For my final dinner, I went to the outdoor restaurant near the Five Oceans and had fried rice. I hadn't been to the place since leaving the 716th MP Battalion 18 months before. It was the first local establishment I had ventured into, and I thought it was an appropriate place to have my departure meal. I ended my last evening quietly reading in my room.

Finally, it was the "wake-up," the day most Americans in Vietnam lived for. I took a taxi to the Tan Son Nhut main gate and caught a shuttle bus from there to the international terminal, which serviced both civilian flights and the military charters bringing in and taking out troops. I checked my baggage and went upstairs to a restaurant-bar. Most of the tables and the bar itself were occupied with EMs and officers apparently waiting for the same departure flight as I was. I found a small unoccupied table in a corner and ordered a Ba Moui Ba. The alcohol spread its warm glow over me, and I tried to savor, and prolong, the moment. My war was about to end. The future was uncertain, and unappealing. Two and a half years. Faces, smells, sounds, the heat, the fear, the adrenalin-rush, all played at the periphery of my consciousness.

I ordered another Ba Moui Ba. The din from the conversations at the other tables and the bar provided a background buzz for my thoughts and my incipient intoxication. A third Ba Moui Ba was soon on the way.

At long last for most, too soon for me, an American voice blared over the loud speaker: "Announcing the immediate loading and departure of flight Bravo Two Alpha Four for Kadena, Japan, and…"—there was a pause—"Travis Air Force Base, San Francisco."

The roar was loud and sustained, and the rush to the stairs immediate. I remained seated, sipping my Ba Moui Ba. Through a window, I could see the line at the departure gate one floor below. There was much friendly jostling and back-slapping. One at a time, papers were checked and individuals let through the gate for the walk—run in many cases—across the glare of the concrete to the plane, a brightly colored Braniff 707. Slowly the line grew shorter. Finally, when only a handful of troopers remained, I finished off the Ba Moui Ba, rose, and reluctantly went to join my fellow soldiers.

Epilogue

The United States Air Force Academy, Colorado Springs, Colorado, May 2000—The graduation was pretty special, particularly if you like a little military pageantry every now and then. The events were stretched over four days, giving observers a sense of the desire for it to be over that the cadets of the Air Force Academy had lived with for four years. But the preliminaries enhanced the anticipation and also served to steel the audience for the final individual granting of diplomas to over 900 cadets. The last ceremony, at the Academy stadium with the cadets on the field and the audience in the stands on one side, began with several mercifully short speeches, and then the names commenced. Each cadet marched across the stage from the side, saluted and shook hands with the Secretary of the Air Force, descended to the front, turned, and saluted the next descending cadet. The weather was hot, but it was the dry hot of the West. The air was clear. On one side, the Front Range of the Rocky Mountains rose abruptly to the deep blue sky. On the other, the Great Plains began their thousand-mile journey to the Mississippi River.

Family members and friends of each cadet cheered when his or her name was announced. I, my wife, Rhonda, and my youngest daughter, Kedron, were among the audience. The cheering quickly became competitive, with each group of supporters attempting to outdo the preceding group. Horns and other noisemakers contributed to the cacophony. After the top ten percent of the class—the distinguished graduates, a group that included my oldest daughter, Ada—received their diplomas, the presentations were by squadron. There were almost 40 squadrons. The announcement of each squadron also produced an escalation in the level of vocal expressions. Ada's future husband, Ben, was among the graduates.

252 VIETNAM, A MEMOIR

About mid-way through the names, youngsters began filtering down to the field. Their goal was to acquire the hats the cadets would be throwing in the air. The hats were not only an attraction in their own right: the cadets put money in the headbands. As more and more kids made it out of the stands to the edge of the field, the Air Force Security Police were increasingly challenged to keep things under control.

So the activity, noise, exuberance, and sense of anticipation mounted. And then in the distance came rumblings. The first thought was that the noise was thunder. But the sky was cloudless. Slowly the realization dawned that the noise was the Thunderbirds, the Air Force's precision flying team, preparing for their performance. The rumblings grew louder.

Finally, the last squadron and then the last cadet were called. The cheering was deafening. Solemnity briefly returned as the cadets were given en masse the oath of allegiance as officers in the United States Armed Forces. After the oath, the band played a rousing rendition of the Air Force song. A pause followed, a pause of barely constrained anticipation.

Then came bedlam. From the west, over the Front Range of the Rocky Mountains, the Thunderbirds, echoing their name, thundered overhead, the sound vibrating way down in your being. Nine hundred-some new second lieutenants, giving a collective roar that had been building for four years, threw their caps skyward. A thousand frantic kids charged the field. And 10,000 or so spectators let go a Super Bowl-Final Four-World Series-class cheer. The bedlam continued for almost an hour as the Thunderbirds performed overhead, the loudspeakers blared such songs as Bruce Springsteen's *Born in the USA*, and noisy exuberance prevailed.

The next day I went for a run along a portion of the Falcon Trail, a cross-country trail that explores woods and ridgelines to the south and east of the Academy's central academic complex. I found a clearing on a wooded ridge. The spot had a good view of the architecturally renowned complex, and the parade field to its east. The Front Range of the Rockies rose majestically in the background. The sky was deep blue, with a few high puffy cumulus clouds.

There, in the solitude, I gave the Academy, and much, much else, a salute.

978-0-595-38036-7
0-595-38036-0

Printed in the United States
42421LVS00004B/106-120